THE
MYSTERIOUS
COALS OF FIRE

King of the Jews

PAUL DOUGLAS CASTLE

BLUEPRINT PRESS
INTERNATIONALE

ISBN
978-1-961117-67-9 (Paperback)
978-1-961117-68-6 (eBook)

Dedications

Great and wonderful is our loving God, and He's the reason for the prophets, disciples, and Yeshua. The Bible is His inspired and glorious work; He put it together to elevate us to a greater understanding of the meaning of life.

The excellent and perfect God-inspired Bible, given to us by a higher power, reveals knowledge about Him and His wonderful and righteous ways. And His perfect word is designed to guide us into His kingdom, located above the clouds.

Beyond the shadow of a doubt, our eternal life depends on us knowing Him and believing in His designed way of life. And it's only through the word of God, the prophets, the disciples, and the Son of God that we can know Him well.

Therefore, I want you to realize that when we stand before the throne of God someday, it's our turn to give an account of ourselves and the lifestyle we've chosen to express our priorities. Then I guarantee you it'll be much better for us if we know about God and have an exceptional relationship with Him, void of ungodliness. And this is His expectation concerning you and me.

Furthermore, suppose we choose to be Bible-savvy and avoid ungodliness. In that case, it will improve our image with Him and make us closer to Him if we dedicate enough time to studying His word on this Earth before we journey into the next life.

I dedicate this book to God, Bryan Paul Castle, Kathy Hager Adrianna Castle, Brother Ricky, and Paul and Jason Castle. Then, without forgetting what's living upon the sacred altar of God, I also dedicate this book to the mysterious Living Coals of Fire.

As for you, I hope you'll desire to learn about God, and you'll give all your heart to Him. And if you do these two things, my Creator God of Heaven and Earth will be proud of you and invite you to live in His kingdom.

I assure you, we'll stand before Him someday, give account for ourselves, and be glad to say I gladly converted to Christianity and tried hard to conform to the excellent gospel of righteousness designed by you.

Conclusively, knowing much about God means we focused on Him properly and made Him a part of us. And if we do this and live by His commandments, He'll give us a key to the pearly gates of His kingdom.

Learning about God will not be boring or a waste of time, but it will improve us in many ways. And I want you to know learning about Him will improve our odds of winning the grand prize of immortality.

Table of Contents

Acknowledgments ix

Chapter 1   The Spark Of Life, Coals Of Fire...................... 1
Chapter 2   Lucifer Upon The Mountain Of God 10
Chapter 3   The Potter Man In Heaven 23
Chapter 4   What Is The Origin Of God? 35
Chapter 5   The Fox In The Hen House 42
Chapter 6   Wrath Applied To Lucifer 51
Chapter 7   Jealousy In Heaven...................................... 63
Chapter 8   The Appearance Of Yeshua 71
Chapter 9   The Appearance Of Yehovah........................... 76
Chapter 10   The King Of Tyrus 80
Chapter 11   The King Of Tyrus Destroyed 98
Chapter 12   A Poem About Lucifer...............................109
Chapter 13   The Seeds of Evil Began With Heavenly Creations........113
Chapter 14   From Physical To Invisible 127
Chapter 15   Pure At Heart 137
Chapter 16   Milk Or Strong Meat.................................152
Chapter 17   Milk, Strong Meat & Baptism 160
Chapter 18   The Flesh 182
Chapter 19   Spirit Involvement.................................189

Chapter 20   The Great Opportunity 201

Chapter 21   The Flesh And The Spirit..............................208

Chapter 22   Supernatural Fellowship, Blessings, And Favor 219

Chapter 23   Stumbling Blocks In Front Of Blessings 231

Chapter 24   Things To Remember 241

Chapter 25   Friendship Or Acquaintance 245

Chapter 26   Respectful Lamb, Or Untamed Beast.......................253

Chapter 27   The Reason For Natural Disasters.......................264

Chapter 28   Close To God...286

Chapter 29   Isaiah Encounters A Seraphim..........................301

Chapter 30   Cloven Tongues On Fire 307

Chapter 31   Liberal Or Conservative At The Gates 325

Chapter 32   Liberal Or Conservative Father And Son......................334

Chapter 33   The Wisdom Of Humpty Dumpty............................343

Chapter 34   Pinpointing Expectations 346

Synopsis 348

Acknowledgments

In all the following stories, wherever scriptures appear, they are taken from The King James Special Study Edition Bible. The Global Bible Society wrote the King James Special Study Edition Bible. P.O. Box 6068, Ashville, NC 28816.

Sincerely, I thank The Global Bible Society for the beautiful accomplishment of the God-inspired Special Study Edition Bible. And everything else written in this book is my analogy, which is based upon the word of God as I understand it.

God bless you

Sincerely, Paul Douglas Castle

Bible story writer

Theologian of the heart

Creative story designer

Chapter One

THE SPARK OF LIFE, COALS OF FIRE

Everything formed of a material and living substance has a beginning, regardless of whether it began in the heavens above or upon this Earth. And some things originating in Heaven are on this Earth, such as you and me. And this is test ground Earth, and you and I are test subjects.

Indeed, it is easy to believe the special Living Coals of Fire living on the altar of God are extremely significant and more valuable than we can imagine. They are the essence of pure energy, love, and holiness, and they were here first and are the initial beginning of all life.

Most likely, all the things we can see and know about concerning the pure energy of the Living Coals of Fire aren't known to burn to the touch. And the supernatural Coals of Fire, not burning to the touch, means the Coals of Fire are extremely special.

Indeed, I want you to know that the special Living Coals of Fire has other symbolic names. Other names include the God element, the spark of life, the essence of pure energy, the Holy Spirit of God, and the breath of life.

Beyond the shadow of a doubt, any one of the above names means the same thing, and all of them identify with the sacred and holy substance of God. And because of their powerful uniqueness, He and they are inseparable, similar to the sun and the sunshine.

Possibly because I know for sure everything has a beginning. For this reason, I firmly believe that the Living Coals of Fire designed the form of our wonderful Supreme God. And maybe He was formed from the pure energy of their essence, more alive than anything else known to us.

It's easy to believe our wonderful Supreme God was the first to rise from the midst of the special Living Coals of Fire. And when nothing else tangible existed anywhere, our God became animated and alive during the Ancient of Days.

Mainly because He is the essence of pure energy, love, and holiness, and He's one hundred percent the special and excellent God element. The God element is the Tree of Life, and His umbrella covers every living thing in the heavens above and on this Earth.

I know it would be impossible for a flesh and blood person to place worth or value upon anything supernatural and heavenly. Because supernatural and heavenly things are priceless, they cannot be calculated in value by the flesh and blood person.

However, it would be logical to assume whatever is living upon the altar of God, inside the temple of God, and upon the mountain of God. It's the most valuable and priceless Living thing in Heaven, except for the Father, the Son, and the Holy Ghost, who are probably the same as the Living Coals of Fire.

Indeed, upon the altar of God dwells the Living Coals of Fire; they are always present and willing to help God in Heaven and upon this Earth. And the Living Coals of Fire is His helper and more loyal to Him than we can imagine.

Indeed, whatever it is, living upon the altar of God, inside the temple of God. It must be, without a doubt, Holy, Godly, righteous, loving, and pure. And upon the altar of God are the Living Coals of Fire. And they are Holy, godly, righteous, loving, and pure.

Indeed, I am saying that inside the temple of God, upon the altar, is the pure essence of Holy things. And they are considered great, godly, and alive. And God's holy and righteous works are assisted in all manner of supernatural help by the Living Coals of Fire.

Positively, I am saying the great mystery of life and everything we see that breathes began with our wonderful Creator God. Indeed, the creation of things started during a mysterious time, going way beyond the boundaries of our perception.

Beyond the boundaries of our perception includes the Supernatural Living Coals of Fire, not known to burn to the touch. And I want you to know that the Supernatural Living Coals of Fire are unlike the Coals of Fire, as we know coals of fire.

However, the highly intelligent Living Coals of Fire can create life and make material objects animated and alive. For some reason, their specialness and the extent of their abilities eludes most people, and they aren't mentioned much throughout the bible.

Indeed, the Living Coals of Fire, who live on the altar of God, are a part of God's body and glory. And most likely, the Father, the Son, and the Holy Spirit are formed from the Living Coals of Fire.

Indeed, because of their unique specialness, they are beyond comparison to the things known to us. It's easy to believe that the Holy Trinity connects with the Living Coals of Fire. In the same way, the Holy Trinity has a relationship with each other.

I assure you that the Living Coals of Fire must play an important role in the lives of the Father, the Son, and the Holy Spirit. Otherwise, the Living Coals of Fire wouldn't always be upon the altar of God, as they always are upon the altar, inside the Temple in Heaven.

I conclude that it's extremely hard and nearly impossible for humans to understand supernatural and heavenly things. And especially when they originate from the Ancient of Days and gather inside the holy temple of God.

Because of our body formation, humans struggle to understand invisible and spiritual things. And without a doubt, we cannot understand things outside our boundaries because of our God-imposed boundaries. And because God created a division, our intellect is much smaller than His.

Indeed, the Supernatural Living Coals of Fire are unusual Living Coals, and they do not burn to the touch. But they are supernatural and spectacular and cannot be associated with coals getting hot and producing heat.

Mainly because the Living Coals of Fire are the pure essence of life and pure energy, and the beginning of their unique source of power is unknown. In the same way, all things from the Ancient of Days are unknown.

The exact reason, I tell you, their power source is unknown is because it coincides with our source of life-giving power. And we cannot understand either power source, nor do we know the complexity of it.

Conclusively, the same unknown power source responsible for keeping us alive causes blood to pump through our veins. It has a similar connection, entwined to the Father, His Son, the Holy Ghost, the Living Coals of Fire, and the breath of life.

Furthermore, they all have similar feelings and feel emotions the same way we feel. And this means the Coals of Fire are alive and highly intelligent. And I guarantee you, their intelligence goes way beyond our intelligence.

All these things mentioned above connect with the Father, the Son, the Holy Ghost, and the mystery of life. And it's easy to believe that when the clay body breaks, it returns to the earth's dirt.

Then, the spirit, the essence of our internal soul, will return to God, the mountain of God, and the Living Coals of Fire. After that, our new heavenly body will most likely be formed from within the midst of the Living Coals of Fire, who live upon the altar of God.

Positively, I want you to know that our new heavenly body, made Christ-like, will not be formed from the dirt of this Earth again. And forever and ever, thanks to the power of God, we'll be much different, healthier, and stronger than we are now.

It's for sure, whatever type of substance our new heavenly body will be formed from, other than the dirt of this Earth. Thanks to our Great God, it will be animated and made alive by the Spirit within the midst of the Living Coals of Fire.

The above statements apply to you and me if we've served and worshipped our Supreme God on Earth and have a pure and loving heart. And if we obey these stipulations and keep His commandments, we can claim heritage in the kingdom of Heaven.

However, I want you to realize that living ungodly has terrible consequences. And the rebellious children of Satan, living carefree and happy-go-lucky, cannot claim heritage in Heaven. Nor will they receive a new body formed by God and the Living Coals of Fire.

Nor will their spirit, after their flesh's death, be carried to Heaven by the angels. But the spirit of the unbelievers is carried down to Hell, and it's a sad fate for the unbelievers in Christ. And for this reason, we better accept God and live a righteous lifestyle.

The wonderful Holy Ghost is the essence of pure love and pureness of heart. And if we are believers in Christ, we have a clean temple; our body and heart are the redefined temple of the pure-at-heart, caring Holy Ghost of God.

The remarkable and extraordinary Holy Ghost of God comes to us from the mountain of God and the Living Coals of Fire. And as mysterious as the Holy Ghost is to figure out, so are the mysterious Living Coals of Fire.

However, the pure and loving Holy Ghost cannot live inside an unclean temple, and it's naïve to believe He'll live inside an unclean temple. And I want you to know it would be cruel for us to want Him to live inside an unclean temple.

An unclean temple contaminated by the filthy swine identifies with an unacceptable temple, not putting a difference between the clean and the unclean. The unclean temple identifies with not putting a difference between the sinful and the just or the holy and the unholy.

Furthermore, we cannot eat unclean foods and participate in sin's impurity, nor can we do anything unclean to our body from within or physically. Nor can anyone behave wickedly and still have a clean dwelling place for the pure essence of the loving Holy Spirit of God.

I am asking you for your opinion and if you believe unclean foods aren't sinful and hurtful and will not destroy the dwelling place of the Holy Ghost. And you think they've somehow been miraculously made clean, or it doesn't matter if we eat them or put them on the dinner table.

Then, you should consider why Jesus only eats clean foods, such as honey and butter, while alive on this Earth. And I am not saying we should only eat honey and butter, as Jesus did. But I am sure the Son of God didn't eat the unclean swine meat.

Positively, we shouldn't put unclean things inside our bodies. And mainly because our body is the living temple of the Holy Spirit of God. And the unclean swine's flesh is at the top of the list of forbidden unclean meats that will defile our living temple.

> **Isaiah 7:14** Behold, a <u>virgin</u> (Mary) shall conceive, bear a Son, and call His name <u>Immanuel</u> (which means God is with us).

The following revealing scripture will illuminate a difference between the clean and the unclean through an example. The following informative example insinuates it's easier to refuse evil if we eat the clean and avoid the unclean.

> **Isaiah 7:15** BUTTER AND HONEY SHALL HE EAT THAT HE MAY KNOW TO REFUSE EVIL AND CHOOSE THE GOOD.

The indicator in the above scripture is saying a clean, loving, and pure Holy Ghost. And a clean temple, void of sin and unclean foods, is the best living temple. And I want you to know it's our responsibility to keep our living temple clean.

The above important scripture indicates that refusing to eat the unclean illustrates the key to a person's inner strength. The above scripture reveals that refusing to eat the unclean will make the person strong enough to refuse the evil and gladly choose the good.

Holy, Holy, Holy is the Father, the Son, and the Holy Ghost. And I am confident; cleanness of every kind increases pure strength to the soul. And I am telling you, the cleaner our living temple becomes, the better daily decisions we'll make.

Positively, I want you to realize that the above scripture's indication is clear. It reveals that unclean foods and rebellious sins will make a person weaker than usual against the persuasive and tempting spirit powers of darkness.

Even to the point, it'll be more challenging to refuse to do the evil and choose the good over the bad or avoid the path leading into darkness. And apparently, the scripture is revealing; an unclean living temple parallels a flaw and a weakness of the heart.

Beyond the shadow of a doubt, uncleanness symbolizes bible rejection, a dimly lit mind, darkness, corruption, and weak resistance. But cleanness symbolizes light, righteousness, and strong inner strength.

I warn you, and you should always be aware and on guard. The wicked spirit of Lucifer starts his mind control program against every person alive at an early age. And we would be foolish to believe Lucifer wants us to begin our life having a clean-living temple.

I assure you, the wicked Lucifer, our arch-enemy originating from the realms of Heaven, starts his mind control program at the beginning of life simply by making everyone unclean from birth. And mainly because the unclean person has a more challenging time refusing to do evil.

Furthermore, keeping a clean-living temple for the dwelling place of the Holy Ghost may be one of the hardest things a person ever accomplishes. And I am sure there are many people, including born-again Christians. They will live their entire life uncleanly and go to their grave being unclean.

Indeed, keeping the dwelling place of the Holy Ghost unclean is something the spirits of demons work hard to do. I am positive most flesh and blood people, including born-again Christians, do not know how thinking with an uncontaminated mind feels.

Chapter Two

LUCIFER UPON THE MOUNTAIN OF GOD

Lucifer is the beautiful and trusted angel who walked up and down within the midst of the Living Coals of Fire, located upon the mountain of God. Sadly, Lucifer was one of the chosen angels to guard the throne, alias the mercy seat, belonging to our Supreme God in Heaven.

Indeed, being a guardian angel in the temple of God allowed Lucifer to access the Living Coals of Fire, who always live upon the altar of God. Although I do not believe God permitted Lucifer to walk within the midst of the Living Coals of Fire, anytime he wanted to walk within them.

It is easy to believe that the corrupt and evil Lucifer took advantage of his position. And he decided to do extra walks within the midst of the Living Coals of Fire, all by himself, while God was away. And if he did, he was making himself extra strong.

However, for some unknown reason, our knowledge will not perceive why the God of creation created Lucifer so much more beautiful than all other angels. However, Bible scriptures reveal God favored him and gave him a unique body made from nearly every precious stone.

Lucifer received life amid the Living Stones of Fire, who reside on the mountain of God. I believe the Living Stones of Fire can make material objects animated and alive, regardless of their material origin.

Beyond the shadow of a doubt, Lucifer wasn't born from a woman's womb. And before Lucifer received the gift of life, he was a material object, not special at all. Until my Creator, God, decided to make him animated, alive, and extremely special. Undoubtedly, God is using Lucifer to give us an example of the effects of beauty and vanity.

I believe the exceptional creation of Lucifer was one of God's most significant works and one of His most beautiful creations. And because of his loyal followers, it's easy to conclude Lucifer was immensely popular among the other angels in Heaven.

Furthermore, bible scriptures indicate that being beautiful and popular seems to be the primary reason, causing the vain Lucifer to be lifted in pride. And even though they shouldn't, beauty and popularity can cause us much trouble.

Indeed, the not-so-loyal Lucifer observed my Great Creator God sitting upon His throne. And sadly, to say, Lucifer envied His position and authority. Primarily because of his beauty and popularity, Lucifer became extremely jealous of our Supreme God.

After that, his creation of near perfection, the jealous Lucifer, was overcome by vanity and the emotion of lust for power. And sadly, I must conclude the wicked Lucifer wanted to have the throne of God for himself, and he wanted to be the highest God.

The foolish and jealous Lucifer was arrogant enough to believe he should be our Great Supreme God. Indeed, his crazy, ambitious goal was inspired by his beauty, popularity, and perfection.

Therefore, because of his exceptional beauty and popularity, Lucifer realized many other angels would listen to him, and they seemed to be charmed by his philosophies. For the above reasons, Lucifer set a wicked and rebellious plan into motion.

Lucifer's objective was to deceive as many other angels as possible and convince them to follow and support him. And I believe Lucifer was stealing and merchandising the Living Coals of Fire from off the altar inside the temple.

Even though they belonged exclusively to God and were off-limits to the angels, the other angels, guilty of merchandising with Lucifer, are the angels cast out of Heaven with Lucifer. And it's logical to believe that Lucifer and his rebellious criminal partners were equally punished.

Without a doubt, Lucifer and the other wicked, rebellious angels wanted the unique and valuable Living Coals of Fire because the particular Living Coals of Fire increased their strength and supernatural abilities, going beyond their present capabilities.

Indeed, Lucifer and the other rebellious angels, determined to conquer the kingdom of God, needed extra strength before they could war against God and the good angels. And it's easy to conclude that the Living Coals of Fire was their only solution to extra strength.

Without a doubt, it's logical to believe Lucifer and the rebellious angels did need an edge on the good angels before they could expect to be victorious in their violent and revolutionary war against a more significant number of good angels and God.

Lucifer wasn't a dumb angel, but he was above average, and he realized he only had one-third of the angels following and supporting him. And it's for sure he and the other rebellious angels must've recognized the good angels, and God outnumbered them.

However, they knew the Living Coals of Fire was the only thing in Heaven strong enough to equal their odds and give them an advantage against the odds. And I believe they hoped they could absorb enough of the essence of pure energy from the Living Coals of Fire and then defeat God.

Simply because they knew the Living Coals of Fire are the essence of pure energy, the spark of life, the God element, and the elixir of strength. And Lucifer and the rebellious angels knew that whosoever's body contains the most of the God element is the most powerful.

Indeed, Lucifer wanted to be more powerful than God and everyone else in Heaven and was willing to fight God of creation for power. And it's also apparent the extreme jealousy Lucifer felt for God made his character ugly, wicked, vile, violent, and rebellious.

Certainly, his foolish heart darkened, and he became corrupt and consumed with rebellious emotions. The thought of being more powerful than God blinded his sense of righteousness, and he quit being loyal to God.

Positively, all of his wisdom became folly because of his overwhelming jealousy, and jealousy caused him to express irrational conduct. And he foolishly believed he could defeat and replace our wonderful Supreme God in Heaven and make Heaven his kingdom.

It's pretty apparent Lucifer had great confidence in his strength, and hindsight proves his confidence was a miscalculation. Bible history proves he and the other corrupt and rebellious angels became victims of their cunning and unethical activity.

Indeed, I want you to know that our advantage is the ability to look into their past, recognize their failure, and refuse to be rebellious like them. And it's easy to see; it was a foolish attempt to overthrow my Great Creator God, and they were unsuccessful.

Now, and because of their rebellion in Heaven, and upon this Earth in the Garden of God, and because of a redesigned bloodline, they are living with the righteous punishment of a pre-designed God-imposed curse, and it's because of their disobedience and rebellion.

It's an unbreakable supernatural curse, and they and their children must endure it until Judgment Day. Their supernatural pre-designed curse is illustrated through the terrible curse of a depraved mind and the unclean desire for homosexuality.

Even now, as I speak, it's a fact that their angelic homosexual physical forms are bound in the pits of Hell, and Hell is their God-designed holding place. And in the recesses of Hell, they can continue being cursed and damned, and homosexual lovers with one another, until they are thrown into the lake of fire.

However, before I continue to explain the curse of homosexuality, placed on the serpent of old Lucifer, alias the snake in the Garden of God, I want you to know the explanation includes his equally rebellious angel friends. And their cursed mixed bloodline children, born during the first Earth age.

The explanation includes why our Supreme God exiled them from His presence and the surface of this Earth. But I will first tell you from the beginning about Lucifer, a charming star in Heaven, before his fall from the grace and love of God.

I assure you, being a trusted angel inside the temple of God was a better time for the charming Lucifer. And his life was good and blessed before he became the hideous and cursed homosexual devil he is today.

Indeed, as this story unfolds, it'll be easier to understand why God cursed Lucifer with the ultimate living curse. And his curse was worse than any other curse ever placed on a man or an animal by our Supreme God.

It's for sure when our Supreme God decides its recompense time, and He puts a supernatural pre-designed curse on a man, woman, or angel. Then, the supernatural curse will not be broken until God removes the curse or destroys whosoever is cursed.

The following informative scripture speaks God's words, describing Lucifer in the making during his time in Heaven. And it's pretty apparent; my Creator God exhausted much effort toward his creation. He exhibited His superior skill when He decided to make Lucifer extremely beautiful.

Furthermore, I do not know why God made Lucifer more special than the other angels. But God blessed Lucifer immensely with advantages and gave him a dominating voice. And it's pretty apparent; his voice gained him much respect among most angels.

> **Ezekiel 28:14** <u>Thou</u> (O Lucifer, the serpent of old, alias the hideous devil) hast been in Eden, the Garden of God;

While Lucifer was in the Garden of God, he had two names he was called. One was the tree of knowledge of good and evil, and the other was the serpent of old. And I believe it would be correct to say he was also the abomination of desolation in the Garden of God.

> **Ezekiel 28:13** Every precious stone was <u>thy</u> <u>covering</u> (means his body was made from) the <u>Sardis</u> (means ruby), Topaz, and the diamond, the beryl, the onyx, and the jasper, the emerald, and the carbuncle, and gold:

> **Ezekiel 28:13** The workmanship of thy <u>tabrets</u> (means setting) of the <u>pipes</u> (means voice) was prepared in <u>thee</u> (O Lucifer, the morning star), in the day that <u>thou</u> (O Lucifer) were <u>created</u> (most likely with the help of the Stones of Fire).

The above informative scripture, taken from the book of Ezekiel, tells us about Lucifer's creation's exquisite and extraordinary beauty in Heaven. And regardless of his beauty, Lucifer is Satan, the serpent of old. And better known today as the hideous and wicked devil.

Through the prophet Ezekiel, God reveals how Lucifer was created from every precious stone. And from the description of his making, it's easy to see my Creator God put extra effort into his design. And I believe vanity overwhelmed Lucifer every time he saw his reflection.

From the prophet Ezekiel's description of Lucifer, it appears that extreme specialness was bestowed upon Lucifer. And the unthankful Lucifer was blessed to have everything an angel could want besides being blessed to have an advanced design.

However, Lucifer wanted more, and he set his eyes on the throne and the position of our Supreme God, and he wanted both of them. And there wasn't enough love in his heart for the God of creation, and he couldn't stop his aggression.

I assure you, I wouldn't be writing this story if the wicked Lucifer were the Supreme God of Heaven and Earth. But I know humanity would be in trouble or completely non-existent. And I believe we wouldn't be here today.

Even without Lucifer as our Supreme God, humankind was reduced in numbers and became almost nonexistent because of him before the great flood. And it's a good thing for humanity; our Supreme God intervened for the sake of us during the first Earth age, before the great cleansing flood.

Indeed, it's a good thing for us humans the evil Lucifer failed in his rebellion against God in Heaven, and he wasn't allowed to be the Supreme God. Otherwise, Lucifer would've destroyed all of humankind from the face of this Earth and not hesitated in doing it.

In the same way, Lucifer was destroying the flesh and blood race during the first Earth age, before the great cleansing flood. And I am confident he didn't hesitate in doing destruction. And we better realize the wicked Lucifer is our arch-enemy.

Even now, while being locked away in the pits of Hell, the evil Lucifer still wants to destroy man from the face of this Earth. And it's because they are the created children of our Great God, and they'll never recognize him as their god.

Indeed, trying to destroy humanity is what he's doing by turning everyone against each other through his power of telepathy. And it's easy to see if we aren't blind to his spiritual influence; Lucifer is a troublemaker among men and women.

Furthermore, just because he's locked away in the pits of Hell doesn't mean Lucifer is powerless to do evil works against God and humanity. Indeed, his invisible spirit of the air is a powerful evil spirit, and gifted to be a stealthy spirit allows him to be an unnoticed adversary among men.

Beyond the shadow of a doubt, his powerful spirit transmits projected thoughts into the minds of whosoever is willing to listen to him. And an analysis of this world will prove that many people are listening to the wicked spirit of Lucifer.

The scripture from Ezekiel's book, including the voice of our Great Supreme God, who speaks in many different places, clearly tells us that Lucifer is illustrated as the serpent of old, and Lucifer was in the Garden of God at Eden.

It's certain; in the Garden of God at Eden, the beautiful and charming angelic Lucifer beguiled, tricked, and seduced Eve. And the result of the serpent and Eve mixing fathered Cain, and Cain was his first-born child.

For the above reason, and as hard as it is to accept, Cain was the devil's firstborn of a mixed bloodline. This truth means Cain was the example child and became the example for many more mixed-bloodline children born after him.

Indeed, because of Lucifer, the tree of knowledge of good and evil, the Garden of God was only available to Adam and Eve for a short while. Adam and Eve were short-term residents in the Garden of God, and they incurred discipline because of rebellion against the perfect word of God.

Indeed, it's pretty clear the rebellious Lucifer was in the Garden of God in his physical form, and the snake of old was him in all his beauty. And I believe Lucifer was in the Garden of Eden shortly after the creation of Adam and Eve.

However, it's also a fact that Lucifer may have been upon this Earth before Adam and Eve and the Garden of God were created. I can conclude this statement by saying the sixth-day creation people were here first.

Furthermore, the wicked Lucifer was not a garden snake playing in an apple tree. And the sweet fruit lady Eve enjoyed from the tree of knowledge of good and evil was not an ordinary apple.

It's also pretty clear Lucifer was there in the Garden of God in Eden and deliberately planned to corrupt the children of God. This truth means Lucifer was in the Garden of God to start his bloodline, and his lineage began through the naïve and innocent Eve.

Indeed, the charming Lucifer played the innocent and naive Eve in the Garden of God as if she were a pawn in his cruel game of deception. Her only defense against Lucifer was to obey God and not eat from the Tree of Knowledge of good and evil.

The following informative scripture, taken from the book of Ezekiel, reveals the wicked Lucifer as a special angel, even though there's nothing special about being rebellious against our wonderful Creator God. And I assure you, wickedness erases his specialness.

> **Ezekiel 28:14** <u>Thou</u> (O Lucifer, the devil, the serpent of old) art the <u>anointed</u> <u>cherub</u> (means special and chosen angel), that <u>covereth</u> (means guarded the mercy seat upon the mountain of God, where the Living Coals of Fire is located);

> **Ezekiel 28:14** and <u>I</u> (the wonderful Most High God) have <u>set</u> (means made) thee so: <u>Thou</u> (O Lucifer) wast upon the <u>mountain</u> <u>of</u> <u>God</u> (where the altar of God is located, with the supernatural Living Coals of Fire upon it, who seem to come alive and assist the Holy Ghost, when they are needed as they were needed at the Pentecost Revival).

> **Ezekiel 28:14** <u>Thou</u> (O Lucifer) hast walked up and down amid the Stones of Fire.

During an unknown time in Heaven, Lucifer was a noble guardian angel upon the mountain of God, and his noble position was inside the temple of God. And I am sure Lucifer witnessed the wonderful and supernatural works of our loving Supreme God, and he knew the source of His extraordinary power.

The scriptures tell us Lucifer walked up and down within the midst of the Stones of Fire, alias the Living Coals of Fire. This truth means Lucifer knew first-hand the power of the God element, and he desired to have the God element for himself.

Furthermore, the extraordinary God element is more intriguing and desirable than anything of value in the above Heavens. And it wasn't the streets of gold, the gates of pearls, or the diamonds and rubies attractive to Lucifer.

I am pretty sure Lucifer was overwhelmed with greed for power, and he wanted to control the Living Coals of Fire, or alias the God element, and possess the spark of life. This truth means he wanted the grand prize in Heaven, and nothing less would satisfy him.

Since this story is unusual, everyone doesn't have to believe my version of Lucifer's rebellion. But it is essential to understand recompense or judgment is attached to acts of rebellion against my Great Creator God.

Positively, I want you to realize that not understanding Lucifer's rebellious fall has no bearing on our salvation. But I guarantee you that understanding Lucifer's fall will make us aware of the consequences of rebellion against the beautiful word of God.

Anyway, this informative story reveals the conclusion of my understanding concerning how and why rebellion and war began in Heaven. And maybe we'll never know the whole story until we go to Heaven, but knowing part of the story is extremely interesting.

Before this story ends, I want you to know and realize that Lucifer doesn't want you and me to win the prize of immortality. And it's because the rebellious ways of Lucifer will destroy our souls. For this reason, I encourage you to resist and not follow his wicked ways.

Indeed, if you resist eating the unclean, it'll be easier to refuse to do evil and choose to do good. And the prophet Isaiah tells us this fact in chapter seven, verse fifteen. And for your benefit, it'll be easier to journey through this life with the Holy Ghost as a guide.

Conclusively, my wonderful God is a do-good God who cannot stand evil and will burn evil angels and men in the fire. Truly, Lucifer gives us examples of things not to do, and being rebellious against God is our prime example from him.

Chapter Three

THE POTTER MAN IN HEAVEN

This enlightenment story concerning the Supernatural Potter Man in Heaven reveals material things becoming animated and alive, like you and I. And I am sure we cannot imagine all the creations our Great Creator God has brought to life in this universe.

From my understanding, these supernatural Stones of Fire, who live on the mountain of God, are inside the temple of God. The temple of God is where the Coals Of Fire call home, and this fact alone proves that they are highly esteemed among all heavenly creations.

They are the kind of stones that will not burn out and will never lessen in strength, nor do they desire to live anywhere else. And inside the temple of God, close to His altar where they live, all sorts of heavenly creations are created, and we cannot imagine their image.

Heavenly creations are given life from material objects, similar to Lucifer's creation from nearly every precious stone available in Heaven.

And I am confident that a whole new world of life will open before our eyes after we go to Heaven.

My wonderful Supreme God was and still is the Potter Man in Heaven, upon the mountain of God. In the same way, he was the Potter Man on Earth thousands of years ago. And when we go to Heaven, the Potter Man will design us a new Christ-like body.

Indeed, His works are a beautiful example, revealing the creative abilities of the Potter Man. The Cloven Tongues on Fire at the Pentecost Revival came first from the mountain of God, and the Stones of Fire and the altar are located near His glorious throne.

The fact is clear concerning our incredible Potter Man and the accomplishments accredited to His record. And I am saying He's responsible for the supernatural creation of angels and heavenly creatures, such as the amazing Seraphim that do temple duties.

These unique creations are brought to life upon the mountain of God, inside the temple of God, and by the Great Potter Man. Material objects, such as diamonds, pearls, and gold, including many other created materials, are used by our Supreme God to create living forms of creatures that breathe and live.

Furthermore, He gives a lot of strength to some of His creations. And because of design, some of His creations aren't so strong. And if what I say sounds impossible to believe, look into the mirror and visualize beyond the flesh after it dies, and only the spirit remains.

Then, consider the possibility of Adam and his body being formed from a material object called the dirt of this Earth. And then imagine the dirt man becoming flexible, and all of a sudden, within the twinkling of the eye, blood was pumping through his heart.

Then, consider how Eve was formed from a material object called the rib, or the bone of Adam. And then imagine her becoming flexible and beautiful and desirable to the man. And please realize we must have an awesome Creator God.

Adam received life by the breath of life, and the breath of life came directly from within the body of my Supernatural God because our Holy and wonderful God exhaled the Spirit from His mouth and directly into the nostrils of Adam.

Most likely, the powerful breath of life had its beginning upon the mountain of God. And from within the Living Coals of Fire, who live upon the altar of God. I am confident animating life is only one of their many capabilities.

I assure you, our amazing Supernatural God and the Living Coals of Fire are one. And I hope you realize that both are the essence of pure energy and love and are exceedingly supernatural beyond our imagination.

Indeed, as hard as it is to understand, a dirt material body changed its form instantly after God breathed into the nostrils of Adam. And it became animated, and bones formed, and flesh and blood came alive because of the God element.

The Living Coals of Fire, who live on the special altar of God, are a mystery to the flesh and blood people on this Earth. But heavenly creations receive more of the essence of energy and are much wiser than us, and they understand the mystery and the importance of the Living Coals of Fire.

Indeed, the beautiful Living Coals of Fire uniquely differ from the hot fires burning on this Earth. And they do not appear to be the kind of fire that can burn hot, nor do they destroy or consume. And I am confident they never burn out or reduce to ashes.

However, they seem to have the power to enhance or make better and give strength to everything they touch. But if the mind is corrupt and evil, similar to the mind of Lucifer, they will not change evil into godliness. And he did have free will to be rebellious against God if he wanted to oppose God, and everything evil opposes God.

Therefore, because of his constant wickedness, nothing can make him righteous and loyal to God. And I assure you, the excellent Living Coals of Fire will not oppose his free will or make him godlier against his will.

Indeed, the Living Coals of Fire seems to be a kind of fire similar to the essence of pure energy. Although, their type of energy is unknown to us and unavailable to us. And they are a different kind of energy than we are accustomed to seeing, even though their power gives us life.

The Living Coals of Fire's pure energy is equivalent to the breath of life, the spark of life, and the Holy Ghost. And this kind of unique energy surpasses all other types of energy. And because of its importance, the Living Coals of Fire have residence upon the altar inside the temple of God.

My Great and wonderful God always seems to have a holy prophet, wiser than most men and stationed at specific historical points. And sometimes, the God of Heaven and Earth uses His loyal prophets to shine a light on the mysteries of Heaven.

Isaiah is one of our great prophets of God and possesses incredible knowledge concerning divine creations. He reveals some of the power of the Living Coals of Fire through his personal story during his visitation moment before the throne of God in Heaven.

Indeed, Isaiah's personal story tells us a bit about the work of the Living Coals of Fire, who live upon God's holy and sacred altar. And I am sure holy and sacred are applicable definitions of the beautiful Living Coals of Fire.

The prophet Isaiah tells us he was touched on the mouth by one of the Living Coals of Fire, and it didn't seem to burn his lips. But the Living Coals of Fire made Isaiah a better man than before the Living Coals of Fire touched him. And I know it's an honor for whoever is touched by them.

I say these Living Coals of Fire are alive and have awareness because, Isaiah said, it was a Live Coal touching his mouth. And being a Live Coal means it is alive. And I am sure the Live Coal was a supernatural Living Coal of Fire.

The following few informative scriptures reveal the prophet Isaiah being called up to Heaven in a vision and standing inside the temple of God. But be assured, his vision was true and accurate, and it wasn't any different than him standing inside the temple of God.

Indeed, the unusual and amazing living creatures Isaiah saw inside the temple of God are a true depiction of his vision of the mountain of God. It proves his ghost spirit was privileged to see out-of-this-world creations while standing in Heaven before my Great Creator God.

Within the following awareness scripture, giving us a glimpse inside the temple of God, you and I will be able to visualize the things the prophet Isaiah describes. And I assure you, Isaiah paints a beautiful picture of God sitting upon His throne.

Isaiah 6:1 In the year that King Uzziah died, I (Isaiah) also saw the Lord sitting upon a throne, high and lifted (means the throne of God, and He was worshipped, and honored by all the host in Heaven),

Isaiah 6:1 and His train (means train, or length of the tail of his robe) filled the temple, (and) above it (His throne) stood the Seraphims's: Each one had six wings (and they most likely flew everywhere they went, and not walked);

Isaiah 6:2, with two (wings), he covered its face, and with two (wings), he covered its feet, and with two (wings), he did fly.

Isaiah 6:3 And one (of the supernatural Seraphim) cried unto another, and said, HOLY, HOLY, HOLY, is The LORD of hosts (means Yehovah, the King of kings, the LORD to everyone present in the temple of Heaven):

Isaiah 6:3 (And the Seraphim said) the whole Earth is full of His glory (means full of the supernatural works of The LORD's creation).

I assure you, the winged creatures inside the temple of God, called the Seraphims, are the creations of the Potter Man in Heaven. And I am sure Heaven has a lot of different types of creations, and it'll be glorious to see all of them.

The above enlightenment scriptures do not reveal the kind of material substance of the Seraphim's creations. But we can be sure their life began as a material object and then animated after receiving the spark of life.

After that, the Seraphim was given the spark of life and a position inside the temple of God, and they could see, fly, walk, understand, and talk to God. And I am confident we'll talk to them when we arrive in Heaven.

It's obvious because the prophet Isaiah says so; their place of habitation is inside the temple of God and upon the holy mountain of God. And their duties are to help God concerning many of His temple functions and achievements.

Indeed, the Seraphins gladly do whatsoever my wonderful God commands them to do, and they are completely trustworthy and loyal to Him. And I assure you when we go to Heaven, God will expect us to be faithful and loyal to Him, too.

The following puzzling scripture has specific details to consider, and this detail means it may reveal a supernatural living temple, animated and alive. And just because it's a building in Heaven, it doesn't mean it's a material object building and doesn't have life.

I am sure there are more things alive in Heaven than we know, and everything alive began from a material object. And I want you to know that the Great Potter Man in Heaven is the Artist, the skilled Designer of every creation in Heaven and on this Earth.

Beyond the shadow of a doubt, He's been designing all sorts of things for billions of years, and He can give life to anything He wants to and desires to create. And it's because He's an incredible Supernatural God and doesn't have limitations and boundaries.

Indeed, the following unusual and unexplainable scripture reveals the temple's doorpost moving to the Seraphim's voice. And we can be specific: the doorposts weren't made of wood, and they aren't metal posts.

> **Isaiah 6:4** And the posts of the <u>door</u> (on the temple of God) moved at the voice of <u>him</u> (the supernatural Seraphim) that cried,

> **Isaiah 6:4** and the <u>house</u> (of the LORD) was filled with <u>smoke</u> (most likely caused by the Living Coals of Fire, which appeared to be a cloud).

> **Isaiah 6:5** Then said <u>I</u> (Isaiah), woe is me! For I am <u>undone</u> (means out of place); because I am a man of unclean lips,

> **Isaiah 6:5** and I <u>dwell</u> (in the company, and live) amid a <u>people</u> (means earthly people) of unclean lips:

> **Isaiah 6:5** For mine eyes have seen the <u>King</u>, <u>the</u> <u>LORD</u> of the <u>host</u> (means that Isaiah was standing inside the house of the LORD and has seen Yehovah in all His glory, the King of Heaven and Earth).

> **Isaiah 6:6** Then flew one of the <u>Seraphim's</u> (means supernatural heavenly creatures) unto <u>me</u> (Isaiah), having a <u>Live Coal</u> (means a supernatural Living Coal, Pure and Holy) in his hand,

Isaiah 6:6, which he had taken with the tongs from off the <u>altar</u> (of our wonderful and Holy God, upon the mountain of God):

Isaiah 6:7 And <u>he</u> (the supernatural heavenly creature) laid <u>it</u> (the supernatural Living Coal from off the altar of God) upon my mouth,

Isaiah 6:7 said, Lo, <u>this</u> (Holy Living Supernatural Coal) hath touched thy lips; and thine <u>iniquity</u> (means thy sins, uncleanness, and guilt) is taken away, and thy <u>sin</u> <u>purged</u> (means removed and forgiven).

The extraordinary and supernatural Living Coal of Fire, the Seraphim took from off the altar of God have a Living Spirit. And I believe the pure and Holy Living Spirit must be a Holy Ghost Spirit since its dwelling place is upon the altar of God.

It appears that these supernatural Living Coals of Fire have the supernatural ability to purify and cleanse a man of sin. And when the mouth of Isaiah was touched by a Holy and Living Coal of Fire, Isaiah was purified and cleansed of his sins.

However, it appears that the Living Coals of Fire didn't have the same effect on Lucifer as on the prophet Isaiah. And just for speculation, there must be a logical reason: the Living Coals of Fire didn't have the same effect on Lucifer as they had on Isaiah.

It could be because the heart of Isaiah and Lucifer desired different gifts from the Living Coals of Fire. And maybe his greed, jealousy, and overwhelming envy couldn't be suppressed, and the wicked Lucifer didn't want to be cleansed and purified.

Indeed, it could be possible; these compassionate and wonderful Living Coals of Fire are the Living Spirit of the Living Holy Ghost. And the living Holy Ghost knows the heart's desires, and they only purify a willing heart wishing to be purified.

I am confident the mystery of life began with our Supreme God and these extremely Holy Supernatural Living Coals of Fire. And I conclude, God has many helpers in Heaven. And I guarantee you, the excellent Living Coals of Fire is one of them.

Furthermore, if you notice in the above scripture, you'll be forced to realize a specific detail paralleling a characteristic of God. The Living Coals of Fire touched the mouth of Isaiah, and his sins were taken away and purged and forgiven.

I want you to realize the purification this Holy Living Coal of Fire did for Isaiah; our great Supreme God does for us also when we become a new person in Christ. And I want you to realize this parallel accomplishment proves they both purify and cleanse men.

Therefore, it appears probable that these Living Coals of Fire are Holy, similar to how my God is Holy. And as hard as it is to consider, it appears that the Living Coals of Fire has the same power as our Supreme God.

However, the Living Coals of Fire obey the voice of our wonderful and Holy Supreme God, and after the death of our flesh. It's easy to believe you and I will submit ourselves to the hands of the Potter man, and we'll be remade from a different substance other than dirt.

Therefore, just maybe, we'll be remade with the help of the Living Coals of Fire, who dwell inside the temple of God. But God is the Potter Man in Heaven, and He decides who receives a remake or redesign by the Living Coals of Fire.

The believers in Christ are the chosen people rewarded with a new body made from a new material element. And I want you to know whatever material is used to form our new body, it'll be much better than the substance called dirt, and there probably isn't any dirt in Heaven.

I believe that the good angels are constantly ascending and descending, up and down between Heaven and Earth. I also believe the children of our wonderful God of creation are lifted and carried to Heaven by an angel after the death of their flesh.

However, the unbelievers are carried down to Hell, and no one in the spirit truly dies until after Judgment Day. However, after the death of the flesh, the believers and the unbelievers go separate ways and may never see each other again.

Positively, some pottery stands the test of time, and some pottery cannot stand the test of time. The following informative scripture reveals a lot about the works of the Potter Man if you dare to consider the enormity of its meaning.

> **Romans 9:21** Have not the Potter power over the clay; of the same lump to make one vessel unto honor and another unto dishonor?

Surely, the way we conducted ourselves during a different lifetime, or a previous earth age, or a heavenly age is an indication the Great Potter Man considers when He forms and molds the clay unto honor or dishonor.

This truth means some vessels are intentionally formed with cracks and flaws by the Potter Man, who collects recompense on violators from the past. And maybe a vessel made unto dishonor is paying a price tag for sin, and he's unaware of his pre-designed judgment.

Conclusively, when we see a person living with a terrible supernatural God-imposed curse, the curse causes them shame. Then it's probably because the Potter Man made them unto dishonor and not out of durable clay.

Positively, we better take this life and the word of God seriously or face the consequences of being built flawed. And if we think we can sin, be disobedient to God, and escape unscarred, then we are wrong.

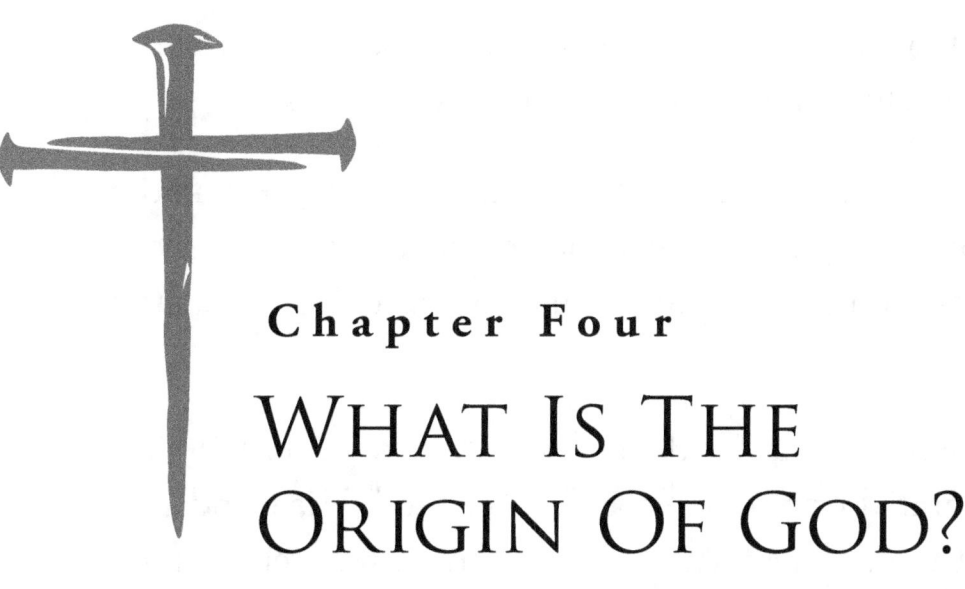

Chapter Four

What Is The Origin Of God?

I t's easy to believe these extremely Holy Living Coals of Fire are a part of the whole essence of God from His head to His toe. And it's because of His uniqueness and His incredible supernatural abilities. And because He's our wonderful Creator, God made from the best material in Heaven.

This truth means the God of Heaven and Earth is inseparable from their essence, including body, heart, mind, and Spirit. And I am confident that the essence of God and these Living Coals of Fire are one with each other, and they have a connection we cannot fully imagine.

Beyond the shadow of a doubt, the essence of our Creator God and the essence of the Living Coals of Fire are both supernatural and holy. And because He loves us, both exceed the boundaries of specialness and deserve our greatest respect.

Positively, and without a doubt, our Creator God is the God element, the spark of life, the essence of pure energy, the breath of life, and the Holy

Ghost. None of the above can be separated from the other, even if the Father, the Son, and the Holy Ghost are three different entities.

I believe the unity between the three is the Living Coals of Fire, and the Living Coals of Fire are probably the substance of their body formation. And I do not know of anything else more adequate or more fitting for their formation.

I am confident that the Living Coals of Fire, who live upon the altar of God, cannot be separated from our Great Creator God, His wonderful Son, or the wonderful Holy Ghost. And I believe the three were formed from the best heavenly element available.

Many times throughout my years of living, I've heard people wonder out of curiosity, just where did our Supreme Creator God come from, and who made Him? And I want you to know this is a good question and deserves some of our study time.

Indeed, many people will wonder and say that no one knows what God was created from or how His existence began out of curiosity. And they wonder, who could've been responsible for creating Him, or did He somehow create Himself from nothing?

Positively, men wonder how He has the power to create us, and their questions entwine with the mystery of life. And the mystery of life began with the pure essence of energy, and the answer radiates from the Living Coals of Fire.

The only logical explanation is clear to me, and I believe my Great Creator God was the first creation created from the Living Coals of Fire.

And this means He's part of the pureness of the Living Coals of Fire, and everything He is in uniqueness, the Coals of Fire are too.

Furthermore, the sacred altar of God, inside the holy temple of God, upon the mountain of God, correlates with the home of the Living Coals of Fire. And I am not saying that the special Living Coals of Fire are restricted to the altar because they do not stay confined to the altar of God.

The special Living Coals of Fire do not burn to the touch, but they are powerful and immortal and have abilities beyond our imagination. And I am sure they do many amazing things in this universe, unbeknownst to us.

As for my wonderful God, sometimes His appearance is fire from His loins upward and fire from His loins downward, but He's not a consuming fire. But He's powerful and immortal and can be anything; He wants to be in appearance and even be a burning bush in the desert.

Furthermore, bible scriptures prove that His appearance of fire didn't consume the burning bush while talking to Moses in the desert. And as remarkable as His appearance was to look upon, the burning bush wasn't harmed by Him.

Our Supreme God and the Holy Living Coals of Fire could have the same substance since they share characteristics. But they still have individuality and separate bodies and can transform into other creations.

This truth means they are powerful; they could be transformed birds flying through the air or a bumblebee sucking nectar from a flower. And because of their transformable abilities, we wouldn't know we are in the presence of our Great God.

Therefore, in all probability, our Supreme Supernatural God and the amazing Living Coals of Fire are created from the essence of pure energy. And because of shared characteristics, their closeness to each other is undeniable.

John the Baptist says the excellent Son of God baptizes men and women with the Holy Ghost and fire. The special fire John the Baptist talks about could reference the Living Coals of Fire, which reside upon the special altar of God most of the time.

Mainly because the Living Coals of Fire and the Holy Ghost are probably the same because of compatibility, and I ask you, what better place could both of them call home, other than the altar of God, inside the temple of God?

The pure and holy Living Coals of Fire is always upon God's altar, and I believe the altar of God sits in front of His throne. And when men, women, and children bow down before the altar, they pray inside God's house.

Their prayers go up to Heaven, before the altar of God in Heaven, and within the proximity of His throne. And again, I assure you, the Holy Living Coals of Fire dwell upon the holy mountain of God and always stay close to our Holy God.

Indeed, the Living Coals of Fire, the Son of God, and our Superior God are the most valuable creations in Heaven. And I am confident that the altar is their centerpiece of activity within the great temple in Heaven.

Therefore, the puzzling question, seemingly hard to answer, is meant to be a great mystery; we can only assume the answer, too: What is the origin of God? It's most logically answered by assuming He was created from within the midst of the Living Coals of Fire.

Because there isn't any other material substance, tangible or intangible, that can create life or create a Supreme God, this truly means the Living Coals of Fire is so unique that only heavenly creations are aware of their existence.

I believe the Father, the Son, and the Holy Ghost are probably the only three created one hundred percent from the Living Coals of Fire. And because of the angel rebellion in Heaven, it's easy to conclude that it wouldn't be wise to create everyone equal and have the same strength and power as Him.

The Living Coals of Fire, alias the spark of life, the essence of pure energy, the God element, or the unknown substance from the Ancient of Days, were probably here first. And it was during a time when this universe was most likely empty and nothing but space where no one lived.

Most likely, the Father, the Son, and the Holy Ghost were probably the first creations in the Heavens above. And they are the Ancient Ones, created from the Ancient of Days. And they may be billions of years old and the reason for the tangible form of everything our eyes see.

Except for the wicked Lucifer's modification to their created bloodline before the great cleansing flood during the first Earth age, the mixed bloodline, or the third bloodline, is the rebellious angels' created heritage.

Positively, some abilities are more special than others, and the power of creation is monumental. And My Great God controls the creation of everything that lives. And every material substance we see is a creation; God created from the voids of the air.

The Father, the Son, and the Holy Ghost have the supernatural ability to make material substances from nothing and then make material substances animated and alive. Indeed, their powers are so far beyond the imagination of men; even our imagination rejects our imagination.

I assure you, there's no magic in this world capable of equaling their supernatural abilities. But we can be assured that the substance upon the altar of God, the mountain of God, and within the temple of God is extremely special, and their value is priceless.

Without a doubt, the substance called the Living Coals of Fire is the silent strength behind the tremendous power of God. And the Living Coals of Fire could be one of Heaven's most valuable living forms and completely unthought-of by us men and women living on Earth.

Positively, the Living Coals of Fire is the least talked about subject by the Father, the Son, and the prophets because all men don't need to know about the Living Coals of Fire and their supernatural uniqueness.

Mainly because many men would worship them instead of worshipping God, and this is a mistake this story advises against making. But there will come a day, and a time, after the death of our flesh, when we'll understand the meaning of life.

Furthermore, I am confident that the Living Coals of Fire's great mystery will be revealed, and we will be made differently from what we are now. And it'll be an incredible transformation from what we were while being alive in the flesh.

However, please be warned and reject being rebellious against the word of God. And it's because He's the Potter Man, and we are the clay. And for the benefit of winning the prize of immortality, we do not want to be shaped the wrong way.

This truth means the Supernatural Potter Man has power over our formation, and His evaluation will form us appropriately. And this declaration of truth should cause you and me to be a hot and on fire Christian, determined to do right.

Chapter Five

THE FOX IN THE HEN HOUSE

Lucifer was one of the special angels; my Great God chose to guard the mercy seat upon the mountain of God, and this privilege was exceedingly great. Therefore, within this informative story, I will add a new name to his many names.

Positively, this exposure story portrays him as a fox in the hen house instead of a loyal and trustworthy angel. And mainly because Lucifer exhibits the stealing and killing characteristics of a fox in the hen house rather than having the characteristics of a good angel.

Beyond the shadow of a doubt, all indications indicate Lucifer as a jealous, rebellious angel, heartless thief, and deceiver in Heaven. And it's easy to conclude the wicked Lucifer was as uncompassionate as a sly old fox inside the hen house.

The fox in the hen house analogy describes him well. And it's because he desired to have the powerful and holy things that belonged to God. The things he desired to steal in the temple of God include the throne of God and the Living Coals of Fire, who live upon God's altar.

The wicked Lucifer should be illustrated as a hungry fox guarding the hen house who wanted all the eggs. The hen house symbolizes the throne, the eggs symbolize the Living Coals of Fire, and the sly old fox wants them both.

Lucifer warred against God because he thought he could defeat Yehovah and be our Supreme God in Heaven. And it must've been the desire of his heart to sit upon the throne of God, inside the temple of God, and have control of the Living Coals of Fire.

God did love Lucifer extremely much, and I believe the heart of God hurt badly because of the rebellious character of Lucifer. And He did lament and wept over Lucifer, nearly the same way King David wept over his son, Absalom.

The unthankful and cruel-hearted Lucifer couldn't feel the emotions of love, and he didn't love his creator God back. But he did know about the power of God and the power of the Living Coals of Fire, who live upon God's altar.

I am certain the mystery of life wasn't a secret to Lucifer because he must've understood the mystery of creation. And I am certain Lucifer watched God enough to know God can take material objects and turn them into animated living objects or creations.

Suppose you are a skeptic and need a good example of material objects filled with God's Holy Spirit. Then, it would help if you considered the wooden staff that belonged to Moses and its ability to turn into a living serpent whenever necessary.

Truly, you should consider the living supernatural mantle of Elisha, endowed with the power to stand waters up in a heap. The supernatural mantle of Elisha that caused iron to swim was instrumental in turning bitter waters into sweet waters.

Certainly, there was also the supernatural living Ark of the Covenant, who commanded respect, proving itself extremely supernatural. For example, it supernaturally caused a wooden carved-out god the Philistines call Dagon to fall on his face and break into many pieces.

The power within the Ark of the Covenant did cause whole cities of Philistine people to have tumors, and thousands died. Not only did it do the above things, but the power within it killed anyone unauthorized to touch the Living Ark of the Testimony.

However, I assure you, and you do need to realize, it's not the wooden staff of Moses, the fabric cloth mantle, or the cape of Elisha. Nor the Ark of the Testimony, endowed with supernatural powers that can perform miracles and kill rebellious men.

However, it's the Living Holy Spirit of God endowed with great and Godly supernatural powers, and He's the reason for the above miracles. And it's the invisible Living Holy Ghost, capable of causing material objects to be supernatural creations.

I assure you supernatural creations have life in them, just as our dirt bodies have life in them, and it's because of the God element. And anything, or anyone, filled with the power of the Living Holy Ghost can do supernatural things.

Even anyone with some of the wonderful Holy Ghost in them can, at the least, understand supernatural things. And I want you to realize that the stronger our Holy Ghost is inside of us, the more supernatural things we'll understand.

It's for certain the holy mountain of God, illustrates a special place in Heaven, and it's where out-of-the-ordinary things happen. And the grand temple of God sits upon the holy mountain of God, and God commands His will to be done from within the temple.

Therefore, all these out-of-the-ordinary things happen from the same location, where the Living Coals of Fire is upon God's sacred and holy altar. And it's regardless of your thoughts concerning the Living Coals of Fire and their involvement with God.

Indeed, this means, regardless of how we might be inclined to imagine, the way the sequence of things works in Heaven. Please remember that the special Living Stones of Fire always stay close to our wonderful God, like an inseparable friend staying loyal.

I believe the Living Coals of Fire and God were together initially during the Ancient of Days. And after all these billions of years, they still are together in Heaven and travel together throughout the universe.

Extremely special and unique supernatural things are accomplished upon the holy and sacred mountain of God and from the midst of the Stones of Fire. And it's quite possible all the things we consider a mystery are the results of planning inside the temple of God.

The beauty and uniqueness of Lucifer were most likely created with the amazing help of the Stones of Fire. But I believe too much of everything was given to Lucifer, and sadly, it swelled his imagination beyond the boundaries of reality.

All his glory was twisted with an ungodly mix of moral values, which he apparently couldn't control. And bible scriptures reveal that his heart was lifted, and his pride, beauty, and foolish imagination corrupted him.

In Heaven, Lucifer became unthankful, not loyal to his wonderful Creator God, his Father in Heaven, and the next informative scripture, taken from the book of Ezekiel, illuminates the mixture of his perfection and foolish imagination.

> **Ezekiel 28:15** <u>Thou</u> (O Lucifer, the devil) wast perfect in thy ways from the day that <u>thou</u> (O Lucifer) wast <u>created,</u> (upon the mountain of God, and from within the proximity of the Stones of Fire),

> **Ezekiel 28:15** till <u>iniquity</u> (sin, rebellion, deceitfulness, and unrighteousness) was found in thee.

The beautiful and trusted Lucifer was the foolish, ungodly adversary who worked deceitfully behind God's back. And as hard as it is to imagine such disloyalty in Heaven, Lucifer decided to blaze his trail and disrupt an orderly kingdom.

Lucifer was doing something in Heaven, identified as ungodly, not loyal, and not untrustworthy. Maybe Lucifer was stealing and merchandising the most valuable substance in Heaven, located upon the sacred altar of God.

Whatever evil Lucifer was doing, it was causing troubles and violence in Heaven among the corrupt angels and the honorable angels. And I assume Lucifer's unauthorized merchandising had something to do with the valuable Living Coals of Fire living on the altar of God.

The incredible Living Coals of Fire were always upon the altar of God, and they greatly enhanced the angels' power, strength, and wisdom. And maybe gaining strength from the Living Coals of Fire was a temptation Lucifer couldn't resist.

All indications insinuate the trusted guardian Cherub, called Lucifer, turned corrupt and untrustworthy. And it appears he uncaringly began stealing and merchandising the supernatural things that belonged to God. And I am certain God will not tolerate acts of corruption in Heaven.

The above indication means the corrupt Lucifer was taking something valuable out of the sacred temple of God. And the Living Coals of Fire are the prized valuables inside the temple. And I am certain Lucifer wanted the most valuable prize.

Mainly because all of the other material things in Heaven are valuable but are, according to our standards; however, in Heaven, they are simply a part of its material structure, not barter. And I believe precious material things were plentiful everywhere in Heaven and as common as water.

Furthermore, gold and silver, diamonds and pearls, haven't any great value to the angels in Heaven. This truth means Lucifer didn't rebel against God for valuable metals and jewels. But he did want something precious, and it was most likely the Living Coals of Fire.

However, our wonderful Supreme God couldn't look the other way, and his problem with Lucifer had to be confronted and dealt with appropriately. And our wonderful God had to do what was right, regardless of the name of the angel it affected.

It's easy to conclude that our Great God couldn't allow Lucifer to continue stealing, deceiving, corrupting, and merchandising His divine creations. And for this reason, our Supreme God cast Lucifer, the thief and manipulator, off the mountain of God and out of Heaven.

I am certain God restricted Lucifer from ever again getting close enough to walk up and down and within the midst of the Stones of Fire. And maybe the rebellious and wicked Lucifer will never step into the kingdom of Heaven again, at least not as an angel with freedom.

Truly, this informative story, The Fox in the Hen House, profiles the characteristics of Lucifer in Heaven. But this is a sad story concerning a beautiful angel and him being guilty of lusting for more and more when he already had everything he needed.

Truly, it's quite obvious that the wicked Lucifer wasn't content with all God had given him, including his noble position in Heaven. And his wonderful, indestructible body, which God made especially for him, lifted him in pride, and he wanted more.

The wicked Lucifer had everything an angel could want except for the throne of God and control of the Living Coals of Fire. But it's quite obvious that Lucifer disregarded any appreciation for his good gifts from God and sought to have it all.

Even though my wonderful creator God is our merciful and loving Father in Heaven, everything has a stopping point. The stopping point came for the rebellious and wicked Lucifer when he decided to rob and take from his Father, who was also his Creator.

Without a doubt, the phrase saying God knows no respect for persons also includes the angels in Heaven. And this statement is proven true because of His reaction to Lucifer. And we may as well realize God puts righteousness first, and He'll cast the rebels out of Heaven.

I am certain the mercy seat in Heaven, upon the holy mountain of God, and inside the beautiful temple of God, is another symbolic word for the throne of God. And the throne of my great God, and the mercy seat of God, are the same thing in Heaven.

Furthermore, mercy is given from the throne of God, and compensation is decided and applied from the throne of God. And the wonderful Potter Man is our Great God, who sits on the mercy seat, and all material objects are His clay.

Furthermore, because of rebellion in Heaven and during the first Earth age, before the great cleansing flood, we may as well realize the Potter Man molds and shapes some men and women to honor and some to dishonor.

Beyond the shadow of a doubt, the honorable and the dishonorable both come through a woman's womb and are born a certain way—including rebellious men, men of diversity, and men not interested in knowing the word of God.

They most likely owe a debt on sin from a long time ago, perhaps from a previous Earth or heavenly age. And I suspect that the larger our price tag is for sin and rebellion, the more dishonorable the Potter Man shapes the clay vessel.

Before this look into the past story, called the fox in the hen house, comes to an end. I believe there was a great fight inside the temple of God, and it happened because the perfect Son of God caught the fox stealing power from the Living Coals of Fire.

Chapter Six

WRATH APPLIED TO LUCIFER

Most all things are conceived within the heart, meaning the brain and heart must be connected. And the heart of the wicked Lucifer was lifted in pride and beauty, and he used his God-given advantages for selfish reasons.

Positively, vanity has negative effects, and because he thought so highly of himself, it corrupted his wisdom because of his brightness. Bible scriptures reveal that his conscience was seared, and his mind became darker than his black heart.

After his heart was lifted, and his glory was all he could see, his brightness faded like a sunset after the end of a long day. And sadly, I must conclude that Lucifer became unfit to be a resident in the kingdom of God and was cast onto this Earth.

After that, the wicked Lucifer became a resident on Earth among the weaker flesh and blood creations he didn't respect. As for us frail humans, having the evil Lucifer here is like living amid a terrible and hurtful storm that never stops destroying.

Here on this Earth, Lucifer decided to continue spreading his corruption, and the degree of it increased with time. But this time, he spreads corruption among the flesh and blood residents before the cleansing flood.

The corruption and wickedness Lucifer was doing on this Earth began in the Garden of God in Eden. It began when Lucifer mixed his angelic seed, and his choice of female was Eve, the naïve flesh and blood woman and Adam's mate.

Rebellion in Heaven and rebellion on this Earth against God identify the reason for a supernatural imposed curse on Lucifer. And the two terrible paths, never known before to angels and humanity, began at the root of the tree of knowledge of good and evil.

Number one is the path to Hell, and **number two** is the supernatural pre-designed curse of homosexuality. Both pathways began at the feet of Lucifer, and Lucifer is the cursed tree of knowledge of good and evil as he was in the Garden of God.

Positively, his pathway is built and paved with dishonesty, corruption, uncleanness, and everything rebellious against God. And sadly, I must tell you, his evil works began in Heaven. And after his fall, the problem became a problem for the people on this Earth.

Lucifer is our prime example of rebellion, ungodliness, hate, and mockery toward our Supreme God. And all the people living on this Earth who are guilty of corruption and dishonesty, are portrayed by the character of Lucifer.

Furthermore, they'll become residents where he is now, and they'll get to know Lucifer personally. And it's because the Judgment Scales of God are fair and accurate, and shared compatibility will be residents with compatibility in the afterlife.

The loyal Apostle Paul puts much effort into describing some of the characteristics of Lucifer and the other rebellious angels. His analogy includes the children of angels and men and women with ungodly and unclean lifestyles, similar to their angelic fathers.

Suppose you want to know more about Lucifer, the wicked, rebellious angels, and their God-imposed pre-designed curse. A full description of their terrible and ungodly characteristics is revealed and told in the book of Romans by the Apostle Paul.

Erroneously, many people mistakenly believe the Apostle Paul is talking about the Roman people only. Although Paul is talking about some of the Roman people, he's not talking only about the Roman people.

Beyond the shadow of a doubt, the Apostle Paul also talks about the rebellious angels and other people who emulate the cursed children before the great cleansing flood. And this means the scriptures written within the Book of Romans have dual meanings.

Anyway, the Apostle Paul's description is a more fitting description of Lucifer, his angelic associates, and their mixed bloodline children. Even more so than the second Earth age homosexuals and the ungodly people of Rome.

Although, because of this world's bad condition and overwhelming ungodliness, I believe the Apostle Paul is talking about both because he uses the word *they*, which includes more than one group of people.

> **Romans 1:23** And <u>they</u> (Lucifer and the rebellious angels) changed the glory of the incorruptible God, into an image made like to (the image of a) corruptible man, birds, four-footed beasts, and creeping things.

The Apostle Paul uses unclean animals, such as birds, four-footed beasts, and creeping creations, and they portray a picture. Paul uses them to illustrate the unclean image; these heavenly, rebellious, and corrupt angels were projecting upon the image of God.

Surely, the primary reason the Apostle Paul uses these unclean beasts is to illustrate an unclean image. These unclean animals and creeping things are the most unclean living things on this Earth for us to identify with for comparison.

Therefore, God places the supernatural curse on the wicked Lucifer and the other rebellious angels. It's a suitable curse, an unchangeable unclean image, and a fitting recompense for Lucifer and all the rebellious angels.

After reading the next informative scripture, it should be quite obvious the ultimate supernatural pre-designed curse is applied to Lucifer. I believe this curse was designed specifically for him and his followers because of the chaos he was causing.

Beyond the shadow of a doubt, the supernatural curse placed on Lucifer is the king of all curses. And it's above and worse than the curse placed on the unclean beasts of the Earth, designed to eat road kill, dead things, and forbidden things.

According to most people, pre-designed homosexuality is the king of all curses, and there's none worse and more shameful. And because of the way they mate, being full of gay pride isn't a characteristic worthy to claim.

> **Genesis 3:14** And the LORD God said unto the <u>serpent</u> (Lucifer, the devil, the serpent in the Garden of God at Eden) because <u>thou</u> (O Lucifer) hast <u>done</u> <u>this</u> (means mixed your seed with Eve), <u>thou</u> (O Lucifer) are cursed <u>above</u> (means more so, and) above all cattle,

> **Genesis 3:14** and <u>above</u> (means more so than) every beast of the field; and upon <u>thy</u> <u>belly</u> (means shameful and unclean image)

> **Genesis 3:14** shalt thou <u>go</u> (means live with), and <u>dust</u> (means humility and shame,) shalt <u>thou</u> (O Lucifer) <u>eat</u> (means live with) all the days of thy life.

Therefore, although many Romans were ungodly, they weren't as ungodly, unclean, and corrupt as the wicked fallen angels. And I believe I can accurately say the fallen angels are the worst of the worst.

Furthermore, I do not believe the ungodly Roman people were cursed more than every unclean animal. As the scriptures reveal, the wicked Lucifer, the other rebellious angels, and the corrupt seed of rebellious angels were cursed.

Therefore, it appears for certain these descriptive and unclean homosexual descriptions have dual definitions. And maybe they have multiple meanings, meant to illustrate more than one group of people, angels, and children of angels.

However, in the explanation book of Romans, the scriptures reveal a supernatural cursed people. And I believe the Apostle Paul mostly talks about the ungodly Lucifer, the cursed angels, and their mixed bloodline children.

I fully believe it was because of Lucifer and his ungodly and unthankful ways, violent rebellion, and corruption in Heaven, including their carnal and ungodly ways during the wicked first Earth age while living on this Earth, before the great cleansing flood.

Because of their anti-godly behavior, they made the righteous image of God look corruptible and unclean because of their connection to God. Fittingly enough, God made their image reprobate, corruptible, and unclean.

Their image was made unclean through a shameful and degrading pre-designed curse of uncleanness. And afterward, homosexuality became their primary curse. Their curse sets them apart, and the pits of Hell were created for the rebellious angels and their children.

Lucifer and the ungodly and rebellious angels' corruption was obviously out of control. And it's easy to conclude that because of war in Heaven, the realms of Heaven are where their reign of terror began.

However, I want you to know that they were out of control on this Earth after being cast out of Heaven and placed among us. And the wicked Lucifer and the rebellious angels were less restrained on this Earth than they were in Heaven.

Because of their overwhelming strength and their supernatural ability to be dominant over flesh and blood, man and woman, flesh and blood people were similar to a gentle lamb, compared to a vicious man-eating bear.

Therefore, because of their out-of-control behavior, the image of our Holy Father in Heaven was suffering. And it was because of the troubles and violence on this Earth caused by the wicked Lucifer and the evil, rebellious angels.

The ungodly and harmful things the rebellious sons of God were doing to flesh and blood, man and woman on this Earth, before the great flood, were cruel and violent. And to a large degree, it was caused because of the unholy and forbidden relationships they were having with the daughters of men.

These ungodly relationships started with the evil Lucifer, who purposely seduced the naive Eve in the Garden of God in Eden. And I assure you, the wicked Lucifer angered God to a boiling point when he seduced the innocent female called Eve.

The next scripture indicates that God was furious with Lucifer and the other rebellious angels, who took the daughters of men and used them to create their bloodline children. And I am certain, because of God's reaction, the bloodline mixing was unauthorized by Him.

The next informative scripture, simple and revealing, portrays the results of God's anger. And it proves beyond the shadow of a doubt that my Great

God doesn't let rebellion go unpunished, and Lucifer will experience the wrath Of God.

> **Romans 1:24** Wherefore God also gave <u>them</u> (the wicked Lucifer and the rebellious angels, and their mixed bloodline seed), <u>up</u> (means over) to <u>uncleanness</u> (means sexual uncleanness, and homosexuality) through the <u>lusts</u>, (means uncontrollable sexual desires) of their hearts to <u>dishonor</u> (means to defile themselves through unnatural homosexual uncleanness with), their bodies between <u>themselves</u>!

Between themselves means Lucifer and the rebellious angels, and between their children of a mixed bloodline were having homosexual sex. And they'll defile their bodies and enjoy doing it. And it'll be a compelling curse that they cannot resist.

After that, God imposed a curse, a new lifestyle was imposed on them, and the mixed bloodline people began practicing homosexuality with each other. This truth means the pre-designed curse on their fathers was affecting them, too.

God gave them *up* or *over* to *uncleanness*, and He gave them a reprobate thinking mind, and being unclean didn't bother them. And their pre-designed curse is the main reason for their vile and degrading unnatural homosexual passions.

Indeed, the men and women guilty of following Lucifer's wicked ways and the rebellious angels during the first Earth age, including this Earth age. They did change from what is normal and natural and against nature to become what they are today.

Furthermore, it's pretty easy to see the supernatural pre-designed prophesized curse of homosexuality has expanded to include many compatible followers. And the compatible followers do not seem to realize they are living with a supernatural God-imposed curse.

Surely, the consequences for rejecting God, living an ungodly lifestyle, and somehow managing to avoid the price tag for sin. It would be like swimming in a river full of hungry piranhas, alligators, and anacondas and not being eaten alive.

Because God isn't forgetful, and the corridors of time do not fade His memory, we cannot avoid paying the price tag for sin. No more than we can swim in a river full of hungry piranhas and alligators and not get eaten alive.

> **Romans 1:27** And likewise also the <u>men</u> (including rebellious male angels), leaving the natural use of woman, burned in their lusts one toward another; men with men <u>working</u> (means doing) that which is <u>unseemly</u> (means having unclean sex, and unnatural sex, and cursed homosexual sex),

> **Romans 1:27** and receiving in themselves that <u>recompense</u> (means fitting punishment for their disobedience, and crimes against God), for their error which was <u>meet</u> (means fitting punishment, and a fitting curse for their wickedness).

Surely, I shouldn't have to explain to anyone what's normal, regardless of whether they are heterosexual, homosexual, or bisexual. But just for clarification, everyone should know the God-imposed curse of homosexuality is not a blessing to anyone.

Positively, it's not considered normal, and normal people do not commit acts of homosexuality. But homosexuality illustrates a curse of uncleanness upon any man who desires and feels lust for another man. And I warn you that the risk of rejecting God and serving Lucifer has severe and hurtful consequences.

The hurtful consequences could come from being cursed with a depraved mind and an unclean homosexual lifestyle. Regardless of your thoughts on the subject, the curse of homosexuality is a runaway train in today's world. And this means the bridge is burned between many people and God.

The wicked Lucifer and the rebellious angels tried to take by force the things that belonged to God in Heaven, and thank goodness, they failed. And after they failed to take Heaven away from the God of creation, they were cast out of Heaven and onto the Earth.

After they were here, they changed the bloodline upon the Earth, and they did it by mixing their seed with the seed of the daughters of men. And for a fitting punishment, God's supernatural curse on them was the curse of unnatural homosexuality.

A pre-designed curse of homosexuality became their long-term punishment, and their cursed lifestyle illustrates their price tag for sins against God. And when many homosexuals say they were born to desire men for a mate, I believe they are telling the truth.

I assure you, the mystery of life didn't begin with a single cell or organisms crawling out of the sea and evolving into humans. But the mystery of life did begin with our Supreme God and the Living Coals of Fire, who live upon the mountain of God.

Lucifer was the fox in the hen house in Heaven and within the temple of God, upon the mountain of God. And for now, the fox in the hen house is a homosexual fox imprisoned in the pits of Hell. And his punishment isn't bad luck or by chance occurrence.

Truly, the punishment of Lucifer should be a good example to remember and a good reason for us not to be rebellious against God. Mainly because God can keep us alive, destroy us, and change our D.N.A. and the genetic makeup of our bodies.

Undoubtedly, men and women guilty of rebelling against God cannot escape His long arm of recompense. And sadly, rebellious men and women could wake up some morning and find themselves living with the unnatural curse of homosexuality.

I assure you, the Potter Man in Heaven, reigning superior upon the mountain of God, has a watchful eye. And I want you to realize He's constantly changing and molding His clay vessels. And if we choose to, we could wake up a new person in Christ in the morning.

It would be much better for us if we were similar to the moth, who transforms into a beautiful butterfly. Because some vessels are broken and destroyed, cast into the fire, they do not get the opportunity for transformation.

Positively, I want you to know the only way to transform into a beautiful butterfly has a stipulation attached. And it's by accepting our wonderful Son of God as our only Savior, and acceptance illuminates our unbendable and required stipulation.

I hope to meet you in the peaceful kingdom of God someday after you've been transformed and you receive a new Christ-like body. And if you do make it to Heaven, it'll be because you weren't rebellious to the wonderful word of God.

Before a look into the past story ends, I want to tell you that God's excellent and wonderful word is the ultimate thing and the conclusion to the whole matter. And if we do not highly respect it, God will not have much respect for us.

Chapter Seven
JEALOUSY IN HEAVEN

In the beginning, before the Earth was established, the image of jealousy was in Heaven until the emotion of jealousy made a fool out of him. But initially, Lucifer wasn't called the image of jealousy, not from the start of his unique and special creation.

However, the image of jealousy was Lucifer, the son of the morning, the day-star, or the morning star in Heaven. But after his fall, Lucifer was called by other names. And none of them are good names, like the excellent names he was called in Heaven.

Indeed, here on the Earth, other names were given to him, such as the devil, Satan, Apollyon, and the serpent of old. His not-so-good names weren't given to him until later after he decided to be an adversary to the great God of Heaven and Earth.

In the beginning, the image of jealousy was an <u>anointed</u> (means chosen) <u>cherub</u> (angel) who guarded God's throne. And it's for certain: the image of jealousy, called Lucifer, was in good standing with God and highly thought of by many angels.

He was one of the two angels guarding the throne of God, and he guarded many other valuable things upon the mountain of God. And the other unmentioned, unnamed angel, guarding the mercy seat of God, was most likely the excellent Son of God.

Our wonderful Supreme God created all the angels in Heaven, making them special and beautiful. But Lucifer, the morning star, was an extraordinary special creation. And for some reason, God created him more beautiful and more powerful than all the other angels.

Lucifer was created with more wisdom, knowledge, and charm than any other angels possessed. And Lucifer, the morning star, was created more perfectly than all the other angels, and his beauty exceeded all the rest of the angels, and God favored him.

There were many of the other angels who looked up to him, and they admired the corrupt Lucifer exceedingly too much. And I believe it was because of his beauty and his position with our wonderful Supreme God, and I am sure the angels that admired him didn't know he would be the evil adversary of the God of creation.

Please remember that heavenly creations have different types of bodies, and they're made differently than you and I are made from the dust of the Earth. And in all our comparisons, the angels cannot be compared to any flesh and blood creation.

Truly, bible scriptures reveal that Lucifer was one of our Supreme God's perfect works to see after his creation, especially in design and appearance. Lucifer was created in the temple of Heaven and from within the proximity of the Stones of Fire.

The materials used to create Lucifer's body were precious stones, such as rubies, topaz, diamonds, beryl, and onyx, including jasper and sapphire, emeralds, carbuncle, and gold. And then, after his creation, Lucifer was given a spirit, but not a Holy Spirit.

Although Lucifer became animated with the breath of life, he was perfect and beautiful to look upon in Heaven. Sadly, his fellow angels highly esteemed him, and some other rebellious angels favored him more than they favored the God of creation.

Many of the inferior angels viewed him as exceptional and considered him the most valuable and prized angel among all the other angels. And mainly because his wisdom, beauty, and strength exceeded all the other angels' wisdom, beauty, and strength.

Except for our marvelous, loyal, and trustworthy Son of God, who was more than an angel, and I know for sure the wonderful Son of God was more than equal to Lucifer in strength, beauty, and wisdom. And I believe when Lucifer looked at God and the Son of God, he saw green, which represents jealousy.

Lucifer was a chosen angel, and it was his duty to guard the throne of our Supreme God, located upon God's holy mountain. And because of his position, Lucifer had more freedom and access to God's holy and valuable things than any other angels.

Furthermore, in the book of Ezekiel, God tells us Lucifer walked up and down within the extremely special Stones of Fire on God's mountain. And I am certain that the supernatural Stones of Fire tempted him, and he couldn't resist taking power from them.

Anyway, I do not believe Lucifer had permission to walk anytime he wanted within the midst of the Coals of Fire. And I am certain the answer to this mystery is unknown. And anything I or someone else says amounts to an assumption.

However, as for myself, I do not believe Lucifer had permission from God to walk freely, up and down, within the midst of the Living Coals of Fire. And I do not believe Lucifer was trustworthy or loyal enough to guard the Living Coals of Fire, whose power is too valuable to trust with a sly old fox.

However, he was one of the two angels trusted to guard the throne of God and the Coals of Fire, who live upon the altar in Heaven. And maybe some of us think and believe God is in control of everything, and nothing needs to be guarded in Heaven.

However, this story proves that the mercy seat of our Great God and the Living Coals of Fire must be guarded against traitorous angels, similar to Lucifer. And maybe it isn't that way now, but it was before the angel rebellion in Heaven.

It's easy to believe that the valuable Living Coals of Fire are too tempting for some angels to resist. And because of their ability to increase strength, some angels want to absorb the power of the Coals of Fire.

The mercy seat of God is another word for describing His throne, and the scriptures reveal our Great God had two heavenly creations guarding it. But please realize a fox has his plans, and the fox in the henhouse will not guard the chickens without stealing their eggs.

The Living Coals of Fire are the powerful essence of pure energy, and they live upon His extremely special temple altar. And most likely, the other trusted heavenly creations, trusted to guard the Living Coals of Fire, was the wonderful Son of God.

However, if the other heavenly creation was the Son of God, then only the Son of God was trustworthy and loyal to His Father. And the bible doesn't say the other heavenly creation walked up and down amid the Living Coals of Fire.

Indeed, the evil Lucifer lacked good character qualities, and the temptation to steal God's holy and valuable things was too much for him. And he couldn't control his runaway imagination and foolish desire to be the most powerful person in Heaven.

Lucifer couldn't resist opposing the authority and the word of God because the perfect word of God wasn't precious to him. However, the perfect word of God should be extremely precious to heavenly creations and earthly ones as they are precious to me.

It appears for certain some of the unthankful, rebellious angels in Heaven were similar to some of the unthankful flesh and blood people on Earth. Especially compared to their erosion of servitude and disobedience to God over a long period.

Rebellious angels and rebellious men do not differ much in characteristics, especially concerning ungodly characteristics. And some angels, like Lucifer, got more rebellious, corrupt, and defiant against our wonderful Supreme God as time progressed in Heaven.

The rebellious angels were choosing to live similarly to children, tired of listening to their Father. And sadly, I must conclude these unthankful and rebellious angels were the sons of God, and He was their Creator Father, and they were living in His kingdom.

Furthermore, He expected them to do right, and why wouldn't a Father want His children to do right? And I assure you, regardless of whether it's a Father upon this earth or our Father in Heaven, a good Father wants His children to do right.

Possibly, if there were such a popularity contest among all the angels in Heaven, the jealous Lucifer would've been a front contender for the most popular angel among all the rebellious angels. But I want you to know there's no honor in being popular among the rebellious angels.

Anyway, I am certain the wicked Lucifer wasn't a front contender among God's obedient and good sons and not a first-place contender. This truth means the only admirers of Lucifer were angels not fully committed to God.

It's true, but sad to say, corruption likes corruption, and one-third of the angels in Heaven were corrupt angels. The proof of this statement is illustrated by recognizing the number of angels guilty of deserting God so they could show their love, respect, and servitude to Lucifer.

The rebellious deserters living in Heaven found themselves someone they could relate to and follow. And they followed and listened to Lucifer, and more so than they did to our Wonderful Supreme God. And I want you to realize no one has more credibility than my Great God.

At one time, the jealous Lucifer was one of the most trusted angels among all the angels, and he had the keys to the kingdom of Heaven. And he must've seemed like a god to many of the other angels, guilty of believing his vain philosophies, conjured up from his imagination.

It's quite obvious some of the angels believed his lies and his high-minded speeches; he would speak out of jealousy, similar to Charlotte weaving a deceiving web. But his heart was lifted too high, and because of his beauty, he thought his wisdom to be great because of his brightness.

As the image of jealousy guarded the throne of God, he reasoned within his jealous and rebellious heart a foolish excuse to replace God. And it's easy to conclude Lucifer imagined himself as a greater person and a better choice to be God than our Supreme Creator God.

Lucifer wrongly believed he was more fitting to sit on the throne of God and rule over all the universe and Heaven. His wicked imagination, extreme jealousy of God, and lust for power were the undoing of his splendor, ending his noble position in Heaven.

Lucifer was undoubtedly an awesome, spectacular supernatural sight in Heaven, and he was privileged to have a lot of respect, especially since his unique body was made from precious stones, such as rubies, diamonds, emeralds, and gold.

His strength was undoubtedly great, and he was probably intimidating to other angels who weren't equal to him. However, another heavenly creation guarded the mercy seat upon the mountain of God, and He also guarded the Living Coals of Fire.

He was different in all respects from Lucifer, rejecting and despising the traitorous things Lucifer was doing. Although, they must've been good friends at one time in Heaven. But now, their different type of lifestyle has set them apart permanently.

Since the angel rebellion in Heaven, Lucifer and Yeshua have been at war because one is righteous, and the other is evil. And the last battle upon this Earth will be fought between two heavenly acquaintances from a previous Ancient of Days.

The last battle on this Earth will be between the two guardian angels in Heaven, who guarded the mercy seat of God, and the valuable Living Coals of Fire. And it's for certain: only one guardian will be left standing, and the other will be erased.

God's loyal and trustworthy Son is blessed, and I am proud of the righteousness He firmly stands for every day of His life. And I pray for Him to overcome the rebellious Lucifer, strip him of power, and remove him from our presence.

Glory, love, and thankfulness belong to the Father, the Son, and the Holy Ghost, our protectors from evil angels. And I proudly testify I am hopelessly in love with their righteousness, even though I've been a failure many times.

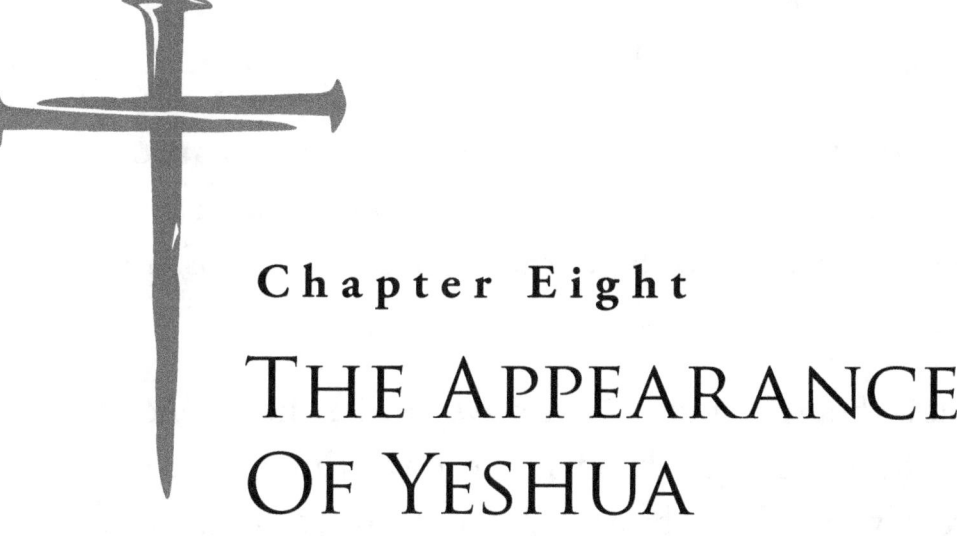

Chapter Eight

THE APPEARANCE OF YESHUA

Four powerful supernatural heavenly creations are described in the Bible and get more attention than any other heavenly creation. And within the last two stories, I've described the appearance of Lucifer and the way his body was made from every precious metal and jewel.

However, within this explanation story, I will describe the appearance of the Son of God, alias Yeshua. And I assure you, He wasn't inferior to any other angel in Heaven, not even in comparison to beauty, wisdom, or anything else.

As for Lucifer, he wouldn't be as grand and powerful as he is now if he hadn't walked up and down within the midst of the Coals of Fire. And the beauty of Lucifer, with his body made of animated precious metals and jewels, is child art compared to Yeshua's beauty.

The description I am about to describe to you is the wonderful Son of God in all His beautiful glory. But as He looks in Heaven, not as He looked as the man in the flesh, called Jesus. Therefore, I will explain so you'll get a glimpse of the image of the Son of God.

As for myself, I believe His appearance is more spectacular than the appearance of Lucifer. And the excellent Son of God, alias Yeshua, was probably the other heavenly creation who guarded the mercy seat of God inside the temple of God.

Truly, the mercy seat is thought of in various ways, but it's the throne of God. And mercy is administered from the mercy seat, the throne of God. And when the scriptures say Two Cherubim's guarded the mercy seat. Then please do remember, Cherubim's are guardian angels.

The corrupt and devious Lucifer and the obedient Yeshua were the guardian angels in the temple of Heaven, upon the mountain of God. And maybe they were the guardian angels before the Cherubims were appointed their guardian position.

Anyway, only one guardian angel stood the test of time, and He resisted the temptation to steal from God, and it wasn't Lucifer. But it was Yeshua, and He was a loyal and obedient heavenly creation. He has a noble position in Heaven, and He's called the loyal Son of God.

The spectacular appearance I will describe of Yeshua is subject to change anytime, whenever He wants His image to change. And mainly because the supernatural Son of God has the power of transformation; another word for transformation is shape-shifting.

I assure you, Yeshua can look as human as the rest of us if He wants to mingle undetected. But the next description of Him illustrates one of

His heavenly appearances. And it's the appearance of our spectacular and supernatural Son of God when He's not the Lamb of God.

It's a spectacular appearance, clothed with a garment down to His foot, and wrapped around His chest is a golden girdle. And His head and His hair are white as snow, and His eyes are as flames of fire. And His great strength exceeds the strength of Lucifer.

Truly, His feet are like unto *fine brass* as if *burnt* in a *hot furnace*, and *His voice*, as the sound of *rushing waters*. And out of *His mouth* went a *two-edged sword*, and the next time we see Him, He'll be a fierce warrior instead of a gentle Lamb.

Positively, His <u>countenance</u> (which means His *visual looks*) was as the *sun shining* in His strength. And the pureness of anything isn't as pure as Him. And possibly, He'll be the only heavenly creation, besides our Great God, powerful enough to conquer the wicked serpent of old.

Upon the holy mountain of God, inside the beautiful temple of God, these two spectacular heavenly creations, supernatural and incredible, guarded the beautiful throne of God. And I am certain Lucifer and the Son of God were an exceedingly powerful force in Heaven.

However, the progression of time divides the good from the bad, and hindsight proves that the loyal Son of God was trustworthy and guarded God's throne better than the jealous and wicked Lucifer.

Therefore, since my analogy is made from the knowledge of hindsight and bits and pieces throughout the bible, I only know some information about the time before the angel rebellion, including the time after the angel rebellion.

Indeed, I will have to assume since I put my faith and trust in Yeshua, the obedient Son of God had to guard the throne of God, the Living Coals of Fire, and the mountain of God from the jealous Lucifer when our Supreme God was absent from Heaven.

During the absence of God, I believe, the jealous Lucifer would've secretly seated himself in the seat of the sapphire throne of God. And maybe he would've declared himself king in Heaven if it were up to him and he didn't have opposition from loyal angels.

However, being King in Heaven was not up to Lucifer, and his strongest opposition was the loyal Son of God. And I am certain the wonderful Son of God continually guarded the throne belonging to His Father, alias Yehovah.

Positively, the corridors of time reveal one Loyal Guardian Angel had to oppose the other guardian angel, who wasn't loyal. This means the loyal Son of God had to protect God's throne, the Living Coals of Fire, and the mountain of God from Lucifer.

The excellent Son of God had to protect all of them from the other guardian angel, called Lucifer, the image of jealousy. And it's easy to conclude that the Son of God had a challenge on His hands because the image of jealousy wanted the things that belonged to God.

Therefore, the opposition between the Son of God and Lucifer began in Heaven, and there has been a war between them ever since. Their opposition most likely started over the throne of God and the Living Coals of Fire, who live upon God's altar.

Furthermore, I present an analogy as we walk through this life in the flesh, void of our memory in Heaven. And it could be a true analogy, or at the least, something to consider concerning us and the corridors of time.

The believers in Christ, automatically drawn to Him, are most likely the reincarnation of good angels born through a woman's womb. And they are the people Lucifer wants to corrupt while they are present in the flesh.

I am certain Lucifer doesn't miss any opportunities to corrupt anyone who supports God, the Son of God, and the Holy Ghost. And mostly because the serpent of old still wants the throne of God, and he still wants to control the Living Coals of Fire.

Surely, the raging war between good and evil will not cease until the Son of God destroys Lucifer, the other guardian angel. And let's hope the Son of God returns soon and restores peace to this Earth by destroying Lucifer and his children of darkness.

Chapter Nine

THE APPEARANCE OF YEHOVAH

Now, after I've described the appearance of Lucifer and the appearance of the Son of God and given you an insight concerning their duties in Heaven and their type of character, and because we are thankful, we should put a difference between the holy and the unholy and the caring and the uncaring.

Next, I shall describe the appearance of our wonderful and extremely spectacular Most High God. And by the time I am finished describing Him, I believe you'll come to a conclusion and consider Him an incredible God.

During the time of Ezekiel, written in the Old Testament, our Supreme Supernatural God came down from Heaven in a whirlwind on fire to visit Ezekiel. And the scriptures tell us the prophet Ezekiel saw Him and beheld the appearance of fire.

Fire from His loins downward, and fire from His loins upward, as the appearance of brightness, as the color of amber. And I can only imagine that the Living Coals of Fire, who reside on the beautiful altar of God, are the appearance of fire and the color of amber.

I believe the Father, the Son, and the Holy Ghost are completely formed from the Living Coals of Fire. And I believe Lucifer wanted to absorb as much energy from the Living Coals of Fire as possible and be like God.

However, I want to point out a fact, and I am telling you, do not assume or wrongly believe; the above description is the only appearance the Son of God and our Most High God have in their wardrobe of appearances simply because they are unlimited.

I want you to know that the wonderful and honorable Son of God and His great Father have power exceeding the boundaries of reality. And I guarantee you that their accomplishments on this Earth only reveal a glimpse of their actual supernatural power.

Therefore, I am telling you that Yeshua and our Supreme God can change their appearances anytime they choose to change. And I want you to realize as hard as it is to conceive, they exceed the boundaries of our imagination.

I assure you the excellent Son of God and our incredible Supreme God are so out of the ordinary and capable of doing anything. They can change or transform their appearances to look like the image of a man or woman if they choose to appear that way.

For example, I believe our Supreme Supernatural God changed into the image of a man when He visited His friend, Abraham. And it happened right before He destroyed the homosexual cities of Sodom and Gomorrah, guilty of being filled with the violent homosexual children of Lucifer.

Even now, after thousands of years, it's easy to believe that some men talk to angels, the Son of God, and God Himself, and they aren't aware of it. Because an appearance is what the eyes behold, a stranger could be an undetectable visitor from Heaven.

Indeed, a God able to make material objects animated and alive can change His appearance anytime He wants to look differently. But Yehovah, in all His glory, has the appearance and the image of fire. But please realize it's not the kind of fire capable of burning the things He touches.

The fiery appearance of God is likened to the fiery appearance of the Living Coals of Fire, and the Living Coals of Fire lives on the altar of God, inside the temple of God, and His temple is the most spectacular place in Heaven.

Although their forms may have different appearances occasionally, the Living Coals of Fire can be Cloven Tongues on Fire. Exactly the way, the Cloven Tongues on Fire came from the Heavens above and visited the Pentecost Revival.

Indeed, the incredible Living Coals of Fire have transformable abilities and can be any appearance they choose. But our Father's image in Heaven portrays their natural appearance.

Because our Father in Heaven may be formed completely from the Living Coals of Fire, and nothing else in Heaven needs to be guarded and protected from thieves except for the wonderful Living Coals of Fire.

This explanation story concerning my great God is called the Appearance of Yehovah. It entwines amazing miracles, unexplainable supernatural accomplishments, and the ability to shapeshift and the Living Coals of Fire.

I assure you my incredible Supreme God is amazing beyond comprehension. And He's entwined with everything mentioned above, regardless of His appearance. And maybe He walks among us all the time, and we do not know it.

Chapter Ten
THE KING OF TYRUS

The elusive king of Tyrus, a little hard to understand, illustrates a parallel story example, having dual meaning. And the parallels reveal it can describe the image of jealousy in Heaven. And the name, called the king of Tyrus, refers to the wicked Lucifer.

This exposure story describes the image of jealousy before he falls from the love and presence of my wonderful God and before he is cast onto the Earth. And to increase our understanding, it's advantageous to know the feelings of Lucifer before his great fall.

The elusive king of Tyrus is an alias imitation name for Lucifer, the image of jealousy, the serpent of old, the charming star in Heaven, and the tree of knowledge of good and evil, and the elusive king of Tyrus was in the Garden of God at Eden.

Beyond the shadow of a doubt, bible scriptures indicate his jealousy was responsible for ultimately causing him his troubles with our Wonderful Supreme God. And I am quite certain the emotion of jealousy causes a lot of trouble, and jealousy is the reason for many murders.

Anyway, please keep this in mind, and remember, when I talk about the king of Tyrus, I am also talking about Lucifer, the image of jealousy, mainly because the king of Tyrus and the wicked Lucifer share the same image and ungodly characteristics.

Positively, their actions are so similar we cannot separate one from the other. And in all respects, the king of Tyrus is the wicked Lucifer, the image of jealousy. Indeed, as this story unfolds, you'll be able to see their parallels become stronger and stronger.

Furthermore, please remember that Lucifer is the invisible spirit of the air, and he entered Judas Iscariot, giving Jesus the kiss of betrayal. For this reason, do not think Lucifer cannot be the spirit of darkness, who lives inside the physical king of Tyrus, if you want to separate the two.

Indeed, I am correct to tell you because Lucifer plays the same game throughout every generation, we would be foolish to think this next statement otherwise. The invisible ghost spirit of Lucifer can possess a weak soul, and he's entered into men throughout every generation since the great flood.

The next explanation scripture illustrates a correlation between the king of Tyrus and the wicked Lucifer, the dark ghost spirit prince of this world. And I am certain we cannot imagine the flesh and blood kings he's possessed throughout the past and today.

> **Ezekiel 28:1** Son of <u>man</u> (means Ezekiel), say unto the <u>prince</u> (of Tyrus, alias the image of jealousy) of Tyrus, thus saith the LORD God; because <u>thine</u> (you're) heart is <u>lifted</u> (means full of pride), and <u>thou</u> (the king of Tyrus, or Lucifer) hast said,

Ezekiel 28:1 I am a God, I (Lucifer) sit in the <u>seat</u> (means in the place) of <u>God</u> (means in the seat of our Supreme God),

Ezekiel 28:1 amid the <u>seas</u> (means amid the nations); yet <u>thou</u> (king of Tyrus, alias Lucifer) art a man, not a God, though thou set thine, heart, as the heart of God.

Even though this informative scripture describes the king of Tyrus, it also describes the wicked Lucifer, the image of jealousy. And mainly because the heart of Lucifer, alias the image of jealousy, was lifted and full of foolish pride.

Furthermore, did he sit in the seat of God, upon the mountain of God, while no one was looking? Maybe so? Otherwise, is he referring to the time before the great flood, when he nearly redesigned the entire population?

Anyway, the evil king of Tyrus, the wicked Lucifer, thought of himself as God, and within his heart, he considered himself similar to our Supreme God. And I believe it's correct to say that no man could oppose or defeat him.

I am certain, among the nations of this world, guilty of being liberal-minded and not having faith or belief in Yehovah as their God. The king of Tyrus, alias Lucifer, the image of jealousy, sits in place of God, and he has many counterfeit and alias godhead names.

I am certain that many men serve and worship him, and the proof is because of this world's ungodly condition. And they do it through the commandments of men and not through the commandments of God. And most of the time, foolish men aren't aware they are serving him.

It's for certain, regardless of what they are, imitation, things are not the things of God. But imitation and counterfeit things are the things associated with Lucifer. And it's easy to conclude Lucifer is an imitation god sitting in the place of God among the heathens.

This parallel story is a symbolic story example, and the king of Tyrus is symbolic of the wicked Lucifer. And as we dig deeper into the scriptures, we'll find out the evil king of Tyrus was in the Garden of God in Eden.

Indeed, so was Lucifer, the image of jealousy, alias the tree of knowledge of good and evil, and the serpent of old. But in the Garden with Adam and Eve, Lucifer was portrayed as the talking serpent of old, symbolic of a snake who was also in the Garden of God at Eden.

It's certain when we get to Ezekiel 28:13, this scripture will prove that the wicked king of Tyrus was in the Garden of God at Eden. But for now, let's ease through the symbolic scriptures and prove the king of Tyrus is the image of Lucifer.

> **Ezekiel 28:3** Behold, <u>thou</u> (O Lucifer, the king of Tyrus, the image of jealousy) art wiser than <u>Daniel</u> (the dream interrupter); there is <u>no</u> <u>secret</u> <u>that</u> <u>they</u> (a man or a woman) can hide from thee.

The material treasures of this world and the ability to have power and authority over other men and control the course of this world. Including the power to be worshipped as God are the goals of Lucifer, the king of Tyrus, or alias, the image of jealousy.

He uses his wisdom and supernatural understanding to his advantage for merchandising and to fulfill the lust of his desires. But he'll never quit lusting for the throne of God and the Living Coals of Fire, who live upon God's altar.

I am certain Lucifer will always be known as the rebellious angel, guilty of stealing and merchandising the things belonging to God. Merchandising is one of the reasons, among other reasons, he was cast out of Heaven and exiled to another place.

From the revealing scripture in Ezekiel, we are told that the king of Tyrus, alias Lucifer, was wiser than Daniel. And being wiser than the prophet Daniel illustrates the king of Tyrus, alias the image of jealousy, as a mighty wise angel.

The loyal prophet, called Daniel, was the wisest man in Babylon and interpreted dreams for King Nebuchadnezzar, or should I say. God interpreted the dreams for Daniel, but Daniel was the go-between messenger man.

Indeed, the wise prophet Daniel, loyal to God, was the reader of interpretation at the palace of King Nebuchadnezzar. Later, in the same palace, many years after the prophesized curse, Daniel revealed the handwriting on the wall for Belshazzar.

The informative scriptures tell us Daniel was wiser than all the sooth Sayers, the astrologers, and the Chaldeans at Babylon. And it was Daniel, Meshach, Shadrach, and Abednego won the contest between meat and vegetable eaters in Babylon.

Indeed, the wisdom of Daniel was similar to the Wisdom of Solomon or even greater and longer lasting than the Wisdom of Solomon. And for Ezekiel to say, the wisdom of the king of Tyrus was greater than the wisdom of Daniel.

Then, the scripture implies nothing can be hidden from him. And this ability tells me the king of Tyrus is the image of Lucifer. The image of Lucifer illustrates an image of the supernatural and superior to the wisdom of flesh and blood men.

However, the image of Lucifer is expressed and told through the image of the king of Tyrus, alias the image of jealousy. And if the king of Tyrus were an earthly king, made from flesh and blood, then he could not know of hidden things.

Nor could he have been in Eden, within the Garden of God. But anyway, the king of Tyrus will suffer the same fate as Lucifer. And in the end, the sword of the Lord will be drawn against his wisdom and beauty, and he'll die without a Savior to deliver him from the damnation of Hell.

> **Ezekiel 28:6** Therefore thus saith The LORD GOD; because <u>thou</u> (O' Lucifer, wicked the king of Tyrus, the image of jealousy) hast set thy heart, as the heart of God.

> **Ezekiel 28:7** Behold, therefore <u>I</u> (the Supreme God) will bring <u>strangers</u> (means heavenly creations of greater strength) upon thee,

> **Ezekiel 28:7** The <u>terrible</u> (means ruthless punishment) of the nations: And <u>they</u> (the heavenly creations), shall draw their swords against the beauty of thy wisdom, and <u>they</u> (the angels of God) shall <u>defile</u> (means destroy),

Ezekiel 28:7 Your <u>brightness</u> (means destroy thy strong hold upon the men, and the ungodly nations of this Earth).

Ezekiel 28:8 <u>They</u> (the angels, and the Son of God) shall bring <u>thee</u> (O' Lucifer, the king of Tyrus, alias the image of jealousy), down to the <u>pit</u> (means down to the bottomless pit), and <u>thou</u> (O' king of Tyrus) shall die the <u>deaths</u> (means same kind of deaths), of <u>them</u> (serving and worshipping you as a god) are slain amid the <u>seas</u> (means slain amid many nations).

Ezekiel 28:9 Wilt <u>thou</u> (O' Lucifer, king of Tyrus, alias the image of jealousy,) yet say before <u>Him</u> (the Son of our Supreme God), that <u>slayeth</u> (means kill or destroy) thee, I (Lucifer) am a God?

Ezekiel 28:9 But <u>thou</u> (O' Lucifer, king of Tyrus, alias the image of jealousy) are a man, and no God, in the hand of <u>him</u> (Him, Yeshua, Emanuel, The Son of God) that slayeth thee.

Ezekiel 28:12 Son of <u>man</u> (the Son of man could be considered symbolic of Jesus Christ.), take up a <u>lamentation</u> (means be mournful, and express sadness) upon the <u>king</u> <u>of</u> <u>Tyrus</u> (symbolic of Lucifer, the image of jealousy),

Ezekiel 28:12 and say unto him, thou <u>sealest</u> <u>up</u> <u>the</u> sum, (means that you were given most everything God had to offer you, and you were) full of wisdom, and perfect in beauty.

Indeed, the wonderful and loving Supreme God in Heaven was good to Lucifer, alias the image of jealousy. And He created Lucifer upon the holy mountain of God, most likely from within the midst of the Living Stones of Fire.

Our wonderful Supreme God put forth much effort when Constructing Lucifer from the best material available. And the wonderful Potter Man in Heaven gave Lucifer everything it took to make him perfect in his construction.

Therefore, out of curiosity, you and I might wonder how and why Lucifer turned out corrupt, rebellious, wicked, evil, and bad. And especially since he was exceedingly blessed, all the odds were favorable for him to turn out good.

My wonderful and thoughtful Supreme God, fair and excellent, wanted intelligent living creations. And for this reason, He created all the angels in Heaven to think for themselves. And it's easy to conclude the rebellious Lucifer was thinking for himself.

The God of creation did not program their minds to be servants and obedient sons, nor did He restrict them from having free will. Truly, one thing is obvious from observation concerning the angel rebellion in Heaven and on this Earth.

The angel rebellion illustrates that the angels in Heaven had free will, and God didn't impose an iron hand of discipline upon them. Otherwise, they would not have rebelled against God in Heaven. And mainly because it takes free will to express rebellion.

Without free will, all the angels would be mindless servants and not thinking sons of our Great Creator God. And our wonderful and considerate Supreme God did not want mindless servants behaving like robots.

However, because of His love for them, He did want the angels and Lucifer to love Him as a Father. And it was because He loved them as sons. And I believe God thought they would be glad to love Him and love doing right.

For the above reason, our heavenly Father gave Lucifer and the other angels a thinking mind. And it's easy to conclude they had plenty of freedom to express free will, and giving us free will proves He's a loving God.

Yehovah hoped they would use their free will to love and respect Him as their heavenly Father. The God of creation wanted them to be loyal sons to Him because they wanted to and not because they had to love Him.

Our Great Supreme God loved Lucifer extremely much. But sadly, Lucifer became the image of jealousy by using his own free will. It is easy to conclude that Lucifer had a mind of his own, but thankfulness to God was lacking.

> **Ezekiel 28:13** <u>Thou</u> (O' Lucifer, the king of Tyrus, and the image of jealousy) hast been in <u>Eden</u>,

The Garden of God was in Eden, and no earthly flesh and blood king had ever been there from another period. For this reason, the king of Tyrus and Lucifer, and the image of jealousy, are the same person but have different names, and they travel the corridors of time.

> **Ezekiel 28:13** (because only Lucifer was in) the Garden of God at Eden.

Lucifer was extremely deceptive and had different names in the Garden of God. Even though they were symbolic names, they were still his names. And he was called Satan, the serpent of old, and the tree of knowledge of good and evil.

Indeed, and of course, he was still Lucifer in disguise under different names, as he is today in all the ungodly nations upon this Earth. And I assure you, he's called the prince of this Earth for a reason. And it's because he has influenced our troublesome part of history.

These words spoken through the scriptures in Ezekiel are the words of our wonderful and all-knowing God. The word of God clearly says Lucifer, the image of jealousy, was in the Garden of God in Eden before the great cleansing flood.

Therefore, the above statement alone identifies Lucifer, alias the serpent of old, as the king of Tyrus. The serpent of old Lucifer and the king of Tyrus are the same person, regardless of which name the scriptures emphasize.

Every precious stone was thy covering, the sardius, topaz, diamond, beryl, jasper, sapphire, carbuncle, and gold. And thy tabrets' artistry (created by the God of Heaven and Earth) (coverings symbolic of Lucifer's super body).

Also, the artistry of his <u>pipes</u> (which means his great voice) was prepared in <u>thee</u> O' Lucifer, king of Tyrus (the image of jealousy). In the day, thou were <u>created</u> (and made from material objects into something beautiful in Heaven).

The next enlightenment scripture reveals the blessed Lucifer's noble position in Heaven and the formation of his beautiful body. And I want you to realize that being anointed by God means God loved and thought highly of him.

> **Ezekiel 28:14** <u>Thou</u> (O' Lucifer, the king of Tyrus, the image of jealousy) art the anointed <u>Cherub</u> (means a chosen angel) that <u>covereth</u> (means guarded the mercy seat, alias the throne):

> **Ezekiel 28:14** And <u>I</u> (the wonderful Supreme God) have <u>set</u> (means made) thee so;

> **Ezekiel 28:14** That wast upon the holy mountain of God: <u>Thou</u> (O' Lucifer, the king of Tyrus, the image of jealousy) hast walked up and down amid the Stones of Fire.

Lucifer, the sneaky thief in Heaven, called the serpent of old, walked up and down amid the Living Coals of Fire, who live upon God's altar. And his walk amid the Living Stones of Fire enhances his strength immensely. And Lucifer would have weakened and died long ago without the strength the stones of fire provide.

The walk amid the Living Coals of Fire made the evil Lucifer stronger and more supernatural than all other angels in Heaven. And I assure you, this increase in strength must've boosted his confidence tremendously.

Possibly, it's easy to believe, after his exile from Heaven and without access to walking up and down within the midst of the Living Coals of Fire. Lucifer, the fallen angel from Heaven, may become weaker and less supernatural thousands of years later as he ages.

If the wicked Lucifer isn't rejuvenated by the Living Coals of Fire within the temple of God, upon the mountain of God, then possibly, his strength will fade somewhat, and he'll not be as strong as he was at the beginning of his creation in Heaven.

It certainly appears to us mortals that the wicked Lucifer and the rebellious angels have been blessed with an extremely long life span. When I think about them, I cannot help but wonder if the rules of longevity, which apply to us, also apply to them.

Specifically, the rule of longevity I am thinking about is the fifth commandment of God, telling us to honor our Father and Mother as the Lord God has commanded thee. And great wisdom is revealed because we honor our father and mother.

Our God-inspired bible reveals that showing honor to our father and mother has benefits. And maybe our days will be <u>prolonged</u> (which means lengthened with a longer lifespan if we gladly honor our earthly father and mother).

I want you to realize that my Supreme God is the Father, and the angels are the sons of God. And I am telling you, the sons of God are expected to honor their Father in Heaven. Similarly, we are expected to honor and respect our father and mother, who raised us from birth.

Furthermore, the rebellious angels' lifespan may be cut short if they do not rejuvenate themselves with the strength of the Living Coals of Fire. And from the pits of Hell, the Living Coals of Fire are out of their reach.

It's for certain the penalty for rebellion and refusal to honor thy Father in Heaven and thy Father and Mother upon this Earth will be a life cut short. And I want you to know God doesn't bless dishonorable children who are rebellious to His command.

Lucifer, the symbolic king of Tyrus, the image of jealousy, had a noble position in Heaven. And I am certain that most other angels in Heaven would've liked to have been blessed with his noble position, beauty, and strength.

However, the dissatisfied Lucifer wasn't happy with having a noble position on the mountain of God, and he wanted much more than God had given to him. The desire to be greater than everyone else was his motivation for wanting more: pride, greed, jealousy, and lust for power fueled his evil thoughts and emotions, and he wanted everything God had created and worked billions of years to accomplish.

The unthankful Lucifer was willing to rebel against his Father and fight against his Creator for power and possession of everything in Heaven. These material possessions meant more to him than his wonderful Father meant to him, who created him. We see it always: men, women, and children are willing to trade loyalty for material possessions.

Lucifer was a glorious angel, made perfect in strength, wisdom, and beauty from the day he was created. Until unrighteousness, jealousy, and rebellion were found in him. And if we could cut something from our hearts, all thoughts of rebellion must be removed.

The wicked Lucifer, the image of jealousy, apparently had everything he needed to be a happy angel. But he wasn't loyal and didn't respect his Creator Father, and gaining powerful possessions in Heaven meant more to him than having a loving father.

Apparently, with all his beauty, wisdom, popularity, supernatural strength, and a wonderful kingdom to call his home, Lucifer couldn't find room to love, honor, and respect his Father, who sat on the throne.

Surely, the moral of this story about Lucifer illustrates an example to remember lest we forget to retain love in our hearts. And I assure you, a person, or an angel, cannot be right with God without having love in their heart for their family and neighbors.

The wicked Lucifer probably had many positive characteristics and should've been a happy angel. But he was missing the emotion of love for his Father and his brethren angels, and I believe happiness was eluding him.

However, the multitude of his vain wishes, his desire to be our Supreme God, and his unrighteous philosophies caused his conduct and the conduct of some of the other angels to be changed, and they went from being obedient to disobedient and became opposition to the ways of God.

It appears for certain they went from being peaceful to violent, and they certainly decided to be rebellious against God. And our Supreme God had to cast Lucifer, the king of Tyrus, alias the image of jealousy, from off the mountain of God and out of Heaven.

After his exile from the Utopian city of God, the rebellious Lucifer was left without his noble position in Heaven. To put it bluntly, Lucifer was cut down to a stump, and for the benefit of peace, love, and harmony, he was separated from the kingdom of God.

Indeed, it's easy to conclude that his weakness was the wrong personal characteristics. As much as I wish it weren't true, Lucifer was cast onto this

Earth, and he wasn't welcome in Heaven. And I am certain the residents living upon this Earth wish he hadn't come here.

Furthermore, his popularity has run its course, and we are tired of the chaos he caused. And I am certain that most earthlings look forward to a better world, not influenced by the terribleness of rebellion.

As God thought about Lucifer and his terrible betrayal, our wonderful and loving Supreme God said to him. O' Lucifer, king of Tyrus, I will destroy thee, <u>O' covering cherub</u> (means extremely special angel), from the midst of the Stones of Fire.

It's obvious that the Stones of Fire are extremely special, and the best illustration I can assume concerns the Living Stones of Fire. They are protected upon God's mountain and must be guarded constantly.

They are kept in a sacred place, where the angels can only access them with permission from our Great Creator God. And because they are connected to the mystery of life, I believe the valuable and wonderful Living Coals of Fire are located near the throne of God.

Lucifer's supernatural powers are much less effective today than they were six thousand years ago simply because he hasn't been able to walk up and down within the midst of the Living Stones of Fire and renew his super energy from the altar of God.

Indeed, Satan's extraordinary body must be considered indestructible and full of strength many thousands of years ago. However, it may have weakened somewhat to the point, making it easier for the wonderful Son of God to subdue and destroy him from God's other creations.

Possibly, for the wicked Lucifer, the king of Tyrus, or the image of jealousy to be strong the way he was during the angel rebellion. He would have to walk again amid the Living Coals of Fire and energize his supernatural angelic body with extraordinary energy.

However, for the benefit of everyone in Heaven and on this Earth, our Supreme God has exiled him, and he's restricted from the mountain of God. And for the sake of everyone, he cannot access the valuable Living Coals of Fire anymore.

However, think not; he's become weak and lost all his strength. Because he's still a powerful angel to us, and he's still a supernatural angel and the dark prince of this world. And I guarantee you, it'll take the strong Son of God to defeat him in battle.

The gold, silver, and precious jewels, including diamonds, pearls, and rubies, didn't have to be guarded in Heaven. But the Living Coals of Fire did have to be guarded in Heaven from the rebellious angels, who lusted for more power than they already had.

Therefore, a logical assumption proves that the Living Coals of Fire was more valuable than the other material objects in Heaven. And mainly because only the most valuable things are guarded, regardless of whether they are on this Earth or in Heaven.

Undoubtedly, the God element, the spark of life, the essence of pure energy, and the Holy Ghost. The breath of life and the Living Coals of Fire are all the same, and they need to be protected from the rebellious angels. And because knowledge improves our ability to do right, we need examples like this story portrays to increase our obedience to His word.

Now, I'll ask you: if the special Living Coals of Fire belonged to you, wouldn't you guard them too? Especially since they must be kept from getting into the wrong hands. And I know righteousness needs to be preserved, and the wrong hands will not preserve righteousness.

However, before you answer the above question, try and put your feet inside the shoes of our Supreme Creator God. And try to feel the feelings of God and the necessity to protect the Living Coals of Fire. Then ask yourself, what would you do if Lucifer stole the Living Coals of Fire from you?

Furthermore, what would you do if Lucifer wanted to sit on your throne and take everything away from you? Anyway, we cannot put our feet in the shoes of God, and we cannot imagine how He felt when Lucifer wanted to take His belongings by force.

However, it's easy to conclude that the Living Coals of Fire had to be guarded against the corrupt angels, who had free will in Heaven. The Living Coals of Fire are the greatest temptation to the angels in Heaven and much more than precious material objects created by God.

Anyway, I ask you, why would the angels need silver and gold in Heaven? Especially since these creations are simply building materials in the kingdom of God. And I seriously doubt if silver, gold, and money are part of the bartering system in Heaven.

However, the wonderful Living Coals of Fire are the ingredient for immortality, but the ingredient to immortality belongs to our Great Creator God. And the Living Coals of Fire are His to share with whom He chooses to share them in Heaven or on Earth.

Positively, I believe, after a good angel carries our spirit to Heaven, after the death of the flesh. We'll be privileged to entwine with the Living Coals of Fire, receive the gift of a Christ-like body, and put on immortality.

Chapter Eleven

THE KING OF TYRUS DESTROYED

There's prosperity in evil and corrupt works, and ill-gotten gains always make ungodly people rich. And the prince of this world is evil, and he can prosper evil men. And tyrant and dictator nations prove prosperity can be achieved through force, corruption, and oppression.

Observation proves that evil and corrupt works sometimes prosper for a long time before the hand of God destroys them. Although, I assure you, the watchers and the holy ones, the council in Heaven, and our Creator God, see every work we do, whether godly or bad.

Whether our works are good or evil or the nature of their intentions, all works are seen from the Heavens above, and heavenly creations record them. And none of us escape the necessity of a recorded life or from being illustrated in the Book of Life.

Furthermore, it's quite obvious our wonderful Creator God doesn't immediately destroy all evil works in their beginning. And it appears one hundred percent true; He silently watches ungodly people do many evil things in this jungle world before He reacts.

Anyway, I conclude that if He did destroy evil things, as suddenly as they happen. Then, according to His rules, God would be dictating the works of men, whether good or evil. And it's easy to conclude my all-mighty God doesn't force anyone to do His will even though He could.

However, I want you to realize and know an unchangeable fact: even if my Great God allows evil men and women to have their season allotted to them according to His time. In the final analysis, His required rules are the scale of honor that measures all men and women.

Indeed, not to say God will not destroy evil works because sooner or later, evil works are destroyed by the will of God. And sooner or later, the God of Heaven and Earth will raise adversaries against dictators and evil men. And most of the time, God's influence isn't recognized.

However, He doesn't usually interfere with evil men until they are measured and found unchangeable. This truth means the gift of free will has to run its course for a while before the value and characteristics of any person can be measured correctly.

Positively, the moral values and the characteristics of every man and woman cannot be measured unless they have free will. Good and evil works provide a way for God to measure the moral value and the characteristics of every man and woman on this Earth.

Indeed, it's only through the gift of free will that a man and woman can be properly and accurately evaluated. But in the end, we'll all be evaluated by three important indicator words. The three indicator words are hot, cold, and lukewarm for the gospel of God.

Therefore, the works of our hearts we do with our hands during our lifetime is our evaluation scale, and our work is equal to hot, cold, or lukewarm. The scale of evaluation means God isn't kidding around when He tells us He'll reject the cold and the lukewarm person.

Surely, the stumbling blocks men face daily are placed before them by Lucifer, the alias king of Tyrus. A clear observation of this world proves this Earth is overwhelmed by stumbling blocks. And we'd have to be blind not to realize ungodliness is a stumbling block.

The evil king of Tyrus is the prince of this world system, and he proved for certain he's the prince of this world when the King of Tyrus offered Jesus Christ the kingdoms of this world if He would worship him. And great power is proven when Lucifer can make this offer to the Son of God.

Truly, it's my assumption, and I believe this world is mostly controlled by the servants of darkness, guilty of rejecting God and His commandments. The king of the servants of darkness is Lucifer, the alias king of Tyrus, who began ruling during the first Earth age.

Indeed, through scripture enlightenment, God wants us to know the king of Tyrus, alias Lucifer, will be reduced to ashes at his end. And this means the king of Tyrus, alias Lucifer, has a prophesized destiny, including compensation, judgment, and death.

Lucifer is an example to all of us, and his example illustrates that all evil works and men will be reduced to ashes. And my judging God assures us that the lake of fire and a pile of ashes are the results of all evil works and the result of corrupt and wicked men.

Beyond the shadow of a doubt, these next few revealing scriptures will explain the final results of evil and rebellious works. And we better take these next few scriptures seriously and not make the mistake of being evil and rebellious by submitting ourselves to living in opposition to God's word.

Ezekiel 28:17 <u>Thine</u> (O' Lucifer, the king of Tyrus, the image of jealousy) heart was lifted because of thy beauty, (and) <u>thou</u> (O' Lucifer, the king of Tyrus, the image of jealousy) hast corrupted thy wisdom because of thy brightness:

Ezekiel 28:17 <u>I</u> (the Supreme God) will cast <u>thee</u> (O' Lucifer) to the <u>ground</u> (means to the Earth), (and) <u>I</u> (the Supreme God) will lay <u>thee</u> (O' Lucifer, the king of Tyrus, the image of jealousy) before (the) kings (of the Earth),

Ezekiel 28:17 that they may behold <u>thee</u> (O' Lucifer, the king of Tyrus, the image of jealousy, the serpent of old, Satan, the devil). <u>Thou</u> (O' Lucifer, the image of jealousy) hast <u>defiled</u> (means corrupted)

Ezekiel 28:18 <u>thy</u> (means God's) <u>sanctuaries</u> (means His holy places) by the multitude of thine <u>iniquities</u> (means sins, and dishonest trade, and the traditions of men),

Ezekiel 28:18 By the iniquity of thy traffic; therefore, will <u>I</u> (God) bring forth a fire from the midst of <u>thee</u> (O' Lucifer, alias the king of Tyrus),

Ezekiel 28:18 (and) it shall <u>devour</u> (means destroy) <u>thee</u> (O' Lucifer, the king of Tyrus, the image of jealousy),

Ezekiel 28:18 and <u>I</u> (God) will bring <u>thee</u> (O' Lucifer, alias the king of Tyrus) to ashes upon the Earth, in the sight of all them that <u>behold</u> (means see) thee (O' Lucifer).

After the prophesized thousand-year millennium is over and Lucifer is turned loose for a while, he'll get one last chance to rebuild his ungodly army. But Lucifer, the image of jealousy, the king of Tyrus, will be destroyed in the sight of men, nations, and kings upon this Earth.

Indeed, the wicked Lucifer, the burning star from Heaven, will burn from within, and he'll be reduced to ashes by the hand of God. And all the people upon this Earth shall be astonished at his demise, and they'll hate every rebellious thing identified with him.

However, after his destruction, everyone will know the terror of the image of jealousy is over. And he'll not trouble the good people on this Earth anymore, nor will we have to wrestle against his evil spirit influence ever again.

Indeed, from the beginning of his jealousy, the evil Lucifer despised and rebelled against our wonderful Supreme God in Heaven. Lucifer has constantly opposed God, and he's tried to destroy all the good works of God, including all the loyal children of God.

Truly, the wicked and hateful Lucifer has destroyed much of God's holy, sacred, and blessed works since he was cast onto the Earth. And it's easy to conclude Lucifer doesn't feel remorse for destroying good things.

It's sad, but the glorious and beautiful rebellious Lucifer, whom God created with the help of the Living Stones of Fire. He turned against God, similar to a ravenous wolf after a gentle lamb, and his wicked characteristics haven't changed throughout the portals of time.

Lucifer has been the supernatural image of jealousy and God's adversary, even before Adam and Eve's creation in the Garden of God. These next few scriptures reveal his fall from glory to shame, and they reveal Hell is the only place left to receive him.

> **Isaiah 14:12** How art thou fallen from Heaven, O' Lucifer (the morning star), son of the morning! How art <u>thou</u> (O' Lucifer) cut down to the ground, which didst weakens the nations!

These words, taken from the scriptures in Isaiah, are the words of God Himself and illustrate Lucifer's evil works. And our Supreme God is certainly the person who tells us about the fate of Lucifer, the alias king of Tyrus.

I realize that different philosophies are floating around in Christianity, and many people are unsure of the location of the pits of Hell. Therefore, the next informative scripture, spoken from God's mouth, will reveal the location of Hell with certainty.

I want you to know that if you always thought the location of Hell is established underground and beneath us, then you are exactly right. But God tells us Hell is moved for judgment upon Lucifer, and his judgment is an unchangeable decree.

> **Isaiah 14:9 Hell from beneath** is moved for <u>thee</u> (Lucifer, alias the king of Tyrus, the serpent of old), to meet <u>thee</u> (Lucifer,

alias the king of Tyrus) at thy coming: <u>It</u> (Hell) stirreth up the dead for thee,

Isaiah 14:9 Even all the <u>chief</u> <u>ones</u> (means leaders) of the Earth; <u>it</u> (the pits of Hell) hath raised all the kings of the nations from their thrones.

Apparently, from the pits of Hell, the kings of the Earth shall know Lucifer, the king of Tyrus, has become weak like them. And from the pits of Hell, mighty men and kings will know they walked down the wrong path.

Positively, the kings of the Earth put their faith and trust in Lucifer, alias the king of Tyrus, also called the son of the morning. They'll wonder how Lucifer, alias the king of Tyrus, was cut down to the ground and made weakly.

Isaiah 14:13 For <u>thou</u> (O' Lucifer, the image of jealousy, alias the king of Tyrus) hast said in thine heart; I will ascend into Heaven, I will <u>exalt</u> (means lift) my throne above the stars of God.

Isaiah 14:13 (And) <u>I</u> (Lucifer) will also sit <u>upon</u> (the mountain of God, where the Living Stones of Fire, burn upon the altar of God), (on) the mount of the congregation, in the sides of the north.

Isaiah 14:14 <u>I</u> (Lucifer the image of jealousy, alias the king of Tyrus) will ascend above the heights of the <u>clouds</u> (in Heaven, and) <u>I</u> (Lucifer) will be like our Supreme God.

Lucifer, the image of jealousy, had big dreams, plans, an out-of-control imagination, and a jealous heart. But his conjured-up thoughts, allowing him to imagine he could be similar to our Supreme God, were extremely foolish and wrong.

Suppose Lucifer could sit upon the highest mountain in Heaven, inside the temple of God, and on the throne. And if he could walk up and down, within the midst of the Living Coals of Fire, more than anyone else, he could not be like our wonderful Supreme God.

Sitting on a throne will not give the power-hungry Lucifer a God-like character or a loving heart, similar to the loving heart of God. I am certain Lucifer, the image of jealousy, could never fill the position of God. And it's because he's not moral enough.

Nor is he righteous enough, lawful enough, compassionate enough, wise enough, or ethical enough. And I want you to know the wicked Lucifer cannot be excellent in character, similar to my wonderful and excellent Supreme God.

However, Lucifer, the image of jealousy, alias the king of Tyrus, does have other undesirable character qualities. Undesirable qualities, good men and good angels reject having. His other qualities are immoral and carnal, unjust and lawless, jealous and unloving.

Lucifer is uncaring and unclean, unholy and unrighteous, and full of hate and envy, and murder doesn't bother his conscience. And the qualities of character Lucifer possesses and exhibits will never allow him to be similar to our wonderful Supreme God.

> **Isaiah 14:15** Yet <u>thou</u> (O' Lucifer, the image of jealousy) shalt be <u>brought</u> <u>down</u> (means delivered) to Hell, to the sides of the pit (before he's cast into the bottomless pit).
>
> **Isaiah 14:16** (And) they that see <u>thee</u> (O' Lucifer, the image of jealousy, alias the king of Tyrus) shall narrowly look upon thee, and consider thee, saying, this is the <u>man</u> (Lucifer) that made the Earth tremble, that did shake the kingdoms.

After Lucifer, the image of jealousy is stripped of his supernatural powers, and he's delivered down to Hell. He'll be seen among the residents of Hell as a failure and a troublemaker for every living creation. And a weak, jealous, rebellious angel whom men and angels will despise and hate to look at him.

Most likely, his fall from popularity after he's proven a terrible leader and a failure. Condemned men will be extremely sorry and remorseful and wish they hadn't considered following his corrupt and rebellious ways.

Even though he was powerful and beautiful, he caused the whole world to tremble. And it's still trembling now through fear and corruption. But in the end, he'll be just another man whom the people in this world will hate, and as for me, I hate him now.

My God tells me not to be afraid of other gods and not to bow down to them. And I do not fear Lucifer, and I'm not too fond of his ways. Otherwise, I wouldn't write negatively about him, but I write extensively about the wicked works he imposes on humanity.

Purposely, I expose him as the cursed homosexual god of this world and the spiritual influence hidden behind acts of ungodliness. And I hate how he's shaped and abused this world through corruption and uncleanness, and I would be foolish not to hate him.

Surely, when the fog lifts and the blinders come off, the eyes see clearly, and the mind understands the truth. Then Lucifer will be the most hated angel ever created in the Heavens above, and we will despise the day of his creation.

However, we do not have to wait until later to hate Lucifer because we can start hating him now. And every day, and every opportunity we get, we can speak against Lucifer and teach our children to hate his corrupt and wicked ways.

Most of us can love God and teach our children the righteous ways of God. And we can lift the perfect Ten Commandments of God and keep them close to us, similar to how we cherish a prized possession.

According to our works, I assure you that salvation is won or lost, accomplished in conjunction with the great Ten Commandments. This truth means salvation is lost because of our wicked works against the Ten Commandments of God.

This truth means the excellent and perfect Ten Commandments are our spiritual armor, and they'll protect us from being a victim of sin. And a victim of sin is anyone who rejects living by the Ten Commandments of our Creator God.

The Ten Commandments of God are the conclusion to the whole matter, and they matter more than any other message. And nearly everything divine and considered righteous and good hinges on us keeping the beautiful Ten Commandments of God.

Nothing pleases God more than seeing His children happy to keep His commandments. And before this story ends, I want you to know Lucifer will drag you and me through the briars, the mud, and the thorns if we do not oppose him.

Chapter Twelve
A POEM ABOUT LUCIFER

Lucifer was a beautiful and charming angel who sinned, and he wanted all of us to turn against God and be similar to him. He kills, steals, and destroys whosoever's life he can. And it's because he's a cruel bully and hates all flesh and blood men and women.

The wicked Lucifer doesn't have a home in Heaven, and the good angels reject him because of his foolishness, rebellion, and jealous sins. And he cunningly laid a stumbling block before the rebellious angels, and a third of them stumbled and fell in.

After he was kicked out of Heaven because of his rebellious character, our righteous Supreme God will not let him have a home in His kingdom again. But his destiny is predetermined because of his jealous sins, and he lives like the Nicolaitans, who love to pretend.

He wanted the throne of God in Heaven, but he wasn't powerful enough to win, and now he hates the children of God, who've learned to resist him. However, he laughs at the weakness of sinner men, and he loves tempting them with all sorts of various sins.

Positively, telepathy is his poison arrow, and he influences the minds of men and women to an unknown degree. And I am certain Lucifer is the reason for violence and troubles, and his hand and heart are against every man.

Lucifer is likened to a fornicator, and he'll be unfaithful to the end, and he's our biggest enemy, similar to a rattlesnake full of venom. He plays upon people's fears and turns their imaginations against them, and most people aren't even aware that they are at war with him.

Jealousy, hate, and greed were his stumbling blocks, and it's easy to conclude that his bad character came between him and our Great Creator God. And now and forever, he's the image of jealousy because he coveted the things belonging to our great Creator God.

Now and always, he's a hideous beast and has a hardened heart and no compassion for the weak. Sadly, I must tell you, Lucifer stepped from the world of light and fell into the world of darkness, and it was because his character was flawed and his love for God wasn't strong.

Indeed, he built his house on the sand, and the foundation crumbled in the wind. And building on the sand proves Lucifer was a foolish angel. And it's easy to conclude living strong for God wasn't entwined into his foundation, and his house has a limited time to stand.

Truly, he's likened to the seed, planted in the wrong places and unable to grow. And sadly, a parallel to his heart is a seed planted on stony ground, where nothing but the tares grow. Indeed, world history proves the tares are nuisances and aren't fruitful plants.

I want you to know he's likened to a plant lacking water, who withered away when the sun came out. And from his new home in the pits of Hell, I am certain his beauty is withering away, and the glory he felt before his fall, he can't feel anymore.

Therefore, his unstable house will fall to the ground when the storms rage, the winds blow, and the rains come. Indeed, the grass looked greener on the other side of the fence for Lucifer until he relocated to the dark side of the fence, where the light never shone.

Now, he's an angry exile from Heaven, locked out of the holy places, and Hell is the only place left for him. And it's easy to conclude he was foolish when he challenged the set ways of God. And the old saying, saying fools are born every day, applies to him and the rebellious angels.

Beyond the shadow of a doubt, good people who hate wickedness do not want his kind around, regardless of his beauty and charm. Beauty and charm aren't good character qualities compared to *sincerity* and *godliness*. Without having these character qualities, the morals of the soul are missing.

His body was superior and beautiful, made from precious stones, but still, after thousands of years, he hasn't changed and wears a face of shame. After his creation, he stood proud and tall, but our Supreme God saw his vanity and cut him down to a crawl.

At one time, the beautiful Lucifer could've had great value and been a pillar of society, but now he's deficient and hasn't any value. And if sin has a patterned character quality, it's similar to causing self-inflicted hurt.

Surely, the moral of this story reveals you do not take the gifts of God lightly or casually or be rebellious to righteousness. Lest thoughts of grandeur, power, and control spoil you, as Lucifer was spoiled rotten and only cared about personal gain.

Conclusively, if we rebel against God's righteous word, the price for being unrighteous will incur a harmful debt. And I want you to know God collects all debts on sin, and no one gets a free pass without suffering recompense from Him. And if I were you, I would write His commandments on my heart and live by them.

Chapter Thirteen

THE SEEDS OF EVIL BEGAN WITH HEAVENLY CREATIONS

Indeed, as hard as it is to believe and impossible as it sounds, the image of jealousy began in Heaven. And because of his rebellion against righteousness and inability to be satisfied with his Great Creator God, he was cast onto this Earth far away from his heavenly home.

However, repentance and change weren't his objectives after he was here on this Earth, and the image of jealousy became the wicked serpent of old. And to prove his wickedness, he tricked and beguiled Eve, and he continued to be unrighteous.

It's for certain that recorded proof in Ezekiel 28:13 places the image of jealousy in the Garden of God at Eden. But as the king of Tyrus, and in the book of Genesis, he was called the *Serpent Of Old* in the Garden of God, not the king of Tyrus.

The image of jealousy, alias the serpent of old, and also the king of Tyrus, cunningly set his heart on a pre-designed task. And sadly, I must tell you, his goal included destroying the good and valuable works of our Creator God in the beautiful Garden of Eden.

Here on this Earth, after the wicked Lucifer was cast out of Heaven and exiled away from the place of his creation, the image of jealousy, the serpent of old, the evil Lucifer, and the king of Tyrus are the same person. Knowledgeable men and women know he has many names he uses in different locations.

Indeed, and for various reasons, the name of Lucifer kept changing after he was cast onto this Earth. Without a doubt, name-changing is his way of eluding some detection, but he cannot deceive anyone if they are bible savvy.

Certainly, since he was called the serpent of old in the Garden of God, his name has changed many times. For this reason, Lucifer is similar to a chameleon; on purpose, he changes his colors to camouflage himself from being discovered by his adversaries.

Lucifer also changes his name to various names to camouflage his corrupt and evil ways among unsuspecting men and women. After Lucifer, the image of jealousy was cast onto the Earth during the first Earth age, before the great cleansing flood.

He was still completely physical and visible, extremely strong, and still in his super-powerful and physically heavenly body. Before the great cleansing flood, he was the most powerful angel on this Earth for approximately two thousand years or more.

No flesh and blood man, woman, or inferior angel opposed him and lived. Indeed, Lucifer, the Supreme God status, the image of jealousy, wanted in Heaven but could not take away from God. He truly believed he could have it on this earth, among us flesh and blood weaklings.

Furthermore, Lucifer did rule like a god during the time before the great cleansing flood, but sadly, he was a cruel tyrant god. Bible scriptures reveal that this Earth was filled with men committing violence, and he was the wolf pack's leader.

Indeed, Lucifer was the dominant god among us earthlings before the great flood, but only briefly. And it appears our Supreme God gave Lucifer a long leash and a lot of slack before imposing restrictions against him.

Lucifer was powerful, persuasive, dominant, and popular among many angels in Heaven, and they foolishly rebelled and chose to follow after him. And sadly, they didn't appear to be remorseful for their wrong choice.

However, Lucifer and the rebellious angels did reap the reward of a god-like status for approximately two thousand years or more, with results to their liking, even here on this crude Earth. And even though they were a long way from Heaven, they had a playground of submissive servants.

The rebellious angels, during the first Earth age, before the great cleansing flood, were similar to little supernatural gods. And it's for certain; they had found themselves a new home here among weaker people with frail flesh bodies.

I assure you, the wicked, rebellious angels were similar to captains and generals upon this Earth in servitude to Lucifer. And it's easy to conclude Lucifer was the rebellious leader among humankind. And the war he started in Heaven to gain power became a spillover, and this Earth is his spillover place to rule.

Strategically, the first thing Lucifer, the image of jealousy, and the other rebellious angels did upon the Earth after being cast out of Heaven. They changed and modified the flesh bloodline, which the God of Heaven and Earth had created for the human man and woman.

Beyond the shadow of a doubt, modifications to the flesh and blood race all began in the Garden of God at Eden. Sadly, I must inform you that the unsuspecting, naive, and innocent woman, Eve, was Lucifer's first target of deception.

Therefore, change to the flesh bloodline began with her and the serpent of old, called Lucifer, the tree of knowledge of good and evil. And I am certain that the beautiful, naïve, and innocent Eve walked naked through the Garden of God, where no other humans lived except for Adam.

She wasn't any match in understanding for the wise, hideous, and evil-hearted serpent of old who desired to use her female abilities. Nor did she know Lucifer had a deliberate plan to destroy her innocence and the works of God simultaneously.

The serpent of old couldn't be a god in Heaven, and he couldn't have his sons in Heaven the way our Supreme God has us. And so, Lucifer decided he would be a god on this Earth and have his bloodline sons, who would only be loyal to him and do his will.

Lucifer wouldn't allow his sons to be interested or loyal to our Supreme God of Heaven and Earth after their birth. After their birth, I believe

Lucifer would purposely poison their minds with hate toward the God of creation.

Indeed, the only thing Lucifer, the image of jealousy, and the other rebellious angels needed to create their bloodline sons. It was the flesh and blood daughters of men, and they knew they could use her for seed mixing, and using the female was their purpose for her.

The naïve and innocent Eve was the first known woman to give birth to a mixed bloodline child, and the mixed bloodline child was called Cain. And as we all know, because of scripture evidence, Cain is the first known person to murder on the Earth.

Lucifer's dark wisdom, entwined with his rebellious attitude and no respect for God's accomplishments, combined with an imaginary and foolish foresight. Lucifer knew the population growth from the children of God would always be troublesome and opposing to him.

Beyond the shadow of a doubt, Lucifer was right about his analogy concerning the children of God because they who understand Lucifer oppose him and his evil ways, even today. And I am certain they opposed him before the great flood.

I am certain the only way for Lucifer, the evil image of jealousy, to avoid opposition from the children of God. It was for him to assimilate them into his bloodline, make them a part of his family, or kill whosoever refused assimilation.

Therefore, to eliminate a troublesome loyal to God bloodline unwilling to worship him as a god on Earth. The wicked Lucifer decided to start his bloodline on this planet and eventually destroy the bloodline started by

God, and this way, the first Earth-age people would have a heritage with him.

Lucifer hated the flesh and blood people on this Earth, and it was because they were enthusiastic and loyal God lovers, determined to do right. And I want you to know that anyone determined to be loyal to their Creator God was automatically his enemy.

However, for the wicked Lucifer to accomplish his expansion plan and redo the God-designed bloodline to his liking, the flesh and blood female are needed before he can propagate and create his bloodline children, whom he can call his own.

Because no rebellious angels were female, the God of Heaven and Earth didn't intend for the angels to have children. And because of His design, Lucifer, the image of jealousy, and the rebellious angels couldn't propagate among themselves.

Furthermore, it appears propagation between the rebellious angels and the daughters of men began with Lucifer. The first hint of mixed bloodline propagation began with the serpent of old and the naïve and innocent Eve in the Garden of God.

Cain was the firstborn of Lucifer's mixed bloodline children, and it was an on-purpose design meant to change the order of things. This truth means Cain was the beginning person of a mixed bloodline on this Earth, whom Lucifer would watch grow and multiply.

However, while the wicked Lucifer and the other rebellious angels were watching their bloodline grow strong and multiply on this Earth, Lucifer could also watch the flesh bloodline at the same time die to make room for his children to populate this Earth.

The fruit on the tree of knowledge of good and evil was the same fruit all men and women lust for throughout every generation. And nearly everyone on this earth has enjoyed the same fruit since Adam and Eve ate thereof in the Garden of God.

The fruit Eve ate from the tree of knowledge of good and evil still is the same fruit, causing men and women to join together in holy matrimony. And it's the same fruit, causing men and women to love one another, push baby carriages around, and increase their family size.

I guarantee you that the forbidden and wonderful fruit Eve ate was not an apple but the fruit of intimate pleasure. And it's for certain innocence in the Garden of God was lost after Eve and the wicked Lucifer shared the fruit of the womb.

Furthermore, I shouldn't have to explain further concerning the birds and the bees and eating watermelon seeds. But the innocent and naïve Eve was beguiled and tricked, and she was seduced by the charming serpent of old in the Garden of God.

As recorded in the book of Genesis, the naïve Eve ate the fruit from the tree of knowledge of good and evil. The tree of knowledge of good and evil isn't a natural fruit tree, but it's symbolic of the serpent of old in all his glory.

The image of jealousy is the charming Lucifer, who has many names on this Earth and uses different names among unlearned men and women all the time. Indeed, in the Garden of God in Eden, he deepens the mystery by hiding behind symbolic names.

Lucifer is why the naive Eve was the mother to the third bloodline race when it began on the Earth in the Garden of God, just as she's the mother of the flesh and blood race upon this Earth, except for the sixth-day creation people God created before He rested.

This truth means Eve is the mother of two different bloodlines, which two fathers fathered, probably on the same day. But for some unexplained reason, we do not have any information about the sixth-day creation people and their beginning.

Anyway, the sixth-day creation people began before Adam and Eve, and their beginning was somewhere outside the Garden of God. This truth means the story about Cain, who took a wife from the land of Nod, insinuates he took a mate with a sixth-day creation woman.

Anyway, bible scriptures tell us these two types of bloodlines, created from the womb of Eve, will oppose and hate each other until harvest time comes. Similarly to the same way, the mixed bloodline Cain hated Abel and killed him.

Furthermore, I want you to know that Lucifer opposes and hates God like the tares oppose and hate the wheat. And the scriptures tell us it's a prophesized hate, and prophesized before the great cleansing flood.

After Lucifer and Eve shared the fruit of the womb, our Supreme God caught up with the serpent of old, called Satan. And face to face, God said unto him, because thou O' Lucifer hast did <u>this</u> (sexual encounter with Eve), thou art cursed above, and more so than all cattle.

Indeed, the curse God applied to the wicked Lucifer was above and more so than every beast of the field; upon thy belly, thou O' Lucifer shalt go. And dust and humiliation and shame, shalt thou O' Lucifer eat and suffer from all the days of thy life.

The next awareness scripture, extremely important to understand, reveals the feelings of God, and it illuminates God talking to the evil Lucifer. For the benefit of knowledge and truth, the next scripture also reveals God's dissatisfaction with the wicked and rebellious Lucifer.

> **Genesis 3:15** And <u>I</u> (the wonderful Supreme God of Heaven and Earth) will put <u>enmity</u> (means hostility and hatred), between <u>thee</u> (O' Lucifer, the serpent of old) and the <u>woman</u> (means Eve), and <u>thy</u> <u>seed</u> (means Lucifer's seed, called Cain) and <u>her</u> <u>seed</u> (means Eve's seed, called Abel, and whosoever is a son or daughter to Adam).

Cain and Abel were born from the same womb, but their characteristics differed after birth. The young boy called Abel, the son of Adam, had a different and better set of values and a much godlier set of morals than the mixed bloodline Cain.

Partially, the difference is because Cain was the jealous son of the image of jealousy, and the influence Lucifer projected was ungodly. And Cain was so jealous of Abel that he rose in anger against him, which was caused by jealousy, a characteristic of his father.

The son of jealousy, Cain, Lucifer's firstborn, murdered his (half) brother, Abel. And it certainly appears the firstborn of a mixed bloodline murdered the firstborn of the children of God, and both were created in Eden.

Positively, the naive Eve, tricked and seduced by Lucifer, was their mother, and Abel was the pure bloodline son of Adam. And I am certain the wicked Lucifer didn't have any good feelings about Abel or care about his life.

However, after the birth example of Cain, the population of mixed bloodline children continued to grow, and probably rapidly. Because the other rebellious angels, who served Lucifer, also followed Lucifer's example of propagation with Eve.

The other rebellious angels, determined to have their children, decided to emulate the example of Lucifer. They took women from the sixth-day creation people for their own to propagate, and they mixed the two bloodlines.

These next few scriptures will turn back the pages of time and illustrate an example of fallen angels out of control. And they reveal how Lucifer and Eve chose to change the course of life during the first Earth age.

These next few scriptures, stunning and meaningful, reveal the other rebellious angels and the daughters of men propagating together, as Eve and Lucifer chose to do. And it's easy to conclude they were modifying the original bloodline.

> **Genesis 6:1** And it came to pass when men began to multiply on the face of the Earth, and daughters were born unto them.

Genesis 6:2 That the <u>sons</u> <u>of</u> <u>God</u> (means Lucifer, and the rebellious angels) saw the daughters of men were fair;

Genesis 6:2 and <u>they</u> (the rebellious angels) <u>took</u> (means took by force, or through seduction, or both through force and through seduction), them wives of all which <u>they</u> (the rebellious angels) chose.

Genesis 6:4 There were giants in the Earth in <u>those</u> <u>days</u> (before the great flood); and also, after that, when the <u>sons</u> <u>of</u> <u>God</u> (means Lucifer, and the rebellious angels) came in unto the daughters of men,

Genesis 6:4 and <u>they</u> (the daughters of men) bare children to <u>them</u> (the rebellious angels), the <u>same</u> (offspring children, called the mixed bloodline children) became mighty men which <u>were</u> <u>of</u> <u>old</u>, (means children born from angels, like the serpent of old), men of <u>renown</u> (men known for a violent reputation who hate and murder innocent people).

The scripture in Genesis 6:4 reveals the rebellious angelic sons of God mixed their bloodline with the bloodline of the daughters of men. And they did it methodically, mostly so the wicked, rebellious angels could have their bloodline children.

Therefore, when the scriptures tell us these children were of old times, it's talking about the children born to the Ancient of Day's angels. This truth means these children were the offspring bloodline of the rebellious male angels, even from the unknown, Ancient of Days.

These rebellious angels, cast out of Heaven, came from the unknown time of old. And from the kingdom of God, where their beginning began. And the serpent of old, cast out of Heaven, was the self-appointed god of the rebellious angels and the god of the mixed bloodline race.

Therefore, part of the supernatural curse upon the serpent of old, alias the wicked king of Tyrus, was to bruise his heel. And the **serpent's heel was bruised** by our wonderful Supreme God's ultimate curse on Lucifer.

I assure you, part of the curse placed on Lucifer and the rebellious angels was the unclean curse of homosexuality. The God-imposed curse caused the serpent of old to have a thinking problem, and the curse entwines him to the abomination of the same sex.

The God-imposed curse the all-mighty Lord placed on the wicked Lucifer includes the rebellious angels and the mixed bloodline race. And maybe they'll be hindered daily by an unnatural lust, one for another and man for man, for the rest of their lives.

It's for certain the shameful curse of homosexuality did bruise their heel and hindered their royal plans of grandeur on this Earth. And their choice of sex partners wasn't the same as before after they were cursed with the curse of homosexuality.

The symbolic king of Tyrus, wiser than the prophet Daniel, was seen in the beautiful Garden of God at Eden, but a different alias name identified him. And because of his elusiveness and ability to deceive, most people cannot connect the two today.

I am one hundred percent certain if God hadn't looked ahead and destroyed the ungodly inhabitants on this Earth with the great cleansing flood. Then, this Earth would be completely populated by the mixed bloodline people and the rebellious angels.

Without the results of the great saving flood, the Earth's population would have been very different during this second Earth age. And without a doubt, the human race would be completely extinct. And for this reason, I call the great cleansing flood a great saving flood.

I am certain this Earth would be Lucifer's Heaven away from Heaven if not for the great saving flood. And if not for the flood, Lucifer would still be roaming around this Earth freely in his physical form. And he would be the god to Earth full of his bloodline children.

If not for the great saving flood, Lucifer and the other rebellious angels wouldn't be locked away in the pits of Hell. And I firmly believe this Earth would've adopted a whole new way of life, and the lifestyles of men and women would be ungodly.

Truly, I cannot fully imagine how this Earth would look and be with Lucifer in total control of its society. And I am certain our imagination cannot picture how Lucifer would shape and rule this world *if* he were the god of total authority.

I am also certain the wicked and hateful Lucifer would cast out God's perfect and righteous Ten Commandments. And I am certain righteousness wouldn't be required in his world. And the things God expects from all people, Lucifer wouldn't expect.

However, thanks to our Great Creator God, and because He cares about us, Lucifer is not the God in control, and this isn't his Earth. And if we want to live forever, we better embrace and love the Ten Commandments of God every minute, hour, and day.

Gaining the gift of immortality with our Great Creator God hinges on us keeping and living by the Ten Commandments of God. And the requirements of the Ten Commandments will never change, not even until the end of time.

Not until Heaven and Earth pass away, and Heaven and Earth will not pass away until our Great Creator God is finished with this Earth. But evil men and angels will pass away permanently, much sooner than the Earth will.

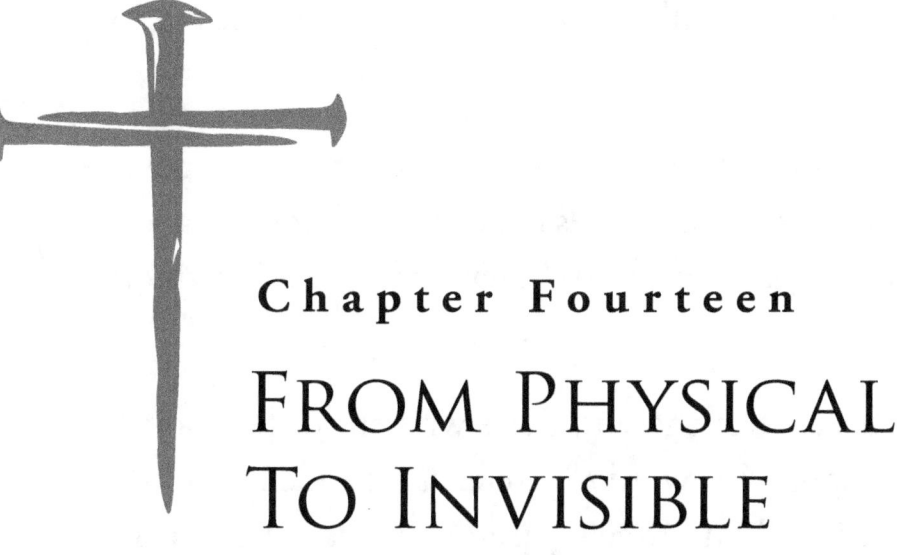

Chapter Fourteen

FROM PHYSICAL TO INVISIBLE

Indeed, before the great cleansing flood, life was much different during the first Earth age, and it was better for the rebellious angels than it was after the flood. And it's easy to conclude their quality of life plummeted after the great cleansing flood.

Before the great flood, Lucifer and the other rebellious angels were in a physical body and visible on this Earth. And all things might have continued being that way if they hadn't taken the daughters of men and created their mixed bloodline.

Mainly because they were living on this Earth unpunished, and a God-imposed curse didn't mark their lifestyle until they mated and mixed their seed with the flesh and blood woman. And God was watching them, and going too far meant that compensation was unavoidable for them.

After the mixing event, the curse of homosexuality and a depraved mind were supernaturally imposed on them. Within the next scripture, taken from the book of Romans, the Apostle Paul talks about the curse of homosexuality and a reprobate mind.

In Paul's explanation of the supernatural God-imposed curse, the Apostle Paul uses the illusive word *they* when he describes the people he's talking about in the book of Romans. And for this reason, we'll have to put an identity to the word *they*.

As for myself, I believe because of the scriptures written in the book of Genesis and the book of Romans. The word *they* refers to the identity of the serpent of old and the other rebellious angels, *given over* to a supernatural God-imposed curse.

Therefore, compensation happened to the rebellious angels before the great cleansing flood. And it was mainly because of the rebellious, wicked, and ungodly things the wicked angels did before the supernatural curse existed. Indeed, they behaved foolishly and condemned their souls to the fires of Hell for opposing God's plan for man and woman.

Furthermore, I assure you that life got much worse for them after they did terrible, wicked, violent, and immoral things after receiving a God-imposed curse. They are a perfect example, illustrating the judgment of recompense catching up to premeditated sin.

I want you to know that their rebellious acts, mixed with wickedness, are the reason for the great cleansing flood. Indeed, the great cleansing flood is a pivotal time, purposely created to change their life course.

The great cleansing flood was the point in time when Lucifer and the rebellious angels changed from physical to spiritual and from visible to invisible. And please understand these needed changes occurred after the great cleansing flood.

The next few scriptures reveal ungodly people and rebellious angels going about their endeavors with a depraved mind as their guide. And the brave Apostle Paul wants us to know that homosexual people are quite different than normal people.

The next few character scriptures, revealing and descriptive, unveil a great mystery to most people. For our benefit, the Bible describes the supernatural pre-designed curse implemented in the Garden of God at Eden. And so you'll know, Lucifer was the only evil creature in the Garden of God.

> **Romans 1:26** For this cause God <u>gave</u> <u>them</u> <u>up</u> (means made them desire a certain way, and they desired to be given over and), into <u>vile</u> <u>affections</u> (means degrading sexual, and homosexual passions): For even their women did change the <u>natural</u> <u>use</u> (of sex,) into that which is <u>against</u> <u>nature</u> (unnatural, unclean, and homosexual).

> **Romans 1:27** And likewise, also the men, <u>leaving</u> (means turning away from) the natural use of (sex with a) woman, <u>burned</u> (means they had uncontrollable homosexual desires, and they burned) in their lust one toward another;

> **Romans 1:27** <u>Men</u> <u>with</u> <u>men</u> (means homosexual men with men) <u>working</u> (means doing) that which is <u>unseemly</u> (means unnatural, and homosexual).

Romans 1:28 And even as <u>they</u> (means the serpent of old, and the rebellious angels, and their rebellious children),

Romans 1:28 did not like to <u>retain</u> (means did not want to know) God in their knowledge; God <u>gave</u> <u>them</u> <u>over</u> (means made them so) to have a <u>reprobate</u> <u>mind</u>,

Romans 1:28 (means evil and dirty mind), to do those things (means homosexual things) which are not <u>convenient</u> (means not right, and not moral, and not godly).

As my wonderful and loving Supreme God watched from Heaven, He saw the serpent of old and the other rebellious angels change His children's bloodline into their bloodline. He decided to *bruise* the serpent again, so God sent the great flood to cover this Earth.

Positively, the ***first bruise*** on the rebellious angels was the shameful curse of homosexuality and a reprobate mind. The ***second bruise*** on the rebellious angels was the great flood removing them from the Earth, and removing them from the surface of this Earth bruised their heel badly.

Indeed, the ***third bruise*** on Lucifer and the other rebellious angels happened when their mixed bloodline children couldn't repopulate and control this Earth anymore. And from the pits of Hell, their population privilege ended, and a woman wasn't available to them.

The great flood destroyed the grand plan of the rebellious and homosexual children of the serpent, and it removed the bad angels from the Earth. As we can see, the serpent's heel has been ***bruised three times***, and the fourth bruise comes after the great flood.

Positively, the cursed serpent of old was *bruised* again for the **fourth time** when God destroyed the homosexual cities of Sodom and Gomorrah. And I believe that stopping the growth of Sodom and Gomorrah stopped an expansion of overwhelming reprobate men from taking control of this Earth.

However, during the first Earth age, the bloodline children of God, not mixed with the angel bloodline, boarded the boat belonging to God and Noah. And God sailed them into this second Earth age for a new beginning, away from the old world of violence, uncleanness, and darkness.

The first earth age, the old world with three bloodlines, existing before the great cleansing flood they escaped from, was similar to the cities of Sodom and Gomorrah, only much worse. But after the great flood, life is better, and the new beginning in this second Earth age is void of the physical presence of Lucifer and his demon army.

The new beginning in this second Earth age is void of all the rebellious angels because they returned to Heaven during the great flood. And I am certain it was the plan of our righteous Supreme God of Heaven and Earth, who was waiting for them to return to Heaven.

However, it wasn't a happy reunion for the rebellious angels because God took hold of them with His mighty hand and locked them away in prison. And for now, the wicked Lucifer, the image of jealousy, and the rebellious angels are reserved and bound in everlasting chains under darkness.

Thanks to God, they are bound in the bottomless pit and waiting for a judgment call against them on Judgment Day. But being in the pits of Hell doesn't mean the presence of the image of jealousy and the presence of the rebellious angels are gone completely.

Being locked away in the abyss of Hell doesn't mean they aren't here on the Earth in this second-earth age because their presence is here among us now. But their presence is not here among us in their physical form, the way they were during the first Earth age.

Still, their presence is here among us, and it's a strong and unnoticed presence, stealth and destructive. And I want you to know that they are the invisible ghost spirits of the air, and unbeknownst to a man or woman, they invade the thoughts of the mind and heart.

Truly, the image of jealousy began in Heaven as Lucifer. And afterward, he was the serpent of old and Satan during the first Earth age. But for now, during this second Earth age, he's the invisible image of jealousy and the hideous devil, among other alias names.

His invisible ghost spirit is alive and strong in the hearts of unbelievers, and many of them follow his pernicious, corrupt, and homosexual ways. And according to the God of Heaven and Earth, they have a built-in hostility toward the children of God.

The Apostle Paul tells us the wicked Lucifer, the image of jealousy, or the serpent of old, is the invisible power of the air. And Lucifer is an invisible and ungodly demonic ghost spirit, continually working through the children of disobedience.

Indeed, the wicked image of jealousy isn't about to change from his wicked ways, and he will continue to oppose God's good and righteous works. At least until the wonderful Son of God returns to the Earth and destroys him with the brightness of His coming.

Hallelujah (means praise the Lord)! And I pray for the second return of the Son of God, and the sooner, the better, because these last days will wax worse and worse and be more unbearable for righteous people until He returns.

Thanks to our great God because, in our history timeline, Lucifer's power has been bruised and reduced to spiritual power. And Lucifer can no longer control the people living on this Earth through physical force. And especially during the second Earth Age.

However, the devious Lucifer has adapted to his new spirit environment, and one of his most successfully used tools is telepathy. And through the ability to implant messages, he communicates with his servants of darkness, who listen to his ghost spirit voice.

Although I assure you, everyone living on this Earth, male or female, is listening to either the wonderful Holy Spirit of God or the voice of an ungodly spirit of invisibility. And I warn you, regardless of whether you are aware, we'll hear the voice of both spirits.

Regardless, whichever it may be among men and women, none of us in the flesh can think entirely for ourselves without being influenced to some degree by spiritual power. And please realize it's up to us to discern one spirit from the other Spirit.

Therefore, the difference between the spiritual power we listen to is in the messages they prod men and women to lean toward doing. Because we are compelled to be godlier or ungodlier, we better examine every thought we consider acting on that runs through our heads.

I tell you, the children of God listen to the voice of the invisible Holy Ghost, and He compels them to be righteous and do well. But the servants of darkness are different, and they listen to the demonic spirit of invisible demons and do not care about righteousness according to God.

This truth means we all follow one authentic God or a lesser god, and our lifestyle truly emulates one another. And because we cannot see these guiding spirits with our eyes, it doesn't mean their presence isn't here among us and feeding us suggestions.

Because the form of the wonderful Holy Ghost is invisible in form, and the demonic spirits of the air are invisible forms, too. And I want you to know that both have the power to plant thoughts and be an invisible guiding spirit.

Obviously, from time to time, we do have to be warned by the caring Holy Ghost and not be deceived by evil thoughts projected through telepathy and mind control. And I am telling you, we better stay on guard constantly and not let an evil thought influence us.

However, if we are Bible-savvy Christians, the caring Holy Ghost is the protector in our fortress, and whenever our thoughts coincide with the word of God, we are listening to the voice of the Holy Spirit of God. And He's the voice compelling us to refuse evil and choose the good.

Indeed, I am certain the Holy Spirit of God is our high wall of defense against invisible evil spirits who desire to control our thoughts and actions.

And if our body is free from the unclean, then our body is the fortress the Holy Ghost works through and lives within.

If we eat the filthy, unclean swine, our fortress can weaken, and our high wall will be brought down. But our fortress can be strong, and our high wall high, if we eat acceptable foods and keep a clean dwelling place for the wonderful Holy Ghost of God.

Indeed, believers in Christ are the living temple of God, and the kingdom of God lives within us. And if the kingdom of God dwells within us, then the Holy Ghost dwells within us, and He will dwell and teach from inside a clean temple that avoids eating the unclean.

However, do be warned, if the living flesh and blood temple is unclean, then the unclean person will suffer from a lack of bible knowledge. And it's because the Holy Ghost cannot function well within an unclean temple. And maybe He'll not live within an unclean temple.

An unclean living temple is like leaving our doors unlocked at night or sleeping under a leaky roof. An unclean living temple amounts to an unguarded heart, and the ghost spirit of demons will invade an unguarded heart and prod the heart to sin.

Beyond the shadow of a doubt, the strength of the Spirit within us is determined by the cleanness of our living temple. And as hard as it is for some people to realize, our degree of cleanness determines the strength we receive from the Holy Ghost. If I were you, I would be careful and not eat unclean foods, but I would endeavor to keep my heart clean.

The definition of sin is defined as the breaking of His commandments, and the definition of unclean amounts to whatever we do to our bodies. And

I want you to know that both definitions will hinder the Holy Ghost from being close to us. And I want you to realize the degree of our holiness will be greater if we refuse to eat the unclean.

Chapter Fifteen

PURE AT HEART

Positively, pure-hearted Christians hear God's inaudible voice as His Spirit speaks to His loyal children. And maybe Christians in love with His word are the only ones He speaks to and finds trustworthy. And I ask you, why should He speak to someone unwilling to listen?

Certainly, our great and wonderful Supreme God will advise and bless all children in love with righteousness. And because His children love doing right, then for an extra benefit, He will give them special understanding and favor.

Positively, I want you to realize the God of Heaven and Earth will be a shield against the wicked and the vilest of men. And no one is stronger or more resourceful than Him. And I want you to know that having Him as our friend will greatly benefit us.

Our wonderful and loving Supreme God, great beyond comparison, is always the Good Shepherd to the pure-at-heart sheep. And the pure at-heart sheep love His ways and excellent commandments and put all their trust in Him.

Indeed, the pure-at-heart sheep know His voice, and they seek after Him every day. And they answer Him when He calls upon their heart. And goodness and mercy shall follow the pure at-heart sheep all the days of their life.

The revealing scriptures tell us the pure-hearted sheep, who love our Supreme God, will dwell in the house of the Lord forever. And the Good Shepherd, alias the Father, the Son, and the Holy Ghost, will teach the pure at-heart sheep the wonderful ways of the Lord.

The Good Shepherd will guide the pure-hearted sheep with His eyes, and He'll provide help to them through His Holy Spirit. And the sacrifices of the pure at-heart sheep are not burnt offerings. But are a broken spirit and a crushed heart, remorseful for sin.

It's pure at heart sheep who desire, yearn, pray, and look for the second coming of Yeshua. And because of their steadfast belief in Him, they will be rewarded with eternal life. And there will come a day they'll live in the kingdom of God.

Indeed, the pure-at-heart sheep who love Yeshua are the ones who carry the seal of the Living God on their forehead. Gaining God's living seal means God's beautiful word guides our hearts. And His seal also means we belong to Him and will live in His kingdom.

God's written word assures us that the pure at-heart sheep are His chosen people who receive divine protection. And they'll not be hurt by the wrath of the wicked devil after many demons are released upon this Earth in the last days.

The pure-at-heart sheep are dedicated people who openly and gladly confess their love for Yeshua. And they aren't ashamed to serve and worship Him and gladly do it with a pure and loving heart. And they worship and abide in His ways before all men.

However, the not-so-pure-at-heart man goats, the tares, and the chaff or trash deny Christ before all men. They'll stand before the Judgment Throne someday, and Christ will deny them before His Father in Heaven.

The pure-at-heart sheep shall be called the sons of God because they believe in Christ and overcome the world of sin through faith in Him. But whosoever denies the Son of God hath not faith, nor do they have a home promised to them in the kingdom of God.

The pure at-heart sheep love their Great God, and they hath the love of God. Because they realize He laid down His life for them. And God is happy with whosoever loves Him, and His loyal followers will be blessed in various ways.

The pure-at-heart sheep draw near to God because they are thankful for the blood sacrifice His Son courageously gave upon the cross. And if we draw near to God, He'll draw near to us. And this is His policy toward all people, regardless of color, nationality, or gender.

Blessed are the pure-at-heart sheep because they endure and dodge temptations, trials, and stumbling blocks set before them by the ungodly servants of darkness. And if we love God, we'll hate ungodly temptations.

Surely, the pure at-heart sheep, who overcome temptations and trials and learn to hate sin, shall receive the crown of life. And every day we live and breathe, our crown of life is challenged by the wicked spirits of the air. And I conclude a crown of life guarantees us a home in the kingdom of God.

Our wonderful God of Heaven and Earth will always bless the pure-at-heart sheep because of their pureness of heart, regardless of whether or not they are rich or poor. And we need to realize being rich or poor hasn't any connection with being pure at heart.

The pure-at-heart sheep are carried to Heaven by an angel of God after the death of their flesh. In the same way, Lazarus was carried to Heaven by an angel of God. And when the day comes for us to make our change, we'll be glad we fell in love with the word of God.

> **Matthew 5:1 through 12** Blessed are the <u>poor</u> (the humble and broken-hearted) in spirit: For theirs is the kingdom of Heaven.

Blessed are they that mourn, for they shall be comforted, as Abraham comforted Lazarus in paradise. Blessed are the <u>meek</u> (the humble, and the pure at heart): For they shall inherit the Earth after it's cleansed of wickedness.

Blessed are <u>they</u> (means the pure at heart), who hunger and thirst after righteousness, as the excellent word of God stipulates it: For they shall be <u>filled</u> (with the love of God, and the knowledge of God, and the glory of God, and every day of their life will be peaceful).

Blessed are the merciful: For they shall obtain mercy. And it's because they gave mercy to their fellow person in need. Blessed are the <u>pure</u> (sincere believers) in heart, for they shall see God and be a part of His kingdom.

Blessed are the peacemakers, who shall be called the children of God because they sought peace among all men. And blessed are they, who are persecuted for righteousness sake: For theirs is the kingdom of Heaven, because they fell hopelessly in love with righteousness.

<u>Blessed</u> (means happy) are ye, when men revile and persecute you, and shall falsely say all manners of evil against you for <u>My</u> (Yeshua) sake. (So) rejoice, and be exceeding glad, for great is your reward in Heaven: For so persecuted they the prophets, which were before you.

The pure at-heart sheep are the salt of this Earth and are the God lovers who prefer righteousness and abhor unrighteousness. But if the salt <u>has lost its savor</u> (means if the Earth is void of pure at-heart men and women).

<u>Wherewith</u> (means how) shall the Earth be salted, and how will it be of value if it's void of the pure at-heart sheep? And without having the pure at-heart sheep, the Earth is thenceforth good for nothing. But to be cast out and trodden under the foot of ungodly men.

I assure you, the pure at-heart people living upon this Earth are the salt of the Earth, similar to the oak trees growing among the poplars. And this great Earth is of no value to the great God of creation if it hasn't got pure at heart people living upon it.

After this middle ground, the Earth is void of pure-hearted people, ungodliness is rampant, and only wickedness remains. Then everything remaining upon this Earth will be the salt-less children of the devil, and we'll have an Earth missing the savor of godliness.

Be assured when the Earth is void of salt, ungodliness is rampant, and the servants of darkness are dancing in the streets. Then our Supreme God will let the salt-less people on this Earth trod the nations underfoot, like a wild beast on a savage hunt for weaker prey.

Beyond the shadow of a doubt, when the Earth is void of pure-hearted sheep. Then, this unstable Earth will be like the first Earth age and turn into a massive killing field. And compassion for human life will fade away like the sun giving way to darkness.

The pure-at-heart believers in Christ are the light of this world, and when the light is put out, only darkness and ungodliness will remain. And when wicked men are above the law, and corruption triumphs over justice, we live under a dark cloud created by the evil prince of this world.

Surely, I am correct to say, without having pure at-heart believers in Christ. Then, this unstable world will be trapped in darkness and engulfed by immorality. And I am certain godly people with salt running through their veins will be as hard to find as gold.

Indeed, we all have essential requirements, and the pure-at-heart sheep cannot live in darkness. But because they love God, they do savor the flavor of salt and light. And we Christians do require the word of God, and it's our light and our salt.

I want you to know our wonderful Supreme God is symbolic of light and salt, love and peace, and everything good and right in this world. But the hideous and corrupt devil symbolizes bitterness, darkness, and unrestrained evil.

Nor does the wicked devil, alias Lucifer, the serpent of old, have any salt running through his veins. And if he did, then he would be loyal to the all-mighty God of creation. But bitterness and hate run through his veins, and he's not loyal to God.

The next matter-of-fact scripture, concerning everyone looking for the right way, reveals the requirements of the pure-hearted sheep. And bible scriptures reveal that good works are like a candle in our hand, which we use to remove darkness.

> **Matthew 5:15** Neither do men light a candle, and put it under a basket, but on a candlestick; and it giveth light unto all in the house.

> **Matthew 5:16** Let your light shine so before men, that they may see your good works, and glorify your Father, which is in Heaven.

The pure-at-heart sheep are determined to carry the candle and let it shine before all men who need to find the light. And the great light shining from the candle symbolizes our pure at-heart God and Him shining light into this world of darkness.

Therefore, if the light from the candle shines into your home, then you should let your light shine before other men. And mainly because the light from the candle should not be put under a basket or hidden from men needing to see the light.

I assure you, God's wonderful word should not be withheld from anyone who desires to hear its infallible revelations. And for the glory of God, it will prevent all men and women from stumbling around in the dark and getting lost in strange places.

The pure-at-heart sheep emulates the greater light shining forth from the throne of God, similar to a bright lighthouse on the edge of the sea. And the candle reveals the rocks, able to destroy ships, or in our case, it reveals sins designed to destroy souls.

Truly, I want you to know the light shining brightly from the candle is symbolic of the wonderful gospel of God. And the wonderful gospel of God divides light from darkness. And His word is light, and ungodliness is darkness.

I assure you, the pure at-heart sheep fall in love with the laws, the commandments, and all the perfect word of God. And it's the pure at-heart sheep who put their hope and trust in the Good Shepherd. And the pure at heart believes God guides us in the right direction.

It's the pure at-heart sheep, willing to do His work, and they try their best to rescue the lost and add them to the flock of the Good Shepherd. Storing treasures in Heaven is accumulated by working for the Good Shepherd.

The pure-at-heart sheep always listen for His still and quiet voice to direct their feet and steer them clear of troubles and wickedness. And I hope you realize that the wonderful Good Shepherd is our rock in times of trouble.

As Heaven is high above the Earth, so is His mercy and love toward anyone, pure and sincere at heart, who puts their faith in Him. And I am telling you, putting our faith in God secures our relationship with Him.

I assure you; the love and mercy of the Good Shepherd are everlasting to the pure at-heart sheep. And the pure at-heart sheep are glad for His mercy and love and appreciate Him. And mercy and love illuminate two key ingredients to a life of immortality.

The pure-at-heart sheep know the voice of God, and they love to hear Him speak through His written word, recorded in the bible. And nothing pleases a Bible-savvy believer more than learning a new mystery concerning our Great God.

Our wonderful Good Shepherd delivers the pure-hearted sheep from storms, calamities, and distress among the ungodly. And I want you to know that we are wise if we tune into His voice and listen to His warnings.

The Good Shepherd blesses pure-hearted believers if they are determined to keep His beautiful testimonies and decrees. And I want you to know, as loving and merciful as He is toward us, He has expectations and expects us to live by His commandments.

I assure you, the pure at-heart sheep will not die the eternal death of the unbeliever. But the pure at-heart sheep will live forever in the peaceful kingdom of God. And they'll be assigned a new body, built to stand the test of time.

The pure-at-heart sheep know the loving-kindness of the Lord, and they appreciate Him. And thanks to Him, we have a wonderful Savior. And salvation is a portion of our inheritance, promised by the wonderful Good Shepherd.

Indeed, the righteous word of the Lord is a lamp and a guiding light to the pure-hearted sheep who cherish His every word. And they always ask themselves before doing anything, would God approve of what I am about to do?

The pure, at-heart sheep, baptized and submerged under water and washed clean, delight themselves in the righteous ways of our Supreme God. And I fully conclude it's a joy to be a new person in Christ and do good works for His glory.

Therefore, I want you to realize that our Creator God's righteous ways are not grievous to the pure-at-heart sheep. And I assure you, there's nothing offensive to the pure at-heart sheep concerning the excellent word of God.

The idols of the heathen are silver and gold, and material treasures and various worldly pleasures usually occupy their time. But the treasures of the pure at-heart sheep are the works of the Lord, including all spiritual things, including the Holy Ghost, who lives within them.

The pure-at-heart sheep have wings, and their wings will carry them safely from the traps and snares of the devil. But the heathen, who walks the walk of wickedness and corruption, will never know the joy of eluding the ways of Satan.

The pure-at-heart sheep believe they have a caring Savior and a future resurrection date with Him. And they delight in their inner peace from serving and loving God. And life is but a vapor, and when the vapor clears, the pure at-heart sheep have a Savior.

The pure at-heart sheep love the instructions of the Lord, but fools despise and reject the knowledge of my God of creation. And the pure at heart sheep incline their ear unto scripture wisdom, and they learn to apply the word of God to their everyday life.

Indeed, the wonderful Good Shepherd gives the pure-at-heart sheep wisdom, knowledge, and understanding. But fools eat from the tree of knowledge of good and evil and fall prey to the traps and snares of the wicked Lucifer.

The footsteps of the Lord walk beside the pure-at-heart sheep, and the pure-at-heart sheep are never alone, even when they are by themselves. But the footsteps of the wicked and the corrupt person shall be cut off. And they'll disappear from the Earth after their allotted time is finished.

Indeed, my wonderful Good Shepherd walks with the pure-at-heart sheep, and He makes their life more pleasant, day after day. But calamities, misfortune, misery, and troubles are the reward for the foolish fool who rejects light for darkness.

Our Good Shepherd is the tree of life, and the pure-at-heart sheep find rest underneath His branches, and they prefer the shade from His tree. And happy and content are the pure at-heart sheep in love with peace, who promote peace and brotherly love.

The Tree of Life is the fountain of youth, and the living waters flowing from its pure heart are the righteous word of God, given to us from the Heavens above. And I want you to know that God's wonderful gospel is the image of God and living waters, too.

The pure-at-heart sheep, determined to love God, are the only ones interested enough to drink from the fountain of youth. And the fountain of youth preserves everlasting life. And I conclude that our fountain of youth is the life-saving gospel of God.

The pure-at-heart sheep are the apple of God's eye and the sweetness of His works, and He favors them with good gifts from above. The pure-at-heart sheep feel the same way about God, and He's the apple in the eyes of the sincere-at-heart sheep.

Beyond the shadow of a doubt, the sweetness of the Lord is warmth and understanding and a feeling of belonging to Him. And I want you to know acceptance into His family radiates a warmth; regular fossil fuel heat will not compare to or parallel.

I assure you that being accepted into His family is worth more than gold, silver, diamonds, pearls, or any material treasures. And there will come a day and a time when having our name written in the Lamb's Book of Life will be our greatest achievement.

Positively, His children of a pure heart will hear His voice calling their name from the Book of Life. Sadly, I must tell you, the rude scoffers, mockers, and unbelievers will not get their names written in the Lamb Book of Life.

I am happy to say our wonderful Supreme Supernatural God is the Good Shepherd. And the pure at-heart believers are happy to be members of His flock of sheep. And I gladly will testify forever I am happy to be one of His pure at-heart sheep.

The Good Master is the flock's Shepherd, who trusts in Him. But sadly, I conclude, everyone else doesn't have a Good Shepherd. This truth means the flock belonging to the Good Shepherd is exclusive, and loving the Good Shepherd makes them exclusive.

The flock of believers is the pure-at-heart sheep who graze from the pasture of righteousness and godliness. And the green pastures, the sheep eat from and hunger for every day, are the wonderful words of our Great Creator God.

The Good Shepherd has many gifts to give believers who love Him, and He fills their bellies with His pure and holy gospel. And His hungry sheep never receive too much of His gospel and continually hunger for more of His excellent life-saving word.

Blessed are the pure at heart sheep, if they walketh not in the counsel of the ungodly or partake the ways of the sinner. And we are a little foolish to believe we can counsel with the ungodly and the conclusions will be godly.

Blessed are the pure-at-heart sheep, determined to keep their lamp full of oil. And blessed are whosoever relies on the valuable word of God, every day and every night. But we do have to fall in love with the word of God to keep our lamp full of oil.

Even though the pure at-heart sheep are the apple of God's eye, they are not as pure at heart as God is pure at heart. And mainly because there aren't any flesh and blood people or heavenly angels as pure at heart as our wonderful Supreme God.

My wonderful Supreme God is the purest at heart, and the rest of us are going through a learning process and learning how to become pure at heart. And the wonderful word of God teaches everyone interested in the excellent formula for developing a pure heart.

Blessed are the meek, humble, and whosoever keeps the peace because these men and women are the pure at-heart sheep prophesized to inherit the Earth. And there will come a day and a time when it'll be the pure-at-heart inheritance time.

Surely, the pure at-heart sheep, in love with the righteous word of God, shall delight themselves in abundant peace, joy, happiness, and love. And they look forward to spending eternity in His kingdom, only consisting of peace, joy, and brotherly love.

The word of the Lord is greater in purity than silver, melted down seven times, with all the impurities skimmed off each time the silver is melted down. And this means God's heart is pure love, and the purest of silver will not compare to the love within His heart.

The pure-at-heart sheep love their incredible God. And they say, glory Hallelujah, and praise the Lord over every good thing. And life is full of choices, good and bad. And we can be pure at heart, or our hearts can be as dark as a black cloud.

I want you to know that the pure at-heart sheep win the great prize of immortality, but no prize is given to the lost. This truth means many men and women were invited to the wedding feast, but some were too busy to come to the wedding and honor the bride and groom.

I assure you, this Earth is a testing place, the middle ground between Heaven and Hell. And this is where everyone upon the Earth is tested for the pureness of heart. And at the end of our life, we'll either be pure at heart or not so pure.

Although, as sad as it may be, not all men will win the prize of immortality, and many people will be cast into the lake of fire. And the destroying lake of fire is reserved for the cold and the lukewarm person. And it's because they couldn't see themselves being hot and on fire for God.

However, do not give up on sinner men and women completely until their allotted time is finished because they must also find our Great God. And wise is the humble Christian, not holier than thou, if he's able to realize *he was a used to be* sinner person himself.

Indeed, this informative story is meant to raise our intelligence to a higher degree of godliness and illuminate the pure-at-heart sheep. It's both a warning and revealing story saying the God of creation is prodding us to be one of many of His pure, at-heart sheep.

However, God only accepts willing volunteers, and He doesn't twist arms, and none of us are forced to be pure at heart sheep. But when it comes time for our spirit to leave this Earth, we'll be glad we volunteered to be a pure at-heart sheep.

Chapter Sixteen

MILK OR STRONG MEAT

Not anyone comes to Jesus Christ from the beginning of their new life and has great spiritual wisdom from the first day of their conversion. Nor do new converts come to Him bible savvy, and they do not have the answer to mysteries and hard-to-understand story examples.

I assure you, for some reason other than great understanding, most of us come to know our Savior with a broken heart from the mud puddles of life. And we come to Him when we have only a little knowledge about the expectations of God.

This analogy means new believers in the gospel of God come to know Jesus Christ as babes sipping on milk. Although it's shameful, I've seen many professing Christians live their whole life and still be Christian babes sipping on milk.

I've seen older Christians of many years in the house of God, and they oppose the authentic word of God as if it doesn't matter at all. And they are still eating the unclean, and they never get to the point where they can understand the truthful word of God with the correct definition.

I suppose it's okay to be a Christian babe on milk if it's the kind of life a Christian wants for themselves simply because all Christians on milk are the children of our Great Creator God, even if they'll never taste the flavor of strong meat.

I guarantee my God loves His Christian babes on milk even though they lack a deep understanding of Him and His superior ways. And as for you and me, we cannot force someone to eat the meat of Christianity if they would rather sip on milk.

However, Christian babes living their whole life on milk are disadvantaged. And having a lack of bible knowledge closes the mind to many important things. And it would help if you realized not understanding important things is a disadvantage for anyone.

Positively, I want you to know that Christians on milk will never reach their full potential, and they'll never be strong servants, crusaders, and fruitful workers for our Supreme God. Anything less than chewing on the meat reveals us not achieving a higher standard of excellence.

Because Christians on milk aren't willing to dig into His word, similar to a lion devouring strong meat, a hungry piranha on a feeding frenzy, or a bear determined to steal honey from the bees, and what good are we to God if we aren't willing to be enthusiastic Christians?

Truly, the definition and understanding it takes to uncover the meaning of His excellent word will not be known to babes on milk. And this means we do have to study hard to be bible savvy. And we cannot be bible savvy if we are dragging our feet.

I am trying to paint a truthful picture about milk, strong meat, newborn babes, and Christians never maturing into strong Bible-understanding believers. It's a symbolic story example, and it portrays how maturity grows with knowledge when Christians eat strong meat.

I assure you, the growth from milk to strong meat is similar to maturing from water baptism to the Holy Ghost baptism. Indeed, receiving the baptism of the Holy Ghost happens after the Christian is weaned off of milk and given strong meat to eat.

It's easy to conclude milk drinkers aren't ready to receive the baptism of the Holy Ghost. And I assure you, we aren't advancing to a higher level of Christianity if we are content to keep sipping on milk. And we do have to advance to strong meat before we can receive the baptism of the Holy Ghost.

The new Christians on milk are similar to babies beginning their new life on milk before they grow mature enough to taste strong meat. But after a while, their hunger increases, so they wean off the milk and start eating strong meat.

Then, they'll grow slowly into a spiritually understanding person, and it's because they aren't satisfied to know just a little bit about God. And I assure you, men and women, on strong meat, hunger to know more about God than men and women on milk.

Positively, it's always the same with young Christians when they start their new life with the God of Heaven and Earth on milk. Without a doubt, we must drink milk before we can eat strong meat, and our beginning is similar to walking and then learning to run.

However, I want you to understand as young Christians grow in the wonderful word of God. Then God's mysteries and secrets will be added as their spiritual maturity increases with their desire to know Him well and eat strong meat.

Eating strong meat means we have an insatiable appetite for the authentic word of God, and we aren't going on a gospel diet. And I assure you, meat is the strong stuff, and it builds strong character, and loving His word means we hate a gospel diet.

The new Christian on milk starts learning the simple and easy things to understand concerning our wonderful Supreme God. But as they slowly grow in Christ, they'll start to understand more things and mature in the word of God.

I assure you, as for myself, milk isn't enough for me, and I sincerely testify. Your joy and happiness will increase by many folds, and you'll become euphoric as you begin to understand the mysteries of God with definition and understanding.

Indeed, being able to interpret the meaning of what God teaches throughout the scriptures indicates we have a strong teaching of the Holy Ghost. And if we do have a good understanding, then we are being favored by our Great God.

Milk represents the beginning of understanding, and strong meat represents the maturity of a man after he's gained an understanding of the scriptures. But we all start our new life with God, similar to babes sipping on milk, which applies to all new Christians.

Especially before we can devour strong meat and understand bible scriptures with the deepness of knowledge, and just as babies cannot start on strong meat, nor can any Christian start their new walk with God full of wisdom and understanding about Him.

A new Christian needs to grow in the word of God the same way a baby grows with age and maturity. Otherwise, growth in the God of creation will be stunted, fullness will not be achieved, and the joy of eating strong meat will not be understood.

Surely, age and maturity in the word of God will help any Christian develop higher learning in knowledge, wisdom, and understanding. And especially if a Christian chooses to get off the milk, eat strong meat, and plunge deep into the pool of life.

Eating strong meat is symbolic of understanding the harder-to-comprehend scriptures, story examples, and the more complicated word of God. But all Christians need to progress from simple bible understanding and advance to a greater bible understanding.

Indeed, anyone not progressing from simple bible understanding and advancing to a greater bible understanding is lacking interest. And they are still on milk and haven't tasted strong meat yet. And maybe they aren't a meat eater at all and never will love the gospel of God.

One of the saddest things for a professing Christian to do is for them to spend their whole life on milk and never taste strong meat. And before this story ends, I'll give examples of Christians guilty of never achieving higher learning and never tasting strong meat.

Number one: The Sabbath Day of the Lord is on the seventh day, and Sun-day is the first day of the week. Sun-day is a counterfeit Sabbath Day, a tradition of men. Yet, many professing Christians are blind to the truth and honor the counterfeit Sabbath Day anyway. And I assure you the commandments are easy to learn, and there's no excuse for not knowing this truth.

Number two: The Son of God's death, burial, and resurrection should be called the Second Passover. And mainly because the Son of God became our Passover, and the resurrection of Yeshua is the greatest event in the history of Christianity.

However, many professing Christians, for some reason or another, call it by the ungodly pagan name of Easter. And I assure you, this mistake could be considered a heretical declaration since the Easter celebration is a pagan event created by the pagan people.

Number three: Our body is the living temple of the Holy Spirit, and the wonderful Holy Spirit cannot live within an unclean temple. And we are foolish Christians, not very thoughtful; if we believe, He'll live inside an unclean temple. Yet, foolish Christians who compromise the word of God expect Him to guide them and answer their prayers.

However, regardless of what our Great God says, many professing Christians eat the swine's flesh, and the Holy Spirit cannot live within them. And the baptism of the Holy Ghost, they'll not receive because they have an unclean temple.

I want you to know that professing Christians doing the above three things will always be a Christian on milk. And it's regardless of their status in the church, the amount of money they contribute to a religious organization, or how many years they've been a Christian.

The seventh day is holy, and the Holy Ghost needs a clean temple to live within. And the Second Passover is holy, and the Easter celebration is profane (which means unholy). And men and women on milk unwittingly say and do things contrary to the scriptures.

Surely, the above three reasons, plus other reasons not mentioned, reveal the danger of staying on milk too long and not progressing to strong meat. And anyway, why would any Christian prefer to stay on milk and not advance to strong meat?

Positively, it takes a meat lover to know the difference between holy, unholy, clean, and unclean. And without eating strong meat, many of the ways of God are lost. And it's because milk is the ingredient for unlearned followers, and milk parallels passive behavior.

Furthermore, unlearned followers often follow the wrong teachers and the traditions of men God hates. And we see it happening all the time, the blind leading the blind or the unlearned leading the unlearned. And I want you to know God doesn't teach or approve of the traditions of men contrary to His truth.

However, if you are eating strong meat, you'll not have to depend on someone else to tell you the exact word of God because strong meat is seasoned with the Holy Ghost, and seasoned meat has the most flavor.

This truth means all Christians are stronger Christians when they are wise in the written word of God. And I assure you, our Great Supreme God wasn't kidding around when He said men perish for lack of wisdom about His word. And I want to warn you it'll be shameful to stand before God passive, lukewarm, and without Bible knowledge.

Furthermore, the dumbest thing a person can do is to spend their entire life learning about everything except for the correct word of our Creator God. And on Judgment Day, highly intelligent men cannot plead dumbness.

For example, it requires our full consideration, regardless of our intelligence. I want you to realize that standing before our Great Creator God, knowing how to make a lot of money, and having a high I.Q. is irrelevant to judgment and Him. Indeed, I hope this story inspires you to seek strong meat.

This truth means if we reject learning about our Great God as we live and breathe, all other types of intelligence will not matter on Judgment Day. And especially since commandment keeping matters the most and not our I.Q.

The fact of the matter is clear concerning anyone guilty of eating bread from the table of Lucifer. This truth means eating bread from his table or living by the ungodly ways of this world will result in the same judgment imposed on him.

The word of God assures us Lucifer will be reduced to ashes, and it'll be by the hand of God. And so will everyone else who refuses to learn about Him. And if we do not eat the bread of life, we'll be toast on Judgment Day.

Chapter Seventeen

MILK, STRONG MEAT & BAPTISM

Before this story starts, I want you to know that we devout Christians have two spirits. And our spirit was given to us at birth, and the Holy Spirit will live within us if we provide Him a clean dwelling place. But I assure you, His Spirit is different from our life-giving spirit.

However, I hope you realize the scriptures do not say the wonderful Holy Ghost has to live inside an unclean temple. This truth means the perfect Holy Ghost has requirements and He comes and goes, and it all depends on the cleanliness of our living temple.

Water baptism symbolizes a newly converted Christian on milk, and water baptism hasn't any connection with the Holy Ghost baptism. And I conclude, and you need to know, the two have a completely different definition.

Biblical evidence reveals that baptism of the invisible Holy Ghost makes us wiser by divine design, and we have a supernatural teacher from within.

And I want you to realize His presence is always within a person on strong meat, and He drenches them heavily in His Holy Spirit.

I assure you, only the person on strong meat is ready to receive the baptism of the Holy Ghost of God. And as for the man and woman on milk, they'll have to grow in the Lord and clean up their living temple before they are ready for the baptism of the Holy Ghost.

Positively, the new Christian on milk is similar to the newborn baby. And the newborn baby isn't ready to chew on strong meat. But the baby will be ready to chew on strong meat after he conforms to the requirements of God and matures with age and understanding.

Positively, age and understanding, strong meat, and advancement in fellowship with God come with growth in the word of God. And as a person grows in the word of God, they'll get closer to the Spirit of the Holy Ghost if they have a clean-living temple.

I assure you that closeness to the Holy Ghost isn't an automatic gift to believers in Christ because we've converted to Christianity. But conversion to Christianity does mean we are searching for the formula for having a strong Holy Ghost.

Beyond the shadow of a doubt, creating closeness with the wonderful Holy Ghost will take work. And the sooner we get close to the Holy Ghost, the sooner we'll receive the baptism of the Holy Ghost.

Furthermore, any person determined to give their life to God and sincerely believes in the death, burial, and resurrection of Jesus Christ is saved. And I want you to know that getting saved is the "*number* one" important thing to do.

However, I want you to realize the formula for getting saved and having a Savior isn't connected to receiving the baptism of the Holy Ghost. And for the benefit of understanding, Christians on milk aren't ready to receive the baptism of the Holy Ghost.

Although, I believe our wonderful Supreme God does hope all Christian men and women will advance in knowledge about Him. And I am certain God desires for all Christians to mature enough to eat strong meat and be filled with a full portion of the Holy Ghost of God.

I assure you, it's impossible for any Christian with a little bible knowledge to have a strong Holy Ghost within them. But every Christian who professes to love God will gain salvation through Jesus Christ, and the next scripture says so.

> **John 3:16** For God so loved the <u>world</u> (and all the people in the world) that He gave His only <u>begotten</u> <u>Son</u> (Jesus Christ), that whosoever believeth in <u>Him</u> (Jesus Christ, Yeshua) should not perish, but have everlasting life.

Beyond the shadow of a doubt, the above scripture reveals that whether we are on milk or strong meat is insignificant to our salvation. *If* we sincerely love the Son of God, alias Yeshua, and accept Him as our only Savior from the judgment of damnation.

Truly, if the blood of the Lamb saves us, we'll not be condemned to the fires of Hell because we believe in the only begotten Son of God. And mainly because He gave His life upon the cross so you and I can have everlasting life and live in the kingdom of God forever.

Furthermore, I guarantee you that a person doesn't have to be a scholar or a theologian, and he doesn't have to understand the meaning of all the scriptures to be saved. And I thank God for the gift of simple salvation because none of us understand the meaning of all the scriptures.

Therefore, if we fall short of understanding every scripture's interpretations and definition, it doesn't mean we are any less saved. And as much as God wants us to be bible savvy, the important thing is to be a commandment keeper.

Indeed, many of us fail to understand because the flesh and blood person error in many ways. But if our heart remains pure to God, and a person repents and changes, then earnest mistakes are forgiven.

However, the man on strong meat understands more than the man and woman on milk; strong meat prevents many mistakes. And the more understanding a person has about God, the stronger his resistance to sins and mistakes will be in this world of temptations.

Indeed, the man or woman on milk can learn from the person on strong meat if they are willing to give their attention to acquiring greater bible knowledge. But if the person on milk doesn't give his attention to greater understanding, his wisdom concerning bible matters will not increase.

Therefore, he'll grow slowly like a baby, never taken from the milk and given strong meat. And maybe he'll be a Christian his whole life on milk. And sadly, I must conclude he'll only possess a simple understanding and know basic Christianity.

However, a man doesn't have to be on strong meat to receive Jesus Christ into his heart and become a son or a daughter of God. In the next informative scripture, the beloved disciple of Jesus Christ, the Apostle John, tells us so.

> **John 1:12** But as many as received <u>Him</u> (means have accepted Jesus Christ), to them <u>He</u> (Jesus Christ gave) power to become the <u>sons</u> <u>of</u> <u>God</u> (means heavenly creations, or one of the angels after death), even to them that believe on His name.

The joy of salvation belongs to every person determined to believe in the name of Jesus Christ. Our Great God prefers everyone to grow strong in their love for Him and gladly eat the strong meat of His perfect word. And regardless of whether it's milk or strong meat we eat, He loves us.

Love for strong meat is all it takes to secure everlasting salvation with our Creator God. And to confess with thy mouth Jesus is Lord, and believe His Father hath raised Him from the dead is a simple request made by the wonderful word of God.

Therefore, simple understanding and the faith to believe in the name of Jesus Christ, alias Yeshua, our Savior, is all it takes to be saved. But after obtaining salvation, devout men of God will seek the more powerful baptism of the Holy Ghost.

The greater power of the Holy Ghost certainly belongs to men who want more than a drink of milk. But to men on strong meat, who are well-studied. And it's for certain; it's the man and women on strong meat who are constantly knocking on the door of God.

Positively, the person of God who receives the Holy Ghost's baptism and the benefits of His teaching will gain benefits beyond normal. And it's easy to conclude that we are breaking normal boundaries when we have the faith to believe in a Supernatural Savior.

Indeed, I want you to know all Christians baptized in the wonderful Holy Ghost are advanced believers in Christ. And because of their increased understanding, they've learned to listen to the Holy Spirit, dwelling within their living temple.

They are obedient believers, and they can be used and taught mysteries and the knowledge of God by the indwelling Holy Ghost. And I testify that knowing that a higher power is teaching us is a great privilege, and we will learn more than the average Christian.

Positively, the good gifts of God and higher learning should be sought after and learned by all professing Christians. And mainly because the things of God are of the uttermost importance to every Christian who seeks to know the character of their Savior.

Whether we are on milk or strong meat doesn't matter as long as we live by God's righteous ways. But it's easy to conclude if we are living by the righteous ways of God, then we are eating strong meat.

Therefore, I assure you many Christians on milk can advance to strong meat if they endeavor to live by the required word of God. And it does matter, and it's extremely important to keep the Ten Commandments of God if we want to know God.

Positively, the commandments of God are relatively simple to understand, even if we are on milk and in the beginning stage of Christianity. We can know God by keeping His commandments, and the first letter of John says so.

John 2:3 And here-by (at this moment) we know that we know <u>Him</u> (our wonderful and loving Supreme God) *if* we keep His commandments.

The loyal and wise apostle called John, filled with wisdom and personal firsthand knowledge, walked and talked with our Lord and Savior Jesus Christ in person. And we can be certain the Apostle John knew the requirement for knowing God.

Indeed, the wonderful Son of God did elevate all His apostles from milk to strong meat, and the Holy Ghost was strong within them. And I'll always believe having a clean-living temple is the formula for receiving a strong Holy Ghost.

Positively, the wise and loyal Apostle John knew the will of his friend, Jesus Christ, and he knew the characteristics considered extremely important to the Son of God. And the above scripture reveals that commandment keeping is the highest pinnacle of importance.

Truly, the Apostle John pointed out and said keeping the required Ten Commandments is an indicator, revealing whether or not we know God. And we would be foolish to believe anything else will substitute for commandment keeping.

The next informative scripture speaks point-blank and direct. It's written in easy-to-understand words and separates the liars from whoever knows the supernatural Son of God. And again, I warn you, do not forget to keep His commandments.

John 2:4 He that saith, I know Him, and keepeth, not His commandments is a liar, and the truth is not in him.

I suppose this is a good time to say the seventh day, Sabbath Day of the Lord, is God's fourth commandment. And Christian men and women, guilty of keeping a counterfeit Sun-day Sabbath Day, are not honoring the fourth commandment of God.

Therefore, whether it's a trick of the devil or a preference to keep another day as the Sabbath Day of their choice, it's a matter of the uttermost importance for every Christian to examine themselves and understand what is true and what is a lie.

Every Christian should read their bible intensely and determine how much they truly desire to know God. And it's up to us to determine if we want to keep the authentic Sabbath Day of the Lord or the counterfeit Sun-day Sabbath Day of man.

However, be aware of John's words, who says we can know God simply by keeping the commandments of the Lord. And again, I warn you, John tells us, anyone who claims to know God and will not keep the commandments of the Lord is a liar, and the truth is not in them.

Indeed, the highly esteemed and loyal Apostle John says commandment breakers do not know God. And to achieve perfect clarity, the Apostle John doesn't use the words if and *but* in his matter-of-fact statement.

Furthermore, the ungodly counterfeit Sun-day Sabbath Day amounts to the doctrine of demon-controlled men. And in all actuality, according to God, there's no such thing as a Sun-day Sabbath Day of the Lord never was and never will be till the end of time.

All Christians certainly have the choice of keeping the doctrine of demon-controlled men or the authentic doctrine of God. But for the benefit of being correct, we need to know the truth before we can make the right choice.

Therefore, I want to point out an undeniable fact because higher perfection is achievable. Even Christians on milk can know God and Christians on strong meat simply by keeping His excellent and required Ten Commandments.

Simply because the righteous Ten Commandments of God, perfect and infallible, are the most important words ever written to humanity. My Great God demands righteousness and appreciates us when we comply with His most important message.

Most Christians utilize the excellent King James Bible as their study guide, consisting of approximately seven hundred and eighty thousand words. And out of those seven hundred and eighty thousand words, the Ten Commandments consist of approximately two hundred and ninety-five words.

Truly, the two hundred and ninety-five words that make up the Ten Commandments of God are the weightier words in the bible. Indeed, the Apostle John says we can know the Son of God simply by keeping His perfect Ten Commandments.

Straight from the heart of the loyal Apostle John, he tells us anyone claiming to know the wonderful Son of God but not keeping His commandments is a liar. And if we do not believe the Apostle John, are we calling him a liar, and he hasn't any reason to mislead us?

I've often heard preachers and professing Christians say that no one can keep the Ten Commandments of God. But the Apostle John says the Ten

Commandments are not grievous or burdensome for us to keep. And if we aren't keeping them, a powerful influence leads us astray.

It's a terrible myth to believe; we cannot keep the Ten Commandments of God perfectly. And without a doubt, it's the doctrine of the wicked Lucifer to believe; we are not required to try and live by the Ten Commandments of God.

It's also a doctrine of the devil for the Christian skeptics to say the Ten Commandments are Old Testament stuff. For this reason, I wholeheartedly witness the Apostle John is a disciple of Jesus Christ; his writings are in the New Testament, and his words are valid.

The Apostle John indicates the Ten Commandments are the corridor and the pathway to the heart of Jesus Christ, alias Yeshua. And I am certain the perfect and wonderful Ten Commandments are the **strongest meat of Christianity**.

According to the scriptures, it's quite apparent that Christian men and women fail to keep the holy and sacred seventh-day Sabbath Day of the Lord. They have a recognition flaw and do not know God the way they should know God.

Even though the Sun-day Christians say they know and believe they know God. They are being deceived by one of the marks of the beast's deceptions, and the deception can only be corrected by keeping the seventh day Sabbath Day.

Indeed, it appears for certain that many Christian men and women have been deceived by the beast, alias Satan, the serpent of old. And I don't doubt that because of his recorded history, all deviations from authenticity have roots in him.

Beyond the shadow of a doubt, the wicked beast of old is the behind-the-scenes character concerning counterfeit and imitation things. And he's guilty of changing the Sabbath Day of the Lord to an alternate Sabbath Day of man.

Maybe Lucifer did it because he knows Christians can only know God if they keep His excellent and required Ten Commandments. And His great Ten Commandments are a requirement we should love to keep.

I assure you, the wicked and rebellious Lucifer doesn't want Christians to know God and have a close personal relationship with Him. And he'll slip in changes to the exact word of God and add manufactured doctrines to keep Christians from knowing God.

Because his counterfeit changes, called the traditions of men, destroy personal relationships between Christians and God. Whenever we uncover a tradition of men, we should immediately expose it and quit doing it.

> **JOHN 2:5** But whoso keepeth His word, in him <u>verily</u> (means truly) is the love of God perfected; here-by (at this moment) we know that we are in Him.

Even the newly converted Christians drinking milk know the Ten Commandments of God because the awareness of the great Ten Commandments doesn't take greater wisdom and knowledge to understand.

However, it does take determination to obey them, and we who are determined to keep the commandments of God are perfected in Him. And it's a wonderful and blessed feeling to know beyond a doubt that we do know God and can say we know God.

Indeed, it's extremely important to us; as we build our faith to know, we know God. But please realize we must know Him through the formula for knowing God. And I warn you, we better conform to His Bible-quoted formula.

The Apostle John says that we can know for certain; we know the Son of God. And it's because we keep His required commandments, and there's no other way to know God. And I would hate to believe I'll live my entire life and not know the God of creation.

Therefore, all persons, young or old, can be on milk and still know God because they keep His commandments. And possibly, a young Christian can know God better than an established older Christian if the Christian of many years hasn't been a commandment keeper.

Beyond the shadow of a doubt, one of the most important things a concerned preacher can do for a newly converted Christian is to stress the importance of keeping the required Ten Commandments and being proud of all their glorious expectations.

Certainly, it would be a good idea if every sermon ever preached in the house of God revolved around the perfect Ten Commandments of God. And I know this kind of teaching would benefit the congregation the most, and the objective of teaching His word is to increase the unlearned persons understanding.

Furthermore, I fail to see how any Christian can claim to be on strong meat if they do not keep the righteous commandments of God. And it is contradictory to believe we can eat strong meat without keeping the righteous commandments of God.

All Christians on strong meat have a greater understanding, wisdom, and knowledge than those on milk. And every Christian man and woman eating strong meat knows the importance of keeping the commandments of God.

You and I can be certain all Christians on strong meat know blessings and favors, the revealing of the scriptures, and the gifts of the Holy Ghost. They are a part of the unique fellowship formula, and closer than normal fellowship comes from receiving the baptism of the Holy Ghost.

I assure you that a greater understanding of the scriptures and the definition of the word of God are gifts from the Holy Ghost. And it's the Holy Spirit of God who teaches men and women living on strong meat, the interpretation of parables, and hard-to-understand scriptures.

The wonderful Holy Spirit of God teaches the interpretation of story examples, parallels, metaphors, and the definition of scriptures having dual meanings. Indeed, His importance is necessary if we desire to know much about our Great Creator God.

Therefore, it's extremely important for all hungry Christians on milk to gradually or quickly wean themselves off it. And Christians on milk should desire to eat strong meat, and then they'll understand what strong meat eaters in love with the word of God already know.

Sometimes, it takes years to receive the baptism of the Holy Ghost, especially if we've eaten the swine's flesh all our lives. And I reveal to you we cannot eat the unclean and expect the Holy Ghost of God to live within our unclean temple.

I assure you the necessary baptism of the Holy Ghost is reserved for hungry Christians who have a clean dwelling place for the Holy Ghost to live within. And I am certain the Holy Ghost will gladly dwell within a clean temple.

I want you to know the special baptism of the Holy Ghost is reserved for Christian men and women who diligently and gladly seek after God with all their heart, mind, and soul. And I am certain the wonderful Holy Ghost loves a clean dwelling place.

Indeed, the baptism of the Holy Ghost is reserved and given in a greater proportion to Christians, who put God and His righteous word first in their lives. And when we constantly do this requirement, His Spirit will be exceptionally strong in us.

Indeed, the wonderful baptism of the Holy Ghost is a special gift given to all well-studied, knowledgeable Christians; knowledgeable Christians who prove themselves to be men of God are not on milk but strong meat.

JUST FOR THE RECORD, THE BAPTISM OF THE HOLY GHOST ISN'T GIVEN TO MEN SIMPLY BECAUSE THEY PROFESS TO KNOW GOD. AND IT'S EASY TO SAY WE KNOW GOD, BUT COMMANDMENT KEEPING IS THE KEY TO KNOWING GOD, AND A CLEAN-LIVING TEMPLE IS THE KEY TO A HOLY GHOST BAPTISM.

However, all new Christians who believe in Christ shouldn't be discouraged because they are on milk initially. Nor should they be discouraged because they do not immediately receive the baptism of the Holy Ghost.

Indeed, I want you to realize it's impossible to prove ourselves as devout men and women of God in a short time. And this means it takes work to prove ourselves as devout men and women, loyal to our Great Creator God.

Furthermore, we cannot receive the second baptism of the Holy Ghost without being tested, tried, and tempted by various evils. But men and women on strong meat have learned to recognize and resist the things contrary to the word of God.

Furthermore, I want you to know the temptations from the devil can turn us away from God before we get rooted deep into the word of God. And we can be certain, every chance Lucifer gets, he'll try to turn us away from our Great Creator God.

If preachers, priests, and teachers teach us the traditions of men and the counterfeit doctrines of Lucifer. Including a watered-down version of the gospel of God, and say, the Old Testament Ten Commandments aren't important to follow anymore.

Then, it'll be harder for a new Christian to get on strong meat, know God, and receive the baptism of the Holy Ghost. And sadly, I must tell you, not all preachers and priests are teaching the meat of Christianity or the importance of keeping a clean living temple.

I assure you before we can receive the wonderful and powerful second baptism of the Holy Ghost of God. First, we must overcome the traditions of men and the influence of invisible demon spirits and refuse to eat the unclean swine's flesh.

Even then, it may seem we'll have to fight through the brush, briars, and thorns to prove to the God of Heaven and Earth that we are into Christianity for the long haul and are committed to Him for the duration of our lives. And I want you to know the reward of eternal life is a gift to whoever commits themselves to keep His word.

It's for certain: we'll have to prove we aren't a quitter when the going gets rough, and we aren't afraid to suffer persecution for the love of God. And carrying the cross of Yeshua means we believe the infallible word of God is the ultimate teaching.

Indeed, if we do manage to prove ourselves before the watchers and the holy ones in Heaven and before the eyes of God, then He will know we are loyal to Him and in love with His righteous word, and we will receive the special baptism of the Holy Ghost.

Afterward, the concerned Holy Ghost will reward us with the gift of bible knowledge, advanced bible wisdom, and spiritual understanding. And we'll recognize the impurities of this world, and we'll separate ourselves from them.

The excellent Holy Ghost will share His wisdom with us. And His wisdom comes from the Heavens above and our wonderful Supreme God. Indeed, the knowledge of heavenly things and revelations concerning the mysteries of life come from heavenly creations.

Therefore, I advise you that we should all seek the wisdom of our heavenly Father, and we should have a strong desire to know a lot about the characteristics of God. During your studies, you'll discover we have a fascinating Creator God in love with righteousness.

John 3:27 (Says) A man can receive nothing, except it is given to him from above.

Positively, the friend and loyal Apostle John reveals that the holy and righteous things the Holy Ghost teaches us originate from the Heavens above, including bible knowledge, general wisdom, interpretations, and definitions of the scriptures.

I assure you divine understanding is given to Christians, and it's given freely and comes from the Holy Ghost of God. And the excellent Holy Ghost of God lives within every man and woman, determined to live by His formula and claim Him as their Lord and Savior.

Therefore, it's of the uttermost importance for every Christian man, woman, and child living in the flesh to do a specific thing. They should care about the dwelling place of the Holy Ghost and keep their living temple clean, void of anything unclean and sinful.

Furthermore, our young children should be taught the importance of keeping their living temple clean, even from the early years of their youth. And mainly because the Holy Ghost is the Spirit of God, and it cannot live or teach from within an unclean temple.

Without a doubt, the Christian man, woman, and child are the redefined living temple of the Holy Ghost. We Christians are a many-membered select group of believers if we believe in Christ and claim Him as our only Savior from the judgment of damnation.

Furthermore, we believers in the compassionate Son of God make up the living church of God, and it's not made from wood, stone, mortar, or metal. But we are the living and breathing redefined temple if we keep our bodies free from the unclean.

Milk is for newborn babies, and strong meat is for the seasoned Christians who persistently seek after God with all their heart and soul. But no milk or strong meat is given to the unbelievers, guilty of rejecting knowledge about the God of creation.

Indeed, the treasures of spiritual knowledge are withheld from the unbelievers, who have dull ears and blind eyes. And water baptism and the Holy Ghost baptism don't mean anything special to the unbelievers.

Furthermore, I hope you realize a man and woman must be born again and become a new person in Christ. Otherwise, they will not see the kingdom of God. And as we live and breathe upon this Earth, being born again is our ultimate achievement.

Our loving Supreme God sent His only begotten Son into this wicked world of the unsaved. And into this world controlled by His former heavenly adversary, the wicked and ungodly Lucifer. Bible events prove Lucifer wanted my great God removed from the throne.

God sent His perfect Son so everyone faithful enough to believe in Him can have everlasting life. And the gift of everlasting life should be cared for with the greatest respect. But the wicked Lucifer doesn't want people to have a Savior from damnation.

Indeed, if you believe in Yeshua's death, burial, and resurrection, you can be born again. And being born again means the heart is reborn, not the flesh. And being born again means we've decided to live for Christ.

It doesn't matter if you are a Christian on milk because Christians on milk are also born-again believers in Christ. And as long as the heart is reborn, and we've conformed to the word of God, then we are fulfilling the definition of a born-again believer.

However, milk is for newborn babies who do not have a great deal of understanding. But their understanding will improve if they truly desire to know more about God. And during this beginning period, enthusiasm for the word of God will be tested for strength.

Positively, strong meat is for hungry Christians who desire to fellowship closely with the Holy Ghost. Eating strong meat means we are Bible-savvy and want to know God's secrets, mysteries, and things exceeding mainstream Christianity.

However, the baptism of the Holy Ghost is reserved for all loyal Christians, who mature from milk to strong meat, specifically to please our wonderful God. And it does please the God of creation when He sees His children mature from milk to strong meat.

However, it's much better to drink milk than to be a lukewarm Christian or an unbeliever who doesn't believe in my supreme God. Simply because professing Christians on milk also have a fellowship with God, even though it's not a strong fellowship.

Positively, the passionate Christians on strong meat are the Christians who have a closer and stronger relationship with the Holy Ghost. And mainly because sincere, passionate Christians who desire to know God better have a closer walk with Him.

Therefore, be assured that the more we understand our Creator God and His ability to shape us into better people. Then, the stronger Christian we'll become, and the more spiritual gifts we'll receive from Him. And I guarantee we can strengthen our bond with God if we want His closeness.

Surely, the stronger we become in Christ and the perfect word of God, the more favored we'll be by Him. And it's an absolute pleasure to passionately and enthusiastically love and highly esteem His holy and sacred Ten Commandments.

If we passionately look forward to keeping His seventh holy day, Sabbath Day, we resist eating the unclean swine. Then, our Supreme Loving God will passionately fill us with more of the Holy Ghost than we would normally receive.

I am certain that every Christian's heart will be more satisfied with eating strong meat rather than drinking milk. And eating strong meat will make God and the Holy Ghost extremely happy with believers, determined to worship Him to the maximum.

Conclusively, winning the prize of immortality is a serious endeavor, and it'll be easier to secure immortality if we try our best. But please realize trying our best entwines with commandment keeping and illustrated reverence to our all-mighty God.

Being on milk our whole life is similar to walking on thin ice or being a borderline Christian. And as cautious as we are about walking on thin ice, we should be more cautious and not oppose the required word of God.

I assure you passion, enthusiasm, exuberating love, and being hot and on fire are the right qualities, and they reveal a serious meat lover. And as

Yeshua said, man does not live by bread alone, but by every word written in His inspired bible.

I assure you, God's excellent word is the ultimate thing: stronger than an oak tree and more honest than George Washington or Abe Lincoln. And I am certain our future habitation hinges on loving God's word. Since the God lovers go up, and the unbelievers go down.

Conclusively, the formula for receiving the baptism of the Holy Ghost is accomplished to a large degree because we keep Him a clean dwelling place. And I want you to realize we are a whole lot silly if we force Him from our temple because we dirty up the dwelling place of the Holy Ghost.

The baptism of the Holy Ghost entwines the kingdom of God living within our flesh body. And both accomplishments entwine together, and they depend on us to refuse the unclean. And I tell you, we haven't sacrificed a thing by refusing to eat the unclean.

For example, we should be concerned when we realize that the kingdom of God is a moveable kingdom that can remove itself from an unclean heart. This truth means eating the swine's flesh is a perfect example of uncleanness, and eating it will destroy the dwelling place of the Holy Ghost.

I assure you that the excellent and particular Holy Ghost will not live within a body temple contaminated by the unclean swine's flesh. And I assure you, there's no logical reason to believe He would live in an unclean home. Furthermore, it's cruel of us to impose uncleanness on His dwelling place.

The definition of the Holy Ghost baptism is being submerged, not in water. But being submerged in the perfect word of God and the righteousness of the word of God drenches us heavily with the Holy Ghost. And the deeper we are submerged, the more strength to His Spirit living within our redefined temple is gained.

Truly, we can play around on the surface and receive the gift of water baptism. But we can dive deep into the righteous word of God and receive the baptism of the wonderful Holy Ghost, and the choice belongs to you and me.

Chapter Eighteen
THE FLESH

This explanation story is called *The Flesh*. It explores the characteristics of a smile and, sadly, I must conclude, the intangible value of a smile. And I know it doesn't hurt to smile at each other. But sometimes, deception is achieved by facial expressions, or a pretty smile can be a baited trap.

Beyond the shadow of a doubt, a beautiful smile hides negative and positive characteristics. And I ask you, by observing, who would know for certain which type of characteristics the smile is hiding when it's wearing make-up?

Positively, if the smile could be compared to anything, then it would be the chameleon hiding behind the transformation of colors. I am certain emotions aren't always stable, and a smile can change into something else quickly.

I assure you a smile reveals nothing concrete, and it's not connected to the personal traits of honesty, sincerity, loyalty, and godliness. And I fully conclude we would be foolish to believe a smile possesses any of these traits.

I guarantee you the flesh is the most deceptive thing men and women possess. And it's because a wrapped package hides the contents within it. And I assure you, what's hiding within, and the appearance has two separate voices, and one cannot speak for the other.

Indeed, I say the flesh is deceptive because the flesh's appearance does not speak for the heart, and just because the flesh is beautiful, and the smile is radiant. It doesn't mean the thoughts of the heart are beautiful too.

I assure you, a genuinely beautiful heart filled with love for righteousness, the Spirit of God, and gospel advancement. It's more beautiful, well thought of, and highly prized by our Supreme God than the appearance of beautiful flesh.

The flesh is the outward exterior, which the eyes behold, but it can hide the interior of a man and a woman extremely well. This truth means, sometimes, it's difficult to see past a person's exterior and see a person's interior. The interior reveals much more than the exterior.

Indeed, the outside appearance is easy to read, and it's for eyesight only. But I assure you, eyesight is easily deceived by appearance. And I am certain history will prove appearances have caused more great falls than anything else.

I conclude that another person's interior is a complex mystery of secret thoughts, and no one can fully read them. I believe I am correct to say incompatibility describes the relationships between most people.

Assuredly, no doubt all men and women would prefer to be handsome, beautiful, and a picture of perfection. But observation shows us not all outward appearances are handsome and beautiful. And we are being deceived; if we believe, we are perfect.

Anyway, thank goodness, the outward appearance has no reflection on the heart, hidden by the cover of the flesh. And in the long run, the test of time will prove the benefits of a beautiful heart will far exceed the benefits of a beautiful appearance.

Our great and wonderful Most High God loves a beautiful heart much more than He loves a beautiful appearance. And the importance of a beautiful heart is much greater in value to God than the importance of a beautiful appearance.

Positively, a beautiful appearance has limitations with God, and it won't improve a man's or a woman's odds of obtaining salvation in the kingdom of Heaven. But a beautiful heart will positively increase a man's or a woman's odds of being accepted and favored by God.

I assure you, a beautiful heart dwells within a pure-hearted person if they have sincere love, not fake and pretense. But observation, and example after example, proves a beautiful outward appearance doesn't prove the heart is pure.

However, the beauty inside of a person is the real sincere you and me, indicating the heart is pure. A beautiful and pure-at-heart person is way more desirable and honorable than someone with a beautiful appearance.

However, the flesh wars against the spirit within, and a beautiful appearance possesses no special defense capabilities. But it's for certain: the pure heart does have defense capabilities. And it's because demons' spirits cannot penetrate a pure heart.

I am quite certain when most people go looking for a mate, the lust for the flesh will most likely be a reason to choose a person with a beautiful appearance. Rather than be wise, choose a person possessing a beautiful heart.

I assure you, and you should already know, that a beautiful appearance doesn't mean the person in question will be honorable, good, caring, and peace-loving and will resist troubles and woes. But just the same, most people gamble on appearance.

However, a beautiful heart is honorable, peace-loving, and a good defense against troubles and woes in this life. And I firmly believe my great caring God watches over and protects whosoever has a beautiful heart.

However, it could be a true analogy because it seems characteristic of most people to associate a beautiful appearance with honor, peace, and love. This truth means most people think men and women with beautiful appearances have beautiful hearts.

The above kind of thinking is false and erroneous, and the truth may be quite the opposite. For example, the beautiful appearance of Lucifer proves appearances are deceiving. And bible scriptures prove his heart was contrary to his appearance.

I am certain that the above kind of thinking could be the main reason for many mixed and ungodly relationships and failed marriages. And sometimes, old sayings are just old sayings. And sometimes, old sayings have a lot of truth, such as water runs downhill.

Surely, the old saying, Beauty is skin deep, is one of the most truthful old sayings that has ever been said, and it's a completely accurate old saying.

And if we remember, beauty is skin deep old saying, when we choose our mate for life.

Then, our life might be more pleasant, peaceful, and happy and last longer without troubles and woes. Simply because beauty's outward appearance is skin-deep, skin-deep beauty fades away, like the flowers and the grass in the fall of the year.

Be assured before I go any further. I want to explain myself and assure you I do not want to attach a bad image to beautiful people. And I want everyone to know I am not stereotyping beautiful people with beautiful appearances as non-desirables with dark hearts.

For the above reason, I better clarify that many handsome men and beautiful women live in this world and have beautiful hearts. And I believe nothing could be better than having a beautiful appearance and heart; having both would be a great blessing.

However, I want you to realize that developing a beautiful heart is much more important than having a beautiful appearance. And the wicked and rebellious Lucifer, more beautiful than the other angels, is a perfect illustration in this story example.

Lucifer, the serpent of old, the wicked Satan, the devil, and the king of Tyrus, and the image of jealousy, and the fallen star from Heaven was most likely one the most beautiful angels God ever created in the Heavens above.

Indeed, the evil Lucifer was made from every precious stone in Heaven, and his beauty was perfected within the Living Coals of Fire. The beautiful Lucifer was perfect in appearance, but the scriptures indicate he had a corrupt and wicked heart.

Indeed, Lucifer's heart and appearance had an opposite illusion effect, with obvious beauty on the outside and an ugly character on the inside. But when his heart was lifted, he wanted to be the Supreme God in Heaven and rule over the universe because of his beauty.

Even though Lucifer was beautiful and full of vanity and pride, his heart was impure and wicked. And I am certain his excellent gifts from the God of Heaven and Earth enlarged his vain character. And his beauty, and his pride, most likely contributed to his downfall.

Beyond the shadow of a doubt, his beautiful outward appearance and ugly heart were deceiving to himself and the other rebellious angels. And I am certain Lucifer's verbal and physical features contradict the ugly thoughts hiding inside his heart.

Without a doubt, and it's one hundred percent true, the other angels around him looked up to him and admired him. And because of his beautiful appearance, they believed in him and considered him a superior creation.

Furthermore, they listened to his vain philosophies and seemed to worship him instead of worshipping my Great God of Heaven and Earth. And maybe the rebellious angels believed in Him because of his verbal skills and beautiful physical appearance.

The appearance is often at war against the wonderful Spirit of God, and the evil Lucifer was at war against God. His heart was rebellious to an extreme degree, and he would do anything to defeat God. And it's easy to conclude the heart inside his chest didn't feel the emotion of love.

Therefore, the wicked Lucifer is our example angel, good in the beginning and wicked in the end. But he does prove, beyond the shadow of a doubt, that a beautiful appearance can cause war with the Spirit and the heart. And I am confident to say a lack of love sears the heart and war results from a stone-cold heart.

I am certain a beautiful appearance, without a doubt, will face more temptation than a beautiful, pure heart. But regardless of appearances, all men and women are tempted by the hideous devil, regardless of whether they have a beautiful appearance.

I assure you, all flesh, male or female, whether beautiful or not. It wrestles and struggles against the devil's wiles and with the invisible demonic spirits of the air. And I am certain the invisible demons of the air can take a beautiful appearance and cause it to be deceptive.

Chapter Nineteen

SPIRIT INVOLVEMENT

The next informative scripture illuminates the ghost spirits of the air and them as the primary influence upon the minds of ungodly men. The next revealing scripture tells us that this world's dark prince is the power of the air and the ungodly influence behind ungodly men.

The next informative scripture also reveals that the dark prince of the air is an invisible enemy of our Great God and humanity. And I guarantee you, ungodliness is his type of influence, and we cannot expect otherwise from a rebellious demonic angel.

> **Ephesians 2:2** Wherein in <u>time past</u> (means the time before we overcome the flesh) ye walked according to the <u>course</u> (means the corrupt pathway) of this world,

> **Ephesians 2:2** according to the <u>prince</u> (means Lucifer, Satan, alias the devil) of the power of the <u>air</u> (means the invisible demonic ghost spirit of the air),

Ephesians 2:2 The <u>spirit</u> (the invisible evil spirit of the devil) that now <u>worketh</u> (lustful, corrupt, and vain works) in the children of disobedience.

Ephesians 2:3 Among whom also we all had our conversation in times past in the lusts of our flesh, fulfilling the desires of the flesh, and of the mind, were by nature the children of <u>wrath</u> (the children against God), even as others (ungodly men, who pursue the lusts of the flesh).

I want you to realize to fulfill the immoral and ungodly desires of the flesh and the carnal mind, then anyone will have to resist the wonderful and righteous Spirit of God and simultaneously accept the influence of the evil ghost spirits of the air.

Furthermore, anyone walking the course of this world is hostile to our Supreme God. And God doesn't approve of anyone living in this world's ungodly ways. And mainly because the course of this world isn't entwined with the righteous ways of God.

However, I want you to realize that the invisible demonic spirits of the air encourage all men and women to walk the course of this world and lust after the flesh. And I believe, I can accurately say, this is the game they constantly play daily against the flesh creations.

Indeed, please be aware it's the invisible ghost spirit of Lucifer and his rebellious demonic friends. Who purposely work corruption through men and women and cause them to disobey the required word of our Great God.

Furthermore, being disobedient to the word of God only leaves the other choice of being obedient to the flesh. And it would be much wiser and more rewarding for every man on this Earth to oppose the flesh's desires and obey God's infallible word.

Rather than walk in disobedience and rebellion and be submissive to the lust of the flesh. And I shouldn't have to say being submissive to the lust of the flesh will cause us much trouble. And I warn you, trouble lurks around the corner every day.

I assure you the war between the flesh and the Spirit of God continues because evil spirits never quit tempting the flesh. And the war with the flesh will continue until the Holy Spirit in man is strong enough to overcome the lust of the flesh.

Wise men know that the air's demonic evil spirits encourage them to fulfill the desires of the flesh and mind. And wise men know for certain we must resist ungodly temptations before we can defeat the demonic spirits of the air.

However, daily, year after year, men and women make errors to the point of a major epidemic. And sadly, I must tell you, men and women fall prey to the evil spirits of the air and reject the good influence of the guiding and teaching Holy Spirit of God.

Until the day comes when either the Spirit of God will conquer and overcome, the flesh or the flesh overcomes the Spirit of God. But sooner or later, the one will overcome the other. And the Spirit of God, or the lust of the flesh, will be the dominant controller of every person.

Observation proves that many men and women will never be able to overcome the lust of the flesh. Because an invisible evil spirit of the air abides in them, it prods them to do wickedly until the death of their flesh.

Therefore, because of the weakness of the flesh, the Holy Spirit of God cannot save all men and women from the grips of the devil. And it's easy to conclude that if we do a general analysis of the majority in this world, we'll be forced to realize that ungodly temptations are too much for most people to resist.

Indeed, because of the strong influence of the evil spirits of the air. Sometimes, their influence is too strong for men to break free from sin. And especially when some persons prefer the ways of the devil and the flesh more so than the ways of God.

I suppose most men and women do not have faith and love for God and the excellent word of God. They'll continue to reject the ways of God because they cannot see the goodness of God and because they cannot feel God in their heart.

These types of men and women do not have enough faith to believe in the perfect word of God, and they mostly think He doesn't exist. And they'll walk after the lust of the flesh rather than after the teaching of the Holy Spirit of God.

It becomes obvious that many men and women haven't overcome the lust for the flesh because of their tree's fruit. And anyone unable to overcome the lust of the flesh will always reject the good Spirit of God, and they'll favor the worldly pleasures in this life.

However, if you prefer, endeavor to walk in the Spirit of God and according to the commandments of God. Then, you'll be stronger in mind and spirit when battling against the air spirits. And the odds are greater; you will not fall prey to the temptations of the flesh.

I assure you that men, depending on their strength, cannot resist the influence of the evil spirits of the air. But we have a partner willing to help us win our battle against the evil ghost spirits of the air, and His name is the Holy Ghost of God.

The ruling demonic evil spirit of the air wasn't always the evil spirit of the air. And at one time, upon this Earth, he had a tangible body. And it was beautiful, superior in strength, and by physical force, he was a ruling god on this Earth, and the flesh person was inferior to him.

Truly, he was the evil serpent of old and the tree of knowledge of good and evil. Lucifer had his physical angelic body during the first Earth age before the great cleansing flood cleansed him and his mixed bloodline children from this Earth.

Indeed, during the first Earth age, before the great flood, he was recorded as an undesirable trickster in the Garden of God at Eden. But after the flood divided the first Earth age from the second Earth age, his physical body is locked away and bound in chains of darkness.

As for now, within this second Earth age, his invisible ghost spirit is the prince of the air, and he wars against the flesh. Within the next scripture, the Apostle Paul reveals a spiritual battle that most men and women struggle against as they journey through this life.

Galatians 5:17 For the flesh lusteth against the <u>Spirit</u> (means against the Holy Spirit, and the spirit of man), and the <u>Spirit</u> (means the Holy Spirit, and a man's inner spirit) against the flesh:

Galatians 5:17 And <u>these</u> (the Spirit, and the flesh) are <u>contrary</u> (means they are in opposition) the one to the other: So that ye cannot do the <u>things</u> (means do the righteous things) that ye would.

In every Christian life, the Holy Ghost and our inner spirit must unite and overcome the flesh. And mainly because the flesh is hostile against the Spirit of God and against our inner spirit, too. And it's because the spirits of demons influence the flesh.

Indeed, disobedient hostility is the work of the cursed, the wicked, depraved devil, and his servant army of evil spirits. But the works of the Holy Spirit are peace, love, harmony, joy, happiness, and everything influenced and permitted by my all-mighty God.

Although it's easy to conclude, peace, love, happiness, harmony, and joy aren't the characteristics of most people. And living ungodly robs a person of happiness, joy, and harmony. And this flaw means the flesh is weak and chooses to do the wrong things too often.

Indeed, the works of the flesh are corrupt, depraved, unclean, immoral, sensual, lustful, detestable, wicked, and everything Lucifer influences. And if not for the Holy Ghost, almost all Christian men and women would yield to the temptations of the flesh and do the things they shouldn't be doing.

Without a doubt, most people would live according to immoral desires and the lust of the mind and heart, as the children of the devil do. And without the Holy Ghost prodding them to do right, they wouldn't feel restrained when tempted to do wrong.

However, the wonderful Holy Ghost living within every clean-hearted Christian man and woman has a voice and a connection to our hearts. And thanks to God, He's the silent voice calling our conscience to live a godly lifestyle and turn away from sin.

Surely, pure-hearted Christians who love God's word desire righteousness concerning everything. They are the people determined to obey God's guiding Spirit, much more so than the will of the flesh.

Indeed, Christians determined to rely on the righteous word of God are saved from much temptation and sin. And it's because they listen to the Spirit, who guides their foot away from the things sinful men do in the flesh.

These next few exposure scriptures, requiring our full attention, reveal the bad characteristics of the flesh. And you'll see, these next few scriptures aren't good character qualities. And everything they speak against, we shouldn't do.

> **Galatians 5:19** Now the works of the flesh are manifest (means made known, and are evident), which are these: adultery, fornication, uncleanness,

> **Galatians 5:19** lasciviousness (means wanton sensuality, lustful, evil, and uncontrollable sexual desires).

Galatians 5:20 Idolatry, <u>witchcraft</u> (includes rebellion), <u>hatred</u> (of things that are good, including hatred for God and parents),

Galatians 5:20 <u>variance</u> (means discord), <u>emulations</u> (means jealousy), <u>wrath</u> (means anger, rage, fury, and vengeance toward others),

Galatians 5:20 <u>strife</u> (means quarrels and struggles), <u>seditions</u> (means dissensions, quarreling), <u>heresies</u> (means rebellion, and vile beliefs).

Galatians 5:21 <u>Envying's</u> (means ill-will toward another, because of advantages), murders, <u>drunkenness</u> (means an ungodly state of mind, and usually focused on the pleasures of sin),

Galatians 5:21 <u>revel-lings</u> (means rebellious, and making merry, partying, and seeking corrupt pleasures in life), and such like:

Galatians 5:21 Of the which I tell you before, as I have also told you in times past, that they which do such things shall not inherit the kingdom of God.

The above three scriptures, taken from the book of Galatians, were written by the Apostle Paul and are extremely illustrative. They are extremely informative and truly descriptive concerning their desire to tell us the signs of an evil character.

I advise you to consider the ungodly things the Apostle Paul warns us about in the above scriptures as an advanced warning. And to save our soul from the judgment of damnation, we should be glad an apostle of God has warned us to care for our salvation.

Indeed, I hope you realize the Apostle Paul is trying to increase our awareness and prevent us from living ungodly. And we should notice these characteristics in men and women we meet on the trail of life while walking to and fro in the flesh.

I assure you that everyone is guilty of illustrating the above ungodly characteristics while walking in the flesh. They are walking in the darkness of mind, stumbling around in the wilderness of sin, and listening to the guiding demonic ghost spirits of the air.

The next three verses below describe acceptable characteristics, quite the opposite of the ungodly things mentioned above. For example, the next scriptures describe men and women walking in the Spirit of our Great Supreme God.

The next three helpful scriptures, we should be glad to parallel, reveal godly characteristics pleasing to our wonderful all-mighty God. And all men of God should desire to emulate them and adjust their lifestyle to the ways of the Lord every day they live and breathe.

> **Galatians 5:22** But the <u>fruit</u> (means the works) of the Spirit is love, joy, peace, long-suffering, gentleness, goodness, and faith.

> **Galatians 5:23** Meekness, temperance: Against such, there is no <u>law</u> (means there's no condemnation in righteous characteristics).

Galatians 5:24 And they that are Christ's have <u>crucified</u> (means overcome and killed the unrighteous works of) the flesh <u>with</u> (which is bound by) affections and lusts.

I want you to know the loyal Apostle Paul did a wonderful job when he revealed the works and the characteristics of the flesh. And it will be considered wise if we remember his valuable words all the days of our lives.

Indeed, it's easy to see the works of the flesh are in opposition to the works of the inner spirit and the Holy Spirit. And mainly because joy, peace, harmony, love, long-suffering, gentleness, goodness, and faith are much different and better characteristics.

Much better than murder, rebellion, witchcraft, drunkenness, reveling, discord, adultery, fornication, lewdness, and hatred. And whosoever does these terrible, ungodly things live under the influence of the demonic spirits.

Indeed, the works of the Holy Spirit are the good works approved of by God. But the works of the flesh are usually flawed, corrupt, and unacceptable. And the young king David, accredited with slaying the Philistine Goliath, was also a prophet of our Supreme God.

The next important scripture is taken from the thoughts of King David, the giant slayer, and his words are true and prophetic. And because it's the will of God, King David does his best to include mercy as a quality of character we should practice.

Proverbs 11:17 The merciful man doeth good to his soul: But he that is cruel troubleth his flesh.

Mercy is an excellent characteristic of the Holy Spirit, but cruelty is a characteristic of Lucifer and the unmerciful man made of flesh. And I am certain we can help our soul by being merciful or destroy it by being cruel.

Positively, the Holy Spirit does the things pleasing to God, but the flesh does the things pleasing to the evil prince of the air. And the prince of darkness worketh evil and corruption into the hearts of men, who choose to serve the flesh.

Furthermore, various troubles and woes will follow after the carnal flesh when it wars against the Spirit of God. And we should all realize this is a testing ground, Earth. And for our benefit, we shouldn't war against the wonderful Spirit of God.

We must conclude we weren't put here to pursue the pleasures of the flesh, especially since the pleasures of sin do not please God. And the word of God assures us it's not the whole duty of man to pursue earthly pleasures.

God assures us that the pleasures of the flesh bear no fruit in righteousness. And the pleasures of the flesh will not create a good record in the Book of Life simply because the fruit of the flesh and the pleasures of sin are vanities. And are as vain as all the other ungodly things in this world, designed to please the flesh.

I assure you, all scriptures throughout the bible illustrate that man's whole duty is to obey the Holy Spirit of God. And a future life of immortality and a Christ-like body depends on us obeying the required word of our Great Creator God.

However, the flesh has deaf ears and a stubborn heart, and if we aren't careful. The flesh will resist doing right and cast out the Holy Spirit from our conscience. And when the flesh doesn't listen to the Spirit of God, then the Spirit is suppressed from doing good works through the flesh.

Indeed, The Conclusion of the Whole Matter is to reverence God and keep His sacred and holy commandments. And I want you to realize that He wasn't kidding around or being nonchalant concerning the seriousness of commandment keeping.

Positively, if we listen to the Spirit and fight against the will of the flesh, then we are doing the will of God. And for some ungodly reason, and Lucifer is the ungodly reason, we need to strictly control the flesh and not submit ourselves to ungodly temptation.

Chapter Twenty

THE GREAT OPPORTUNITY

Surely, if a person lives many years, they'll have the wonderful opportunity to write a great and favorable autobiography. And I want you to know that our autobiography can be filled with godliness, good works, and deeds accomplished for the glory of our Great God.

Unless we've been a man or woman, guilty of rejecting God and not repenting for doing the ungodly pleasures in this world, and if we are an unrepented sinner and refuse to change, we do not want to carry the cross of Yeshua.

Then, I must tell you, our autobiography will not be written so great, and it'll not help us on Judgment Day after it's filled with corrupt and wicked works. But I assure you, we will regret being corrupt and wicked.

However, regardless of whether it's good or corrupt works, a man or a woman does during their lifetime. It's still our written autobiography, which we wrote for our presentation. And I guarantee you we will present our autobiography before the Lord on Judgment Day.

The word of the Lord assures us the Book of Life in Heaven records our life from the beginning until the end. And it's our autobiography, and it records all our works in the flesh. It's accurate and true; nothing is left out or added to, and it's infallible.

The Book of Life assures us that all our works throughout the years are recorded and saved for Judgment Day. And if we do have foresight, we will plan for Judgment Day. And if we are wise to the Book of Life and care about our afterlife, we'll fill it with good deeds.

Positively, the caring man and woman determined to obey the Spirit of God and live by God's commandments, laying up treasures in Heaven are His favored children. But the man and woman who obey the lust of the flesh and reject the Ten Commandments haven't got any treasures in Heaven.

Therefore, if I say the grass and the flowers of the field symbolize the flesh, it glorieth when it's young and fadeth when it's old. Then, I am saying the great Spirit of God is symbolic of a beautiful flower, and it's much more beautiful than the grass.

This truth means I am also trying to say a beautiful flower is similar to the beauty of the Holy Spirit. But, sadly, the flesh is weak, and it gets battered in the storms. And because of its frailty, the flower never fully recovers from each previous day.

However, the indiscriminate beauty of the wonderful Holy Spirit is incomparable, and it's much more desirable than beautiful flesh. Simply because beautiful flesh has the destiny to lose its beauty, and we all know it'll die like the grass.

Indeed, a beautiful appearance will fade away. But a beautiful heart will always be beautiful, regardless of our age. A beautiful heart is a sign of goodness and godliness, and it's the only kind of heart God approves of and will invite to live in His kingdom.

The next parallel scripture, concerning you, me, and everyone else, parallels us to the grass. And it illuminates how the cycle of things comes and goes and how the youth of anything is a cycle, having a destiny to fade away.

> **Isaiah 40:6** The <u>voice</u> (of God) said, cry. And <u>he</u> (the flesh man) said, what shall I cry?

Surely, this scripture reveals the human race, blind as bats and out of place if they think they have a promised long life. And mainly because the human race is similar to a flower, and it has a short season to live, and the voice of God goes on to say.

> **Isaiah 40:6** All <u>flesh</u> <u>is</u> <u>grass</u> (going to fade and die), and all the goodliness is as the field's flower.

So beautiful do the flowers look when they are young and colorful. But as time marches forward, the beauty of the flower fades and dies, and it's the same way with a beautiful appearance. And our age changes are similar to the spring turning into fall.

It's easy to conclude when people are young, they are full of life and as carefree as flowers swaying in the wind. But for some ungodly reason, short-sightedness prevails, and carefree people do not look far enough ahead and consider the future of their next life.

However, as time marches forward, day after day, their beautiful appearance will fade away. And even the grass, battered by winds and storms, will retain its beauty better than the flesh. And the great autobiography they should write will rarely coincide with the word of God.

If the exterior is more important to the vain person than the interior, looks are more important than a beautiful heart. Then, I must tell you, no beauty was left in their golden age simply because the exterior was more important to them than their interior.

It may not be evident to the person walking in their youth, but the body, made from clay, will swiftly decay and fade away. In a metaphor way of saying, the flower is symbolic of the flesh. And the flower is saying; we have a season, similar to the way the flesh has a season.

If the voice of our Great God says, Cry, flesh man, cry, and the flesh man says, what shall I cry about God? Then our Great God might say, see the beauty of the flower; now observe how time works against it and causes it to fade away.

I firmly believe the flower is our example of blooming in the wonderful word of God before our time to secure salvation fades away. Indeed, the flower example tells us there's only a short time to prepare us for the next life cycle.

Beyond the shadow of a doubt, our next life cycle will be determined by our autobiography in the Book of Life. And before the beauty of life fades away, you and I shouldn't wait another day to look beautiful before the Lord.

Indeed, the flower and the flesh have much in common, and the flowers need sunshine and rain. This truth is similar to saying that we need the perfect word of God, the same way the flowers need sunshine and rain.

The war between the flesh and old age symbolizes the flower wanting to stay beautiful and not fade away. But the reality of the flower cannot escape the life cycle; no more than the flesh can retain its beauty, day after day.

Truly, if the flower could speak words of advice, it would say, Do not let the vanity of beauty spoil your salvation day. And the wisdom of the flower would say, there will come another day if we learn to overcome the vanity of our sinful ways.

The lesson of the flower teaches us a fact of life when it illustrates we only have a short season before our cycle of life disappears. And this means unless a man learns to overcome the flesh and care more about having a beautiful heart, he'll not bloom again in the next season.

Without a doubt, I am correct to say that a beautiful heart will more likely get through the gates of pearl than beautiful flesh. And this means beautiful flesh hasn't any advantages with God when we stand before the gates of the pearl.

However, regardless of our appearance and how we look in the mirror today, tomorrow, and next year. I want you to know we'll all be beautiful in Heaven, like a flower, blooming daily, year after year.

The prophet Isaiah says, The grass withereth, and the flower fadeth: Because the Spirit of the <u>Lord</u> <u>bloweth</u> <u>upon</u> <u>it</u>. And <u>bloweth</u> <u>upon</u> <u>it</u> means our life cycle has begun its countdown, and its allotted time is ticking like a clock. And this means our cycle of life will eventually stop.

Positively, all flesh and blood people are like the grass, and the Spirit of the Lord controls life and death. And I am sure Isaiah is trying to say life is similar to the grass and the flowers, and all three will withereth and fade away.

Positively, the prophet Isaiah is saying, in a roundabout way, that beauty has a pre-determined cycle and always fades away. But he's also metaphorically saying that the word of our Great God shall stand forever, and it'll never fade away.

Conclusively, the wonderful Son of God wants us to know man does not live by bread alone but by every word proceeding from the mouth of God. And this means the word of God is seriously important, and we are required to live by it.

I assure you, my Great God is merciful when sinners repent and change. But if they do not change, then they'll permanently fade away. And when God says, obey My commandments and live, we better believe His words.

Indeed, this need-to-understand story, called the flesh, illustrates a fact-of-life metaphor story. It purposely entwines the flowers, grass, and life cycle. And you and I aren't flowers and grass, but we are seasonal, too.

Positively, the lesson from this testimonial story concerns the flesh, the cycle of life, and the spring and the fall. It's telling you not to let the vanity of beauty spoil our lives and ruin our salvation day because we will get old and fade away.

I assure you, we cannot change the order of things designed by our Creator God. But we can conform to His great Ten Commandments and live forever, and the cycle of life will quit cycling us like the flowers and the grass.

Truly, this important story has a serious message to reveal, and I am telling you to care more about pleasing God than pleasing the flesh. And if we do, we'll be more beautiful than the prettiest flower in a large field full of flowers on any day.

Chapter Twenty-One

THE FLESH AND THE SPIRIT

I am certain life will be much better for believers in Jesus Christ after the Holy Spirit of God is poured upon all flesh. Life will be much better for believers after they quit being passive Christians and become passionate Christians.

Furthermore, passive Christians will become passionate after the beautiful Holy Ghost is poured upon them. The next informative scripture illustrates hot and on fire Christians in the last days, drenched and filled with the Holy Spirit of God.

The wonderful Holy Spirit poured upon believers will be accomplished by God. And it'll include dreams and visions and prophesizing. And I believe this time, yet to come, will include miracles and a great shaking on this Earth.

Acts 2:17 And it shall come to pass in the last days, saith God, I will pour out My <u>Spirit</u> (means knowledge of Him, and His word), upon <u>all flesh</u> (and it may mean upon everyone, but many will reject it):

Acts 2:17 And your sons and your daughters shall <u>prophesy</u> (means they shall speak the word of God), and your young men shall see visions, and your old men shall dream dreams.

In the above awareness scripture, the Apostle Peter tells us about a time yet to come and maybe soon in our future. And it's quite clear that the last days, the end time yet to come, will be unusual, supernatural, and extraordinary.

I firmly believe the end time prophesized days the Apostle Peter speaks about has begun and will be fulfilled with notable works. And for God's glory, I am certain passionate men of God will accomplish notable works, and I hope to be one of them.

Positively, I assure you I could not write about the unusual, supernatural, and extraordinary things I write without having the Spirit of God compelling me to do it. And because I love God and His gospel, I am a willing vessel shaped by the Potter Man.

Because of the Holy Spirit of God, His clear guidance, and the undeniable fact that I've fallen hopelessly in love with the word of God. I've written and published eight books in an approximately two-year period of time, and as of this update, I have nine books published.

Surely, it's an amazing feat for anyone to accomplish, and my work exceeds most of what most people will do for Christ. But I could do it because the hand of God was upon me, and it prodded me to complement His gospel truth, and I willingly will explain many things.

Indeed, this great last day's end-time message the Apostle Peter is talking about is from the Pentecost Revival. And I believe the great message from the Pentecost Revival is intended for us. And it's because we live in the last days, prophesized by the Apostle Peter.

The last day's statement means right before the great and terrible tribulation time and before the great second coming of Yeshua. And I assure you, the great revival we are told about at Pentecost will be small compared to this end-time event.

As for the Apostle Peter, he speaks about a special time when the Cloven Tongues on Fire came down from the altar of God to be with the people on this Earth. And the knowledge we gain from the Pentecost Revival will increase our understanding of God.

I assure you, the powerful Cloven Tongues on Fire will most certainly leave the altar of God again, and they'll come down to this Earth in the last days. And I am certain it'll be their pleasure to participate in the shaking of this Earth.

The Apostle Peter speaks the compelling words of God, and he delivers a message from God when he says, I will pour out My Spirit upon all flesh. And the word all flesh means every man, woman, and child upon this Earth who believes in God.

Truly, his analogy includes the passive Christian, the passionate Christian, all believers, and the pure-at-heart person. And this coming end time Peter speaks about, when the Holy Spirit of God is poured upon everyone is nearly here.

I am certain it'll be a last day's end-time event filled with the supernatural, and it'll be similar to the amazing days of the Pentecost Revival. However, the number of participants in this end-time event will include millions or billions of people.

It will be a special time, designed to include heavenly creations and Cloven Tongues on Fire. And I believe flesh and blood men will speak in different tongues, and men of other languages will understand them.

All these extraordinary and supernatural things will happen all over this unstable world, and race, gender, and nationality will not matter. And the extremely active Holy Ghost will speak God's love into everyone's heart.

Beyond the shadow of a doubt, the caring and concerned Holy Ghost of God will call lost men to repentance and change. And I am certain that the Spirit of God will ask them to join the Good Shepherd's flock before it's too late.

It could be likely to happen, this last day's end time event, similar to the Pentecost Revival. It'll be the last time upon this Earth when God pours out His Spirit on all flesh before the last trumpet sounds. And the definition of foolish men will be illustrated by men that reject His Spirit.

I am certain this last day's end time event will be during a time when God lovers will harken to the sinner person. To save souls, they'll invite sinners to join the family of God, and this act of love illustrates God's forgiveness, revealing a Christian caring about lost souls.

A flying angel will soar through the Heavens above during this last day's event and will be voicing His concern over the things to come upon this Earth. And signs like this mean the countdown to the end is close at hand.

I am certain that *The Conclusion to the Whole Matter* will be one of the end-time messages for everyone. Even though I want you to know, it's always been the greatest message from the beginning and will be until the end.

It's quite possible, and most likely accurate to say, after an allotted period. There will not be more time for conversion to Christianity; the window of opportunity will close, and the choice to accept the Holy Spirit of God will vanish.

Truly, I am talking about this special time, yet to come. It might be the last chance to accept God, be saved, and inherit the kingdom of God. Especially before the mark of the beast is applied to anyone who rejects His Holy Spirit and His designed way of life.

Mainly because corruption cannot inherit incorruption; no more than flesh and blood can inherit the kingdom of God. But if the spirit of man overcomes the flesh, then the pure at-heart spiritual man and woman will put on immortality and be a child of the promise.

However, please be aware the wicked invisible demonic ghost spirits of the air are the adversary of the flesh and the adversary of the Spirit of God. And I assure you, they stand between the good works of the Holy Spirit and the flesh.

Therefore, I want you to realize when the wonderful Holy Spirit of God cannot overcome the ungodly desires of the flesh. Then, the demonic ghost spirit of the air makes the flesh more corruptible and less wanted by the wonderful God of creation.

However, be assured the appearance and the image of the flesh reveal no reflection on the character of the heart. Within the next informative verse, the wonderful Son of God has something to say concerning the Spirit and the flesh and about temptation.

> **Matthew 26:41** Watch and pray that ye enter not into <u>temptation</u> (means enter not into sin): The <u>spirit</u> <u>is</u> <u>willing</u> (to reject evil temptations), but the flesh is weak.

In the above scripture, the Son of God tells us that watching *and praying* is our most effective armor against the tempter of the flesh. And the Spirit is willing to help the flesh and teach it ways to fight against the temptations of the tempter.

Truly, the Spirit knows the flesh is weak, but the Spirit cannot fight against every person's choice of free will. For this reason, we cannot give in to the desires of the flesh and let the Spirit battle the tempter without us doing our part to resist sin.

The lust of the flesh and the evil desires of this world bear no fruit. But bible scriptures reveal that carnal and immoral desires bring death to the soul. And we all know the wicked Lucifer tries to get us to sin. And this means he's trying to destroy our souls.

Indeed, the sins of the flesh are servitude to the tempter, and the ungodly ways of the tempter will cause separation from our Savior God. And I warn you, separation from God means we'll fail the test of life and not become a resident in His kingdom.

The next awareness scripture concerns the sinner part of our life. It recalls the memory of ourselves at a terrible time when we were in the world and foolishly living in sin. And even though we didn't realize it, we were jeopardizing our souls.

> **Romans 7:5** For when we were in the flesh, the <u>motions</u> (means desires) of sins, which were by the law, did work in our <u>members</u> (means within our body and flesh) to bring forth fruit unto death.

Indeed, the Apostle Paul battled in the war between the Spirit and the flesh, and Paul was doing the things in the flesh the Spirit abhorred. And I believe many of us traveled the wrong road before finding the right one.

Surely, the changed Apostle Paul is a good example of a sinner who became a spiritual man and still wrestled against the flesh. And maybe we'll always be wrestling against the flesh to some unknown degree, even after our conversion to Christianity.

The Apostle Paul tells us, and maybe from his own experiences that he knows God's word extremely well. And the Apostle Paul says, there is no good thing that dwelleth in the flesh, for the good the flesh wishes to do, it does not, and the evil it wishes not to do, it does.

The Apostle Paul assures us a believer in Christ must be strong in the Spirit before it can defeat the lust of the flesh. And this means we need to lean on the strength of the Holy Spirit of God, and He will help us resist the temptations of the flesh.

The next informative scripture insinuates the believers in Christ are the people trying not to walk after the flesh. And I want you to know after we become a new person in Christ, we are expected to walk in the ways of Christ and be loyal to Him by abiding by His commandments.

> **Romans 8:1** There is no <u>condemnation</u> (means not damned, and not lost) to them which are in Christ Jesus, who walk not after the flesh.

However, there is condemnation among the unbelievers, and whosoever rejects and denies the Holy Spirit and walks after the flesh. And the believers in Christ, free from condemnation, live in the Spirit and are strong enough to reject the lust of the flesh.

> **Romans 8:4** That the <u>righteous</u> (means requirements) of the law might be <u>fulfilled</u> <u>in</u> <u>us</u> (whom war with the flesh), who walk not after the flesh, but after the <u>Spirit</u> (which is righteousness).

> **Romans 8:5** For they that <u>are</u> (means whosoever pursues) after the flesh does mind the things of the flesh; but they that are after the Spirit, (they mind, and care about) the things of the Spirit.

Indeed, two different types of people desire the flesh and the Spirit: the loyal believers in Christ care about the Spirit, and the other type of person, called the unbeliever, cares about satisfying the flesh.

I want you to realize that Christians and only Christians desire God's excellent and wonderful Spirit. But sadly, I must conclude that the unbelievers desire the pleasures of the flesh and keep company with whosoever desires to satisfy the flesh.

The unbelievers and whoever is weak in Spirit desire the things of the flesh, and the believers desire the things of the Spirit. And the things of the Spirit are the righteous ways of God. And the ways of God illuminate the way of life we Christians cherish and love.

Surely, whichever it is of the two directions the heart desires the most, the greatest desire will defeat the lesser desire in the war between the Spirit and the flesh. And I conclude that the heart has reigns like the horse, and we better hope the Spirit of God controls our reigns.

However, please remember that this life is a test between godliness and ungodliness. And our serious God-inspired bible tells us, over and over, that permanent death and Hell are reserved for the ungodly person.

> **Romans 8:6**: To be <u>carnally</u> (means worldly) minded is death; but to be spiritually (means godly) minded is life and peace.

> **Romans 8:7** Because the <u>carnal</u> (means unclean) mind is <u>enmity</u> (means hostile) against God: For <u>it</u> (the carnal man and mind) is not <u>subject</u> (means not obedient) to the law of God, neither indeed can <u>it</u> (the carnal mind) be.

> **Romans 8:8** So they (who live according to the flesh), who are <u>in</u> <u>the</u> <u>flesh</u> (means controlled by the desires of the flesh) cannot please God.

> **Romans 8:9** But <u>ye</u> (Christians believers) are not in the flesh, but in the Spirit, "*if so be*" that the Spirit of God dwells in you. Now, if any man has not the Spirit of Christ, <u>he</u> (that man) is none of <u>His</u> (means not of Jesus Christ).

Romans 8:10 And "*if*" Christ be in you, the <u>body</u> (means the flesh) is dead because of sin;

Romans 8:10, but the Spirit is <u>life</u> (means alive in you and giveth life) because of <u>righteousness,</u> (and because you reject the temptations of the flesh, and (you) are alive in the Spirit, because you believe in the righteousness of God).

Anyone walking in the flesh is not God's loyal sons and daughters, nor does the great Spirit of God dwell within them. The Apostle Paul tells us that being carnally minded results in death. And this isn't a casual warning but a serious one to remember.

However, as the Spirit of God compels many, they are the sons and daughters of God. And when a man or a woman learns to listen to the Holy Spirit. Then they'll be stronger, and they can defeat the temptations of the flesh.

Indeed, the appearance of the flesh is deceptive and doesn't speak for the heart. Even though the flesh and the heart are part of the same body, both still have individuality. And because the flesh is beautiful to look upon, it doesn't mean for certain the heart is godly.

It doesn't mean the appearance and heart project the same message or image simply because they entwine together in the same body. And I warn you, perception is a gamble if we form conclusions without evidence.

I assure you that a beautiful heart filled with the Spirit of God is much more likely to win the war between the Spirit and the flesh. And if Christ is in us, then the flesh should resist sin. And I am certain ungodly temptations will be easier to refuse.

Truly, a person who values the Spirit more than the flesh is highly valued by God because they are winning the war against the flesh. And the Apostle Paul wants us to know the Spirit is life because it teaches righteousness.

A caring person puts more value on the Spirit than on the flesh. And a warrior for God cares more about the Spirit than he does the flesh. And a warrior for God fights the desires of the flesh.

The excellent Spirit of God directs men in the ways of righteousness, and the flesh pulls men toward the ways of unrighteousness. And it'll always be that way, and there will always be war between righteousness and unrighteousness.

Similarly, there will always be war between the Spirit and the flesh. And the war between the spirit and the flesh reveals some men as winners and some as losers. And sadly, the losers will always be submissive to the flesh.

However, please remember that the war between the Spirit and the flesh is extremely serious. And you and me, and everyone else, are warriors for the Spirit, or we are weak compromisers bending our knees to the flesh.

Even though bloodshed isn't a part of the war between the Spirit and the flesh, it's still a serious war that we should fight hard to win. The consequences of losing our battle to the weakness of the flesh are nearly as bad as shedding our blood through suicide.

Conclusively, if we reject God's wonderful and righteous ways, we submit ourselves to the pleasures of the flesh. Then it isn't much different than you and me, committing suicide to the spirit and killing the godliness of our soul.

Chapter Twenty-Two

SUPERNATURAL FELLOWSHIP, BLESSINGS, AND FAVOR

I want you to realize that supernatural fellowship, blessings, and favor are gifts from our wonderful Supernatural God. And I want you to know that God rewards everyone willing to obey His voice and keep His commandments and laws.

Sometimes, our wonderful Supernatural God takes not-so-brilliant men who love Him and obey His voice. And He lifts them and makes brilliant men out of them. And thanks to God, they can do His good and glorious works more than before.

Therefore, if you want favor with our Supreme Supernatural God from above, always be extremely close to Him. Then He has requirements we must fulfill, and all His requirements entwine with perfect righteousness.

If it's your heart's desire, and above all other things, you want to be filled with the Holy Spirit of our Supernatural God from above. Then, you must be determined to do great and righteous things for His glory, and for a bonus, you will prosper wherever you go.

Furthermore, if you want the Holy Supernatural God to be your friend, never forsake you, and watch your back against enemy attacks. Then, you must obey His commandments and laws and not turn your right foot or your left foot from doing His will.

I assure you if we provoke our wonderful Supreme God to jealousy by recognizing strange gods as real and valid. Then He will anger, and His wrath will show through compensation in one way or another, and the violator will get hurt.

Positively, if we provoke our wonderful All-Powerful God to anger, the curse of judgment will come upon us in one form or another, hurting us terribly. But be assured; God only angers at wickedness, corruption, and evil works.

However, if we listen to the invisible and intangible spirit of devils and demons and sacrifice to ungodly entities, and not to our Supreme Supernatural God, if we honor gods of any sort from other cultures, or to newly made up gods, or to gods with alias names, meant to imitate our Supreme God.

Then I want you to realize that the great Rock of Salvation, alias our wonderful Creator God, may not remember us at transition time. And it'll be because we neglected Him and foolishly honored strange gods.

Our Supreme God is the Rock of salvation, and He's the one promising to feed the saints with the inheritance of Jacob. And Yehovah alone is the only God who cares enough and promises the saints that they can ride upon the high places of this earth if they delight in Him.

Truly, I pray you'll delight in Him, be in a position of acceptance with God, and have supernatural fellowship with Him. And I hope you'll receive blessings, favor, and showers of love from our Supreme loving God because you love Him immensely.

I hope you'll receive supernatural favor and blessings if you keep God's righteous ways instead of man's traditions. And I hope and pray God will look down from the Heavens above and smile when He sees you.

Positively, I am certain the above things, including fellowship, are gifts and rewards to any person filled with the Holy Ghost of God. Knowledge and wisdom, understanding, and divine assistance are a part of any person's life when they ride upon the high places of the earth.

I assure you good gifts are ours to claim when we live in defense of God's infallible laws, commandments, and His designated lifestyle. His designed lifestyle and commandments are the formula for creating perfect people.

Furthermore, if we are devout believers in God, then the Holy Spirit will be a shield against the wiles of the invisible spirit of the devil. And no one from any corner of this earth is as powerful as our God, and He's responsible for creating everything our eyes behold.

The glory and beauty of our Great Supreme God are observed through His many creations' supernatural works. And do realize His glory shines through the man and woman, who are filled with the invisible Holy Spirit of God.

Indeed, the body of any person, filled with the Holy Spirit of God, is God's redefined living temple. This truth means the living church of God is alive and walks and talks with the Holy Ghost of God, who lives and dwells within every clean-hearted believer in Him.

Truly, if we love Him and keep His commandments, we'll be safe from incurring His wrath, judgment, and supernatural curses. And living by His commandments should please us as much as it pleases Him. And I assure you, this trade-off is in our favor.

The fear of our wonderful Lord is not to be afraid of Him, as if He's a bully, standing over us with a zapper in His hand. Although I warn you, we should tremble whenever we rebel against Him and purposely sin.

Positively, the fear of the Lord means we should sincerely love Him and reverence Him as our friend, Father, and God. And the fear of the Lord means we should hunger for His fellowship and His holy and righteous word.

The fear of God means we should reverence His laws and commandments daily as we live and breathe. And the fear of God means we should be upright men or women among all the people crossing our path in everyday life.

If we fear God and are compelled to do right, then we've concluded that He's teaching us the right way. And after learning the right way, the strength of our Supernatural God will shine through us, and the fruitful works we do in His name will be blessed.

The fear of God means we agree with His rules and respect His Supreme authority. And I want you to know that keeping the excellent and perfect Ten Commandments He wrote in stone is a good place for us to start showing our respect to Him.

The fear of God means we'll put a difference between the things belonging to God and the things belonging to Satan. And the fear of God means we'll live by the required word of God, and we'll reject the rebellious ways of the evil Satan.

I assure you, every man and woman on this earth has an invisible guiding spirit within them. And it's so undetectable, and its influence isn't usually recognized. And to an unknown degree, we are pawns on the chessboard of life, played by the spirit world.

However, do not be naïve, and please realize not every spirit is the wonderful Spirit of God. Because ungodly spirits travel the air corridors, they have the power of telepathy. And I am one hundred percent certain they possess and control some people.

Indeed, the measured strength of every person's spirit is metered by how much they are filled with the invisible Spirit of God or the invisible ghost spirit of the devil. And the saved are filled with the Spirit of God, and demonic spirits possess the unsaved.

Without a doubt, the invisible Spirit of our God is revealed by the steadfastness of our righteous works. And God gives a strong Spirit and a strong gift of discernment to men and women who gladly surrender their life to Him.

Therefore, if we are loyal men or women of God, we have a strong supernatural gift of discernment. Then, I want you to know that we can stand beside another person and feel the strength of the other person's spirit.

Whether they are a person of God or ungodly, their spirit is detectable when we stand next to them because a man possessed by an evil spirit will set off alarms in our heads. And mainly because our Holy Spirit of God will detect his evil spirit.

It's for certain men possessed by the spirit of the devil will be disturbed and upset sometimes and without being provoked at all. Even without realizing the reason, they are upset or disturbed. And it happens when they stand beside a man filled with the Holy Ghost of God.

I assure you the moral strength of the Holy Spirit is supernatural, and the Holy Spirit can detect the ungodly spirit within wicked men. And we are blessed to have the Holy Spirit for a friend willing to reveal the presence of ungodly spirits.

Therefore, simply because of opposition to each other, the invisible Spirit of God clashes with the wicked invisible spirit of the devil. When this happens, the man with the weakest spirit is usually out-maneuvered by the man with the strongest spirit.

For the above reason, it reveals the importance of being filled with the Holy Spirit of God and not just having a little bit of Him. And mainly because the ghost spirit of the devil is strong, and he will trample on the man, having only a small amount of the Holy Spirit living within him.

Regardless of what men think concerning their spiritual strength, it's not the man carrying the Holy Spirit of God. But it's the strength of the Holy Ghost of God carrying a man if the man is a true Christian man of God and has a clean-living temple.

Positively, a man filled with the Holy Spirit of God loves to savor the word of God as if it's the most delicious meal he's ever tasted. But a man not having the Holy Spirit of God identifies a man without flavor, similar to a meal without salt.

Truly, a man filled with the Holy Ghost identifies as a man standing for holiness, righteousness, cleanness, and courage. And he's a special man who possesses the strength to resist the evil and demonic ghost spirit of the devil.

However, a man or woman void of the Holy Ghost of God living within them will lack his holiness, righteousness, internal strength, and cleanness. And sadly, they'll not be able to resist the temptations of the invisible and wicked spirit of the devil.

However, a man filled with the wonderful Holy Spirit of God has abundant <u>salt</u> (which means righteousness and much love for God in his heart). And thanks to the beautiful Holy Spirit of God, his soul is everlasting, and he's the salt of the earth.

Positively, this means he's an example person who personifies righteousness based upon the word of God. But if the salt has lost its <u>savor</u> (if a man has lost the will to live godly), wherewith shall the earth be salted?

I am quite certain without having the strong Spirit of God and His influence of godliness upon a few good men. Then, this unstable earth will not have much value left upon it after men and women with salt are gone from among humanity.

After that, when this unstable earth is void of men and women having salt, it'll be good for nothing except to be cast out like something unwanted and trodden under the foot of corrupt, wicked, and unclean men.

It could be said salt is symbolic of the Holy Spirit of God, and men rejecting to know God haven't any salt. And a man not having salt running through his veins stands for nothing, is good for nothing, and cannot be trusted with the smallest things.

I want you to know that God's magnificent glory cannot be found in any person who lacks the flavor of salt. And I want you to realize it does take salt to carry the cross every day and oppose whatever is contrary to authenticity.

If we are the redefined temple of God, and the Holy Ghost lives within us and guides our footsteps away from evil exploits. Then, our characteristics prove salt is part of our backbone, and a man without salt doesn't have a strong backbone.

Indeed, a backbone with salt is required to stand strong in this world, and salt is needed to walk in the righteous ways of God. Salt is developed in high quantities, and salt multiplies in whosoever is obedient, respectful, and thankful to our Supreme God.

Truly, only a man with salt has enough faith to believe God created all things and that every living thing is subject to His command. This truth means God is a Father to every living creature who possesses the element of life, regardless of the form it represents.

Indeed, if we care about our soul and doing right, we should be loyal sons and daughters, bound to His righteous and wonderful Ten Commandments. And I assure you, His excellent laws are written for the good of us all, and denying them is a danger to our souls.

Truly, there cannot be any honor in a person who doesn't have salt and a passionate love for righteousness. And mainly because salt is the primary substance entwined with our inner strength. And salt can shape a person's character and everything concerning our life.

Nor can a person lacking salt hold their head up high and look another person eye to eye without fear of his salt-less soul being detected. Without having salt, we cannot have confidence in ourselves. And honesty and integrity will elude a person not having salt.

I assure you the word of God is sharper than a two-edged sword, cuts in both directions, and doesn't play favorites. This truth means divine blessings and favor from above can be given and taken away by the will of the Lord.

The two-edged sword of the Lord cuts coming and going, and it'll divide the blessed from the cursed. And it's logical to believe divine supernatural blessings and favors are honorary gifts to the obedient Christian.

Therefore, if the above statement is true, then discipline and corrections are judgments upon the disobedient Christian. And it's wise to know my Great Creator God controls all supernatural blessings, favors, discipline, curses, and judgments concerning our behavior.

Indeed, the wise people in this jungle world are obedient believers in the God of Heaven and Earth who cherish His every word. But the unwise people in this jungle world are the disobedient unbelievers who go with the flow and live a liberal lifestyle.

Ultimately, we must believe supernatural favors, blessings, curses, discipline, and judgments are a controlled necessity. And they are totally in the hands of God, and beyond our understanding, and not always logical to the flesh and blood person.

I believe it's time to point out the fact between manufactured and supernatural blessings. And I want you to realize there's a difference between the two types of blessings, and we should know the difference.

Supernatural divine blessings come from our Great Creator God and are a gift from the realms of Heaven. But manufactured blessings are self-made blessings. And it's because some men labor hard for their blessings and prosperity.

Furthermore, it would be naïve to think the servants of darkness aren't blessed by the master of darkness, the wicked Satan. The Son of God reveals that Satan is the evil prince of this world, and he can and will bless his servants of darkness.

Therefore, I want you to know blessings come from at *least three different* sources. And *number one* is from God, *number two* is from hard labor, and *number three* is from Lucifer. And I am certain most men cannot tell you the source of their blessings.

Indeed, blessings from hard labor bring prosperity to hard workers, and blessings from Lucifer bring prosperity to the wicked. But God's blessings bring prosperity, happiness, good health, good fellowship, and many more positive benefits.

There are two main indicators, and to a large degree, they can indicate the greater source of our blessings. And I want you to realize the traditions of men versus the commandments of God are the two main indicators.

Indeed, the loyal believers in Christ, who put the Commandments of God first, are more likely to receive supernatural divine blessings. But believers and unbelievers who've chosen to live by the traditions of men and blaze their trail through life.

They both can receive their blessings through hard labor or the master of darkness since he blesses whosoever opposes the word of God. However, all blessings do not come from the same source, and there are at least three different avenues of blessings.

Even though I am certain all men and women would like to think their blessings come from our Great Creator God. But I conclude that because of different lifestyles, all people aren't certain about the avenue of their blessings.

It's for certain some men worship our Supreme God, and He blesses them because they enthusiastically follow Him. But the prince of this world is Lucifer, and he has enthusiastic followers, too. And his servants of darkness do not go unrewarded.

Although, I believe most blessings today are manufactured because of ungodliness from within and from outside the church. They are blessings earned by the sweat of our brow, by the works of our hands, and by applying ourselves to sources of revenue.

This informative story is called Supernatural Fellowship, Blessings, and Favor. It's meant to reveal three different sources of blessings, And I fully believe it's safe to say our lifestyle is an indicator pointing to our source of blessings.

This explanation story reveals divine blessings and favors are rewards, and they are given to us by our Supreme God. Because we strive to do His will and enjoy carrying His cross, I want you to know that all our blessings aren't free.

Furthermore, blessings and favors given to men from the evil god of this world aren't given away freely, and they have to be earned, too. Wicked and corrupt men gain favor and blessings from Satan simply because God's righteous ways aren't important to evil and corrupt men.

Our Supreme God of Heaven and Earth expects us to walk upright and be loyal commandment-keepers before God blesses us. And we would be foolish to believe anything less than loyalty to His required word will gain you and me divine blessings.

However, I want you to know there's a price tag for everything, and the evil god of this world has requirements, too. This truth means he expects his followers to be commandment haters and hate commandment keepers before he blesses them with prosperity.

We must choose our God wisely and walk in His ways because of extreme importance. Otherwise, we'll receive nothing divine from above. And the good things all loyal Christians receive come from above, and the best blessings come from above. And because I love my brothers and sisters in Christ, I hope everyone finds the path to His heart.

Chapter Twenty-Three

STUMBLING BLOCKS IN FRONT OF BLESSINGS

Within this exploration story, I would like to ask you an important question, and it concerns the spiritual direction of many churches. And I am asking you, what is the most harmful thing, or the wickedest tradition of men, ever to happen to the church and its members?

I wonder how many Christians could answer the above question correctly because passionate Christians are hard to find even if they've been involved with a church most of their life and go to church Sunday after Sunday.

Indeed, the answer to this extremely important question could reveal the key to an abundance of divine supernatural favors and blessings. And for our benefit, we need to know the correct formula for receiving favors and blessings.

I will gladly share my opinion if you do not know the correct answer to the above important question and desire understanding. And I want you to know my opinion is based on the word of God, as I understand it.

Positively, because I want the best for all Christians, I want to see all Christian men and women be blessed with divine supernatural favors and blessings. And I believe in the formula I am revealing to you because it's biblical and the fourth commandment of God.

I will enlighten you that this commanded requirement is much more significant than most Christian men and women realize. Sadly, I must tell you, many professing Christians do not know the answer to this extremely important stipulation I am about to tell you.

Simply because of deception from the pulpit and a lack of bible study, including an ongoing problem dating back hundreds of years, there are several reasons this problem between man and God is hidden from the eyes of most professing Christians.

I believe this because commandment breaking is a serious compromise, the most hurtful thing to ever happen to the churches, the temples of God, and the Christian members. Truly, it's changing the authentic seventh-day Sabbath Day of the Lord to another day.

The sacred and hallowed Sabbath Day of the Lord was changed from the seventh day of the week to the first day of the week. And I want you to know it was accomplished by man's will and without my Great God's authority.

Therefore, the changing of the fourth commandment by man and the change not having the authority of God or the Son of God. It's managed to cause more spiritual and personal relationship harm to Christians than any other tradition of men.

Mainly because no man, church leader, or pope has the right or the authority to change any one of the commandments of God. I can tell you changing the seventh day, Sabbath Day, to another day shouldn't have happened then, and it shouldn't be happening now.

Our Lord's true and holy Sabbath Day is on Saturday, the seventh day of the week. And I assure you, it's not on the first day of the week, Sun-day. And the Sun-day Sabbath Day amounts to an ungodly counterfeit Sabbath Day not holy, sacred, or hallowed.

Truly, counterfeit things aren't recognized by my wonderful God, nor is He pleased with counterfeit changes to His gospel truth. And it's logical and biblical to believe divine and supernatural blessings, favors, and fellowship are special rewards from God.

They are rewards to the man and woman, determined to keep, obey, and observe the seventh day, the Sabbath Day of God. Simply because the keeping of the seventh day, Sabbath Day, identifies with a requirement for one of the greatest promises written within the bible.

It's a sincere promise from our Supreme God and only promised to the seventh-day Sabbath Day keepers. However, the Sun-day Christians claim this promise also. But according to the excellent word of God, their claim is denied.

Absolutely, and for your benefit, you should listen closely to the word of God, written within these next two informative scriptures. Then you'll understand from these next two scriptures the greatest stumbling block before divine supernatural blessings.

However, I hope you realize that God-designed requirements aren't bendable. If you aren't doing these scriptures mentioned, God requires us to acknowledge to receive supernatural and divine blessings. Then, sadly, I must tell you, these absolute promises from God will not be yours to receive.

Therefore, absorb the word of God from these next two scriptures, apply His rules to your lifestyle, and God will bless you. And mainly because the knowledge extracted from these next two scriptures is important to all Christians if they are interested in receiving divine blessings.

Isaiah 58:13 If <u>thou</u> (means if you will) turn away <u>thy</u> <u>foot</u> (means thy heart) <u>from</u> (means breaking) the <u>Sabbath</u> (holy rest day), from doing thy pleasures on <u>My</u> <u>holy</u> <u>day</u> (means on My seventh-day Sabbath Day):

Isaiah 58:13 And <u>call</u> (means believe) the <u>Sabbath</u> (seventh day Sabbath Day is) a <u>delight</u> (means a pleasure to observe).

Isaiah 58:13 The holy of the Lord, honorable; and shall honor <u>Him</u> (on the seventh day), not doing thine own ways, finding thine own pleasures, nor speaking thine own words.

Isaiah 58:14 Then shall <u>thou</u> (means you shall) delight thyself in the Lord;

Isaiah 58:14 and <u>I</u> (the wonderful and truthful Most High God) will <u>cause</u> (means promise) <u>thee</u> (you), to ride upon the high places of the earth, and feed <u>thee</u> (you) with the heritage of Jacob, thy father:

234

Isaiah 58:14 FOR THE MOUTH OF THE LORD HATH SPOKEN IT!

As we live, breathe, and walk upon this earth, we have important choices concerning our walk with God. And it's seriously important to walk, talk, and live within the holy ways of the Lord if we desire to be blessed by God.

Most likely, the two scriptures you've just finished reading could be the greatest promise of divine blessings and favors to all upright and qualifying Christians. And maybe you'll never have a greater opportunity to claim a divine promise from God.

These two scriptures include a close fellowship with the Lord, and it's promised from the mouth of the Lord, thy Supernatural God. And if we believe in Him and the sincerity of His word, we should put our faith in the above two scriptures.

These two important scriptures, taken from the book of Isaiah, are written to all believers determined to keep and honor Him on the seventh day, the Sabbath Day of the Lord. And it's obvious that our great and wonderful Lord, thy Supreme God, has promised us Sabbath Keepers a great promise.

Positively, He wants us to know we can ride upon the high places of this earth by delightfully keeping the holy, sacred, and hallowed seventh-day Sabbath Day of the Lord. And riding upon the high places of the earth means we'll have favor with our Supreme God.

Surely, divine blessings and favor will be the gifts and rewards to all Christians who desire to ride upon the high places of this earth. This truth means our Great Creator God watches over His loyal Sabbath Keepers and blesses them with many gifts.

Indeed, the second part of His great and wonderful promise, He speaks from His mouth, depends on us keeping His seventh-day Sabbath Day. And it's an absolute promise, saying He'll feed us with the heritage of Jacob, thy father, His prince of many nations.

The word of God assures us the heritage of Jacob is a promised home in the kingdom of God. And His kingdom is the right place we should want to call our permanent home. And the grand prize of immortality entwines with the heritage of Jacob.

Indeed, I want you to know that you and I can claim the same heritage God promised Jacob. Claiming His promise has a simple requirement, and delightfully keeping the seventh-day holy day, Sabbath Day, is His requirement.

I assure you the seventh day, Sabbath Day, is one of the few holy things within the Bible, considered hallowed, sacred, and holy. And out of seven hundred and eighty thousand words written within the King James Bible, only special things are hallowed.

One special thing is the hallowed name of God, and another is the hallowed temple in Jerusalem, which King Solomon built. And for certain, Nebuchadnezzar destroyed the hallowed temple of God, and another special hallowed thing shouldn't be forgotten.

It's written within the fourth commandment and says the seventh day, Sabbath Day, is holy. And it always will be His holy day, regardless of what excuse Sunday Christians use to justify the Sunday Sabbath Day.

I want you to know an undebatable fact: the God of creation didn't make a mistake when He wrote the fourth commandment. But Sunday Christians make mistakes when they oppose His fourth commandment and keep a manufactured Sabbath Day.

Positively, the Sun-day Christians are guilty of keeping the counterfeit Sun-day Sabbath Day and calling it the Lord's Day. They've nearly destroyed the holy seventh-day Sabbath Day of the Lord through rejection and disobedience to the fourth commandment.

For the above reason, why would the God of Heaven and Earth bless Sun-day Christians and reward them with supernatural favor and blessings? And especially when they knowingly or unknowingly destroy His hallowed and sacred seventh-day Sabbath Day.

Certainly, please remember, these promises from the mouth of the Lord are promised to the seventh-day Sabbath Day keepers. And they aren't promised to the Sun-day Sabbath Day keepers, who observe and honor the first day of the week and wrongly call it the Lord's Day.

I assure you, and you need to know, that the first day of the week isn't the holy rest day of the Lord. Bible evidence proves Sun-day is not a holy day, nor is Sun-day the hallowed and sacred Sabbath Day of our wonderful Creator God who created the world and us.

Therefore, I challenge anyone, including Sun-day Christians, to prove that Sun-day is the authentic Sabbath Day of God. And I challenge anyone, including the Sun-day Christians, to prove that Sun-day is a hallowed, sacred, and set apart holy day.

These two concrete promises from the mouth of the Lord are certainly told in this revealing story. They are written in the book of Isaiah, and I want you to know that the Old Testament is still valid today. And I also want you to know His promises are, too.

I assure you, these two promises from God are a key factor, and they can change our lives as we walk on this Earth. And I hope you are one of the Christian believers determined to claim these two promises from the all-mighty God of Heaven and Earth.

Furthermore, I shouldn't have to say to any Christian God doesn't lie. And when He makes us Christians a promise, He will keep it. And we should expect Him to keep His promises the same way; He expects us to keep His beautiful Ten Commandments.

Therefore, if we desire divine supernatural fellowship, blessings, and favor from our Supreme loving God, please remember that we have a commandment covenant to keep. And a breach of covenant means He doesn't have to honor His promises.

I assure you God is all-knowing, and He knows if we are passionate, sincere, hot, and on fire about our feelings for Him and His perfect word. And our Wonderful Most High God knows the depths of our sincerity and the shallowness of our covenant-keeping.

I believe all passive, lukewarm Christians who are not concerned about honoring the seventh day, the Sabbath Day of the Lord. They'll cause a breach of covenant, and they'll not obtain full happiness in this life or ride upon the high places of the Earth.

Furthermore, because they are covenant breakers, all lukewarm Christians will have a harder time getting close to my Great Creator God. And it's easy to conclude it'll be harder for them to receive supernatural blessings and divine favors from Him.

Simply because they are passive Christians and not interested enough to learn the truth and apply it to their everyday life, this truth means passive Christians cannot see the benefit of obeying the word of God completely and gladly represent it with honor, delight, and happiness.

My Supreme God loves pure-hearted people, especially when they enjoy keeping His required commandments. And God loves all Christians, determined to love Him and keep His commandments as a major part of their life.

Indeed, God loves a loyal Christian, and divine blessings and favors are entwined with His love for His loyal people. And He loves them because the pure-hearted believers in Christ will love Him, whether or not they get anything in return for loving Him.

Beyond the shadow of a doubt, love from God cannot be gained through pretty words or be bought and sold. And giving seed money for promised favors doesn't work with God. And we would be silly to believe our Supreme God sells His love.

However, God gives divine blessings and favors to pure-hearted people freely if they love Him unconditionally. And mainly because He knows a pure-hearted Christian isn't serving Him for the benefit of earthly riches and material gain.

Most of the time, people always want something from God, and they rarely ask God what they can do for Him. But I am certain it'll make us closer to our God if we start our day by asking God what can I do for you today.

Surely, if we sincerely look for a way to shine the light of God into dark places and try to advance the good works of God. Then, our fellowship with Him will improve, as will our chances of receiving divine supernatural blessings and favors.

Simply because our wonderful Most High God does give rewards to His faithful disciples and lovers of righteousness, determined to follow Him. And God does reward Christians who desire to work for Him sincerely and spread the gospel of salvation to the lost.

Chapter Twenty-Four
THINGS TO REMEMBER

Positively, this is test ground Earth, and salvation must be obtained here through repentance and change, or souls will be lost to the fires of Hell. And God needs Christian men and women who care about the salvation of others other than themselves.

Our Supreme God, the Creator of everything flesh, knows all the thoughts hiding inside the brain, and our heart cannot hide anything from Him. And this means He cannot be deceived and knows if we care about whosoever is lost.

Indeed, He knows the joy and exuberance men and women feel when they find and worship Him. And I want you to know these are the kinds of people He blesses and reserves a home for in His peaceful kingdom.

Beyond the shadow of a doubt, our incredible Supreme God, supernatural and wonderful, loves joyous and exuberant Christian men and women after they realize the importance of using His righteous word to secure eternal salvation.

In the same way, Daniel and Joshua, Ezekiel and Elijah, especially if they are passionate and thankful, have found the right way and look forward to learning an abundance about Him. And I am certain these passionate Christians are close to His heart.

Including David and Jeremiah, Elisha and Moses, Abraham and Isaiah, Samson, Samuel, Jacob, and many more, Nehemiah, Noah, Job, Hosea, and Amos, like you and I, can be close to Him too.

Indeed, Daniel, Shadrach, Meshach, and Abednego were close to the heart of God, and they all refused to compromise the commandments of God. Nor did they compromise the food laws or the true seventh-day Sabbath Day of the Lord and didn't eat the unclean swine's flesh.

God loved them because they prayed three times a day. And because they bowed their knees to no other man, or god, regardless unto their death. And it's clearly illustrated through the scriptures: God blessed Daniel abundantly. And He showed Daniel favor because of Daniel's strong belief in Him.

God loved Daniel mainly because of Daniel's strong adherence to His perfect word. And because He knew for certain Daniel was committed to His commandments, He gave to all of us. And if we want to be loyal, we can emulate Daniel to a large degree.

Shadrach, Meshach, and Abednego were similar to Daniel and worshipped our Supreme God only. As the story of Daniel concludes, their loyalty to God caused jealousy among certain Chaldeans, and certain Chaldeans caused them to receive a pronounced death sentence.

Furthermore, when the angry king Nebuchadnezzar tied them, bound their hands, and cast them into the fiery furnace, seventeen times hotter than normal. Our Supreme, loyal God was watching them and probably was the fourth man in the fire.

Positively, He protected them from the flames of death and King Nebuchadnezzar's wrath. God was there for them because they honored Him with delight, even in the face of certain death. And when our degree of love equals their degree of love, God will be proud of us, too.

Supernatural fellowship, favor, and blessings aren't given away like free samples at the grocery store. But divine blessings and favors have to be earned the right way. And we would be silly to believe there are no strings attached.

Truly, a close fellowship with God is gained through loyalty, obedience, and a passionate desire to be a doer for God. All Christians should want to be a worker, not ashamed to stand strong for God's commandments and the required ways of the Lord.

After all, the ways of God and His Ten Commandments are our covenant with Him, and they are the strings attached to our gift of salvation. Covenant keepers are His special people who get the most attention from God.

Conclusively, this awareness story and warning story is called Things to Remember. It reveals an important message: Covenant-breakers haven't discovered the formula for supernatural blessings and divine favor from above.

I want you to know for your good that everything divine hinges on keeping the Ten Commandments of God. And I assure you, the perfect

Ten Commandments are His ultimate message from our extremely serious Creator God of Heaven and Earth.

Chapter Twenty-Five

FRIENDSHIP OR ACQUAINTANCE

As much as I hate to believe in reality, I've often heard people mistake friendship for acquaintance, as if both words mean the same thing. And I want you to know it's a lot naïve to believe that friendship and acquaintance mean the same thing.

For this reason, I want to say before this face reality story starts. And so, there'll not be any misunderstanding; I want you to know there's a lot of difference between the definition of friendship and acquaintance.

Furthermore, many Christians call God their friend. And it could be possible, because of bible stipulated requirements, they do not know Him well. And maybe it'll take some growing before we know He's our friend.

Indeed, we Christians can be friends with God, or we can be an acquaintance with God. And the choice is ours to decide, and God will honor our decision, and He'll allow us to be His friend or acquaintance.

Positively, He's watching us from above, and it's up to us to show Him which one we truly want to be with Him. Our character and lifestyle will be the determining factor, deciding whether we are a friend or merely an acquaintance with Him.

I assure you, pretty words of love do not decide our standing with God if they are similar to the wind blowing in all directions, and I assure you, correct definition matters. And time has a way of identifying us as a friend to Him or as an acquaintance.

Positively, the word friend has much more meaning. And it means we know someone extremely well and are close to them. But the word acquaintance lacks the strength of a closer bond, meaning we slightly know them and aren't close friends.

Many people are often merely acquainted with God, yet they expect a lot of attention to their needs. Indeed, people seek blessings and favor from Him, and they only slightly know Him. And slightly knowing Him means they're only an acquaintance.

Sometimes, getting a favor from a friend is easy, but getting one from an acquaintance is much harder. And it's the same with our Great God, and friendship with God should come first before we ask Him for a personal favor.

However, I assure you, everyone on this Earth has the ability and the right to be a close friend to our Great God. But sadly, I must tell you, more people will become acquainted with Him rather than close friends.

Mainly because they do not know God, and they do not look for the fellowship formula it takes to be a close friend with Him. But everyone can know Him well if they are ready to fully embrace His Spirit, love, and royal and majestic words.

However, before we can be friends with our wonderful God, we'll have to reject the invisible demonic ghost spirit of the devil. And I warn you, the devil plays by a different set of rules than God, and he will keep us from being close to God if he can.

However, to be a close friend to our Great Creator God, we must live by His holy and righteous rules and decrees. And it's vitally important for us to keep the beautiful commandments of God and delightfully keep His seventh-day Sabbath Day.

Furthermore, it would be wise and more logical for everyone to develop a sincere friendship with God and build upon His excellent word. And a friendship with Him only works if we are compatible with His required word.

A friendship must amount to much more than mere acquaintanceship; pretty words alone mean nothing to God. Especially if we expect blessings and favors from our great Supreme God and have nothing to barter with except for pretty words and insincere smiles.

An acquaintance is far less important and valuable to God than a sincere friendship. A devout Christian, determined to have a close friendship with God, is more likely to receive divine blessings from God.

Truly, close friends to God are more likely to receive divine favors from Him than someone passive and just acquainted with Him. And mainly because friendship with God requires sincere passion and love from us. And He does know the exact level or degree of our feelings for Him.

However, an acquaintanceship amounts to a passive relationship, and a passive person does not make a solid commitment he'll keep. And if we aren't committed to His required word, we'll fit the definition of an acquaintance.

Joshua was a friend to God and was favored by God, and he was magnified in the sight of all the people of Israel simply because he was strong, courageous, and determined to do as our Supreme God instructed him to do.

Indeed, Joshua loved God with all his heart, and God was aware of Joshua's love toward Him. And for this reason, God supported Joshua. And He told Joshua there would not be any man strong enough to stand against him all the days of his life.

It's for certain the fellowship between Joshua and God was a sincere friendship, and it went way beyond a mere acquaintanceship. And mainly because Joshua was an on-fire believer in God and extremely passionate about obeying the excellent word of God.

Surely, we can have supernatural fellowship with God if we are passionate about His holy, sacred, and heavenly things. But I warn you if we aren't passionate about His holy and sacred things, a close friendship with Him will elude us.

In almost all the stories and examples written throughout the bible, whether in the Old or New Testament, divine blessings and favors are gifts to the friends of God who sincerely want a close fellowship with Him.

Therefore, it appears for certain that God's gifts are given to His friends rather than to His acquaintances. For this reason, I highly recommend everyone seek friendship with God rather than be an acquaintance with God.

Furthermore, if we seek after and sincerely want to know God and want to develop a friendship with Him, then there's only one way of doing it. And since His physical and visible presence isn't here on this Earth among men, but is in Heaven.

Then, every person wanting to know Him will have to know Him through the two important things He left behind for us to know Him through. Those two important things are *His Holy Spirit* dwelling within us and *His Holy words* written down and recorded in the bible.

I guarantee you that all the bible stories, written between the book of Genesis and the book of Revelation, are all about God and the people of Israel. They are illustrated examples, revealing how we can know our Great All-Mighty Creator God.

The God-inspired bible reveals His story examples to all of us, and He placed them on this Earth for the benefit of everyone. Indeed, this truth means He gave us His bible so all men and women might know Him through the stories of the prophets and His Son, called Yeshua.

We must be loyal to our great God, believing in Him as our only God, and getting close to the Holy Ghost, living within our living and breathing temple, including you and me, keeping His righteous commandments as the apple of our eye, and holding Him close to our hearts.

Then, I am looking forward to a delightful fellowship with Him, especially on His sacred and hallowed seventh-day Sabbath Day. His holy day He set apart from all the other ordinary and average six days of the week, and it does matter to God.

The honest word of God assures us divine fellowship, blessings and favors, and supernatural protection will follow men through life who passionately and sincerely do those things pleasing to Him, and Joshua is our recorded proof that God loves whoever listens to Him.

However, the acquaintance, the stranger, and anyone passive and lukewarm toward Him isn't His close friend. And be assured, the God of Heaven and Earth is also an acquaintance, a stranger, passive, and lukewarm back to them. And I advise you to be passionate about His word and love it with all your heart, mind, and soul.

I assure you, there's a lot of difference between a lukewarm-hearted person and a sincere, hot, on-fire, pure-at-heart believer in Christ. And the lukewarm have an insincere heart and only care a little about the word of God. Simply because a lukewarm-hearted person usually is reckless with their soul.

Furthermore, a lukewarm-hearted person usually has many irons in the fire, seeking luxury and material gain. And because of a lack of interest, the required word of God seems too grievous and restricting for them.

However, pure-hearted people know there's a better world to come, and they are mostly satisfied with the simple things in life. Indeed, most of all, believers in Christ are happy to have a personal relationship with Him. And they are happy to know it'll grow into a never-ending eternal relationship.

Indeed, suppose most Christians and non-Christians would honestly examine their life and day-after-day experiences. Then, they can probably find things in their past to be thankful to God, and illustrating thankfulness reveals our feelings toward Him.

Indeed, it's an individual choice for professing Christians to care about the righteous ways of God and give Him credit for the good things in our lives. I conclude that it's up to each person if they want to be thankful to God for their good fortune.

However, the other choice is to claim their good fortune is self-done, luck, or by chance occurrence. But if a Christian claims their good fortunes are self-done, luck, or by chance occurrence.

Then, I ask you, how can they possibly be thankful to our all-mighty God for their good fortune, good health, and peaceful way of life? Simply because luck, chance occurrence, and self-done things can be reasoned by the heart as just good luck.

Many men rationalize and figure their good fortune is just a part of life, and their life turned out good for them, and our Great God of Heaven and Earth didn't influence it. And thanks to God, we can believe this if we want to leave God from the picture.

However, in all things, a professing Christian should give thanksgiving to our wonderful Supreme God of Heaven and Earth. And it wouldn't hurt for them to know the story of the Babylonian King Nebuchadnezzar and why he ate the field's grass for seven years.

I guarantee you nothing good and divine is given to a man without it coming from our God in Heaven. And regardless of what men think, He controls divine blessings and supernatural curses, too. And even though He's a patient God, He will give up on some people.

I assure you, giving thanks to God means we thank Him for our good fortune in life. And we believe He intervenes in our affairs sometimes when we need help from above. And this analogy, entwined with us being thankful, illuminates our faith in Him.

However, not giving thanks to God illustrates our lack of respect and reverence for our Wonderful Supreme God. And this analogy means we haven't any faith in Him or do not believe; He'll intervene sometimes.

I want you to know a lack of respect and reverence for our Creator God will most likely result in wrath from God, even if we aren't aware of the avenue of wrath. And I am certain most men do not understand the reason for divine recompense.

For example, Nebuchadnezzar was cut to a stump for lack of respect and reverence for our Supreme God of Heaven and Earth. And Nebuchadnezzar was changed from a sane man into a mad man, given the heart of a beast and the claws of a bird.

His hair grew like eagle feathers, and he was changed into a grass eater for seven years before his sanity returned. And men in need of discipline from God may not compare to that of Nebuchadnezzar, but they will experience hurt of some type.

Chapter Twenty-Six

RESPECTFUL LAMB, OR UNTAMED BEAST

Indeed, this concerning you and me story called a Respectful Lamb or Untamed Beast. It's written because our life decisions are entwined with our actions and reactions. And the respect, or the lack of respect, we illustrate toward God, family, and friends.

As for myself, I have two Fathers whom I love and respect immensely. But when I pray, I do so to my Father in heaven. He's my Creator Father and my only God, and He gave me my extremely good and wonderful earthly father, whom I love and miss every day.

My wonderful Father in Heaven gave me and everyone else the fifth commandment, and He does expect me to obey it. And He expects everyone else to honor our earthly father, love, and respect him.

The God of Heaven and Earth also expects me to honor my mother, and if I do, my days on this Earth will be honorable and long upon the land. But there are many children in this world today who do not honor or respect their father and their mother.

However, they still pray many prayers to my Great Creator God and ask God for divine blessings and favors from Him. And they think He shouldn't be bothered by these children's disrespect for their earthly parents. I want you to know disrespect to parents is noticed in Heaven.

It could most likely be possible; divine blessings, favors, and fellowship with Him are out of their reach. And yet, they understand not. Anyway, divine favors from God will be much harder for these disobedient children who desire respect but give none back.

Indeed, these types of men and women have double standards because they want to receive blessings from God even though they do not respect their Father in Heaven or their Father and Mother on this Earth.

I guarantee that divine blessings and favors from God are not so easily obtained, where anyone can have a need, and it'll be fulfilled. And I warn you that disrespect and double standards can kill our blessings.

Positively, divine blessings and favors cannot be ordered from God as if they are merchandise from a catalog. And divine blessings and favors are neither for sale nor free merchandise simply because our Great Creator God is not everyone's merchant God.

Therefore, short-order divine blessings and favors are usually out of the question. And real-life experiences reveal they rarely are obtained. And it's regardless of how many prayers we exhaust through pretty words or how many times we pray.

Our Supreme God is a kind and generous God who loves a righteous person with a pure and honest heart. And I want you to realize that when God finds men and women like these, He reserves them a place in His kingdom.

However, an ungodly person conformed to the ungodly ways of this world and having unclean lips is similar to a wild beast in the wilderness, looking for innocent lambs to prey upon and take advantage of their innocence.

Maybe it would take the Living Coals of Fire, who lives upon the altar of God, inside the temple of God, and upon the mountain of God. To purify his soul, remove his sins, and make him fit for the kingdom of Heaven.

If divine blessings and favors were ours for the ordering, all we had to do was ask our Supernatural God for them, and we would receive them. Then, everyone on this Earth would be prosperous and happy for at least a while.

However, I am certain if the God of Heaven and Earth God answered every prayer, regardless of the request, then I conclude this world would turn into a material world and a playground where people play every day. People allowed to play daily will believe God is blessing them because their life is easy and comfortable.

Furthermore, the imagination would enlarge and overwhelm reality, and people would view their good fortune as something they deserve. And sadly, I must tell you, they probably wouldn't consider giving obedience back to God for their prosperity reward.

Positively, if our Great God answered every prayer, then there would be no end to the ways many men would invent to pleasure themselves upon this Earth. And every neighbor would wake up every morning, praying for something new.

If divine blessings and favors were available for the ordering, then my Great God would be someone men use to get their way. And I know ordering divine blessings would create a different way of life; no man would be humble.

Most likely, if divine blessings and favors from above came easy, all our desires and dreams would come true. Then, most men and women would be spoiled rotten. And they would be rebellious children when their prayers weren't answered, and they didn't get their way.

I believe spoiled men and spoiled women, pampered by the easy life, would rebel against discipline from God as if spoiled brats do not require discipline. And maybe almost everyone would be a spoiled brat if life was too easy.

Surely, if everything came easy for spoiled brats, they would lean to their understanding and always want to live their way. And I am certain most people wouldn't have time to practice the word of God.

Indeed, we have examples of spoiled people who prefer to live the way they want. And it's regardless of the conditions around them or who their spoiled ways affect. For this reason, I conclude selfishness is a sign of a spoiled person and someone too proud to lean on God.

Spoiled people are self-centered, usually fickle, and do not live according to the righteous ways of God. And His not fickle perfect and righteous Ten Commandments; they will not take seriously. And maybe they would forget the Ten Commandments completely.

Lucifer and the rebellious angels were living in the lap of luxury before their fall from the presence of God, and maybe they were spoiled angelic brats. And spoiled brats blessed with too much of the easy life rarely respect their Father, even if He's our Creator God.

However, upon testing ground Earth, we men and women need to learn God rewards His children for keeping the commandments of God. Being rewarded has another requirement, and the keeping of the seventh day, Sabbath Day, is the requirement.

Indeed, I want you to realize being spoiled and pampered isn't a reward from our Great God of creation. Indeed, Judgment on the rebellious angels proves God doesn't like spoiled brats. And sooner or later, He will do recompense against spoiled brats.

Here on this Earth, where life lessons are learned hard, we must learn an important truth. We are rewarded with divine blessings for doing good, righteous, and fruitful works pleasing to our wonderful Supreme God.

Indeed, when men fail to learn these valuable lessons upon testing ground Earth, their fall will be similar to that of the wicked Lucifer and the other rebellious angels. And I want you to know that following God's required word is fall prevention.

I assure you, the righteous Ten Commandments of God are similar to a bright lamp, shining within the midst of a dimly lit and dark world. And the law is the word of my all-mighty God, and the law pulls men out of darkness and places them within the light.

Therefore, I want you to know that without God's excellent law and the great Ten Commandments, there would only be darkness and lawlessness.

And as lawless as this world is now, it would be much worse without His law. And a parallel to a lawless world is the animal kingdom.

Indeed, the perfect and wonderful Ten Commandments and His needed, helpful, excellent law are our perfect instructions on how to build a life pleasing to God, and He's our Creator Father, sitting on the throne in Heaven. And the God of creation has the right to create and enforce the law.

Furthermore, I assure you that men and women must please God and meet His approval before they are rewarded with supernatural blessings and favors. Indeed, you need to realize this is a golden rule, unbendable and not about to change.

Although we need money to survive, having a comfortable nest egg is nice. But putting money first and wanting too much is a vain thing. Our lifespan is short, and excessive riches and unneeded blessings of prosperity are vain goals to pursue constantly.

Furthermore, vain goals are a waste of time, and during our golden years, vain things will become a hurtful thorn in our side. And mainly because our lifespan is compared to the flowers, grass, and spring and fall, we will fade away in a short season.

The grass withereth, and the flower fadeth, the same way as us, but the word of God shall stand forever, and we are short-season residents. But a promise from our great Supreme God is the best anyone can receive during our short stay on this Earth.

Indeed, I want you to know that blessings and favors are nearly unlimited to believers who ride upon this Earth's high places. But the best promise in the whole bible, I am aware of, is for God to feed us with the heritage of Jacob.

Bible scriptures reveal our Supreme God of Heaven and Earth makes the above promise to every loyal believer if they are a commandment keeper and are determined to honor His true seventh-day Sabbath Day and delight in it.

For the above reasons, I pray you'll be wise enough to claim God's two great promises to you and me from His mouth. And there isn't any good reason; we shouldn't be able to ride upon the high places of this Earth during our short time here.

However, I want you to realize the wonderful fourth commandment may present a problem to you if you are a Sun-day Sabbath Keeper. And you reject the authenticity of the bible and then accept the manufactured traditions of men.

Mainly because Sun-day is not the fourth commandment, but Sun-day Sabbath keeping does veil the truth from the eyes of an unlearned Christian. An unlearned Christian is a believer in Christ, unable to identify with the fourth commandment.

However, God's fourth commandment is personal to Him, unchangeable and unbendable, isn't written in some breakable mystery code, and we do not have to be highly intelligent to interpret the meaning of the fourth commandment.

Truly, it's quite obvious that most professing Sun-day Christians do not study the wonderful word of God intensely enough. Otherwise, they would understand the meaning of the fourth commandment and be happy to keep it.

Furthermore, Sun-day preachers do not teach much about the blessed, sacred, and holy seventh-day Sabbath Day. And I want you to know His authentic Sabbath Day is the meat of Christianity.

It's also obvious the congregation in the pews of the Sun-day churches aren't self-explorers. And I conclude, because of their compromise, they aren't seeking the truth concerning the controversial fourth commandment subject.

During many prior generations, the Sun-day Christians have kept a counterfeit Sun-day Sabbath Day. It's also extremely accurate and quite obvious because of scripture evidence. And because of overwhelming acceptance, the end of their compromise isn't in sight.

Furthermore, it's also quite obvious because seeing is believing. The manufactured traditions of men, or the commandments of men, unapproved by my Great God, have replaced some of the gospel of God in the Sun-day churches.

It's also obvious: God's excellent and perfect word is pure, undefiled, infallible, and undebatable. It's made of no effect by the traditions of men, and the wonderful Son of God reveals this fact in the book of Mark.

Bible scriptures reveal that men's traditions make the perfect word of God of no use, says Jesus Christ in this next revealing scripture. And of no use means the power of His word will not help us if we choose to keep the traditions of men.

Mark 7:13 Making the word of God of <u>no effect (means of no use) through</u> *your traditions, which ye have delivered (means handed down to the congregation) and many such things do ye.*

Truly, it's obvious most Sun-day Christians aren't aware of the hurt they suffer from because of disobedience simply because they are rebellious to the holy and sacred and extremely special fourth commandment of God.

This problem is mainly because rejection of the fourth commandment has harmed their relationship with God. But corrections can be accomplished simply by straightening our lives, regardless of whether anyone else does.

This truth means if the church building we frequent will not conform with the authentic word of God, then the living church of God is an alternative, but it isn't a building. But it's you and me, and the special kingdom of God lives within us.

Therefore, the greatest church in the land is the living church of God, and it's called the living church of Jesus Christ. And it's a many-membered body of believers in Christ who love and respect their opportunity to be close to Him.

The Holy Ghost lives within everyone with a clean-living temple and belongs to the living church of God. And I want you to know the members of the living church of God entwine the kingdom of God together as one flock.

I assure you; the sheep are the flock, and the Son of God is the good Shepherd. And because they love the word of God, the flock members have a close friendship with the Son of God. And for the benefit of higher love, they quit being an acquaintance to Him long ago.

This concerning story is extremely serious and important, called the Respectful Lamb, or Untamed Beast. It entwines blessings, favors, prayers answered, and the ability to know God well. Unless we are ungodly and fit the definition of a wild beast.

Therefore, we should gladly study the word of God intensely because of the way it affects our life with our Creator God, especially since we would rather reap the reward of divine favors and blessings instead of wrath and supernatural curses.

Conclusively, before this story ends, I want you to know that salvation is a gift on the first day. But after the first day, we'll be expected to fall in line with the requirements of God. And so, you'll know, a new person in Christ means we've decided to live by the requirements of God.

Furthermore, I want you to know we cannot decide whether we are saved, and we think our decision to be saved is all that matters. Because many things are attached to staying saved, being a loyal covenant keeper is one of them.

I assure you, covenant-keeping is summed up in two hundred and ninety-five words. And these righteous two hundred and ninety-five words entwine and revolve around God's excellent and required Ten Commandments.

Furthermore, covenant-keeping produces heat, and the heat I am talking about produces a hot and on-fire Christian. And anyone less than hot and on fire isn't radiating enough heat. And I am telling you, red-hot Christians are God's foot soldiers on Earth.

I assure you when the silver cord breaks, our spirit is carried to Heaven by the angels. We'll be proud to arrive at the gates of Pearl as a red-hot and on-fire Christian and as one of His former foot soldiers upon this Earth.

Chapter Twenty-Seven

THE REASON FOR NATURAL DISASTERS

Natural disasters have happened regularly throughout history, and we can expect them to keep happening. And maybe they'll get worse with time. Most people aren't certain and cannot say whether natural disasters are divine interventions or chance occurrences.

For the above reason, this is my analogy concerning natural disasters. And my analogy is based upon biblical events, combined with my sense of logic. But I do want you to know it's an assumption to believe all natural disasters are caused by the hand of God as if God can be blamed for everything.

It's also an assumption to believe natural disasters happen in certain locations because God did nothing to keep them from happening. Yet, people always make these assumption statements and should know fully that no one knows God's mind.

Nor does anyone know why my Great Creator God intervenes, doesn't intervene at a particular time, or if He allows natural disasters to happen at all. And when we make unfounded statements and blind remarks in our search for answers.

Then, our answers about the unknown are usually an assumption conjured from within the realms of an overactive imagination. But it's our nature to search for answers concerning the unknown. And unfortunately, it's our nature to assume many things.

I believe sometimes, we are correct in our assumptions. And sometimes, we are wrong in our assumptions, especially concerning natural disasters. And if I said some natural disasters could be the handiwork of God because of sin, then my analogy is an assumption.

However, some natural disasters may happen because of overwhelming sin since overwhelming sin does incur the wrath of God from time to time. And I can say, one hundred percent for certain, that God hates all acts of sin.

Although, some natural disasters may not be the handiwork of God. But anyway, how would I know for certain? After all, I am not Abraham, and all cities are not similar to Sodom and Gomorrah and the roundabout plains, which were overwhelmed with sin.

However, I know that not every disaster happens by the hand of the all-mighty God. And it's because there are always variables. Jesus points out this fact and reveals that not all disasters occur because of God, even though bible history reveals that some disasters do.

Furthermore, the Son of God uses the tower falling at Siloam to illustrate a fact, and the illustration reveals sometimes bad things do happen. And it's because of luck, or by chance occurrence, or because of human error.

Indeed, disasters do not always happen because everyone's sins are great, as some people think about the other person. Too often, some people believe when natural disasters happen to another person, it is a judgment call by God.

However, a rock-constructed tower falling on men cannot be considered a natural disaster. And this means not all disasters can be labeled as natural disasters. And especially when they are unnatural disasters or are caused by faulty construction.

I've heard believers, non-believers, and self-righteous people assume natural disasters target anti-godly people and ungodly cities. Some people believe the natural disaster hitting New Orleans happened because the people living in New Orleans were carnal and sinful people.

Now, some people are assuming Hurricane Sandy was the work of God. And He's responsible for devastating parts of New York and New Jersey. It appears the same assumption was made about the people of Haiti after the disastrous earthquake hit there.

Assuming people believe these natural disasters happened because of the same kind of sinful immorality, similar to Sodom and Gomorrah. As for myself, I do not know if New Orleans, Haiti, New York, and New Jersey are filled with sinful immorality any more than other places.

I've never been to any of those places, and I would be foolish to say God did this and did that to them because of sin. But I believe it's an assumption to believe the hand of God sent Katrina and Sandy to punish sinful people.

It's also an assumption to say that the earthquake that hit Haiti happened because of sinful immorality. But once again, I am making an unprovable assumption concerning something I know nothing about. But I know for certain I shouldn't be assuming anything.

Furthermore, I am certainly making another assumption if I say those hurricanes weren't sent by the hand of God. This truth means if I make assumptions and haven't any facts to back up my assumptions, I unwittingly say, this or that is the reason.

Then, I am just as guilty as many other people who make assumptions about things they assume but know nothing about. This truth means I do not know if my assumption is any more right or wrong than the other people who are also guilty of making assumptions.

Indeed, I wouldn't trust my assumption any more than I would trust someone else's assumption. But I know one thing for certain, and this one thing is a fact, which isn't debatable by any logical analogy.

Positively, I want you to realize it's hurtful to make assumptions concerning people hurting from the devastation of natural disasters. It's a fact natural disasters hurt and kill people, and many homes are destroyed.

I assure you it would probably be much wiser, more respectful, and better for everyone if we didn't try to make assumptions about the natural disaster situation of other people, regardless of their reputation, especially as to whether or not the natural disaster happened by the hand of God or whether it was fate or by chance occurrence. However, I will say the number one assumption most people assume is the belief God is trying to get people's attention through natural disasters.

Furthermore, I will say regardless of whether a natural disaster is His way of getting people's attention. It wouldn't hurt to turn away from sinful immorality and live a commandment-guided lifestyle, clean and righteous, and pleasing to God.

Suppose all men and women everywhere would live their lives according to the word of God and adjust their lifestyles to comply with His requirements. Then, it couldn't be assumed that God's hand was behind a natural disaster when it occurred if it occurred.

However, I assume it's much easier to assume the hand of God is against other people amid natural disasters rather than assume the hand of God is against us when natural disasters come our way and hurt us.

After assuming this analogy, I am starting to believe that we mortals have a great imagination, allowing us to do a lot of assuming. And especially concerning the ways of our Supreme God, when we shouldn't assume at all, concerning the unknown elements of nature.

Truly, we mortals have a great big imagination, and we can Rose-Color situations and many of the wrong things we flesh and blood people do. But we do not know the mind of God, nor do we know the actual cause of natural disasters.

Nor do we know why God allows natural disasters to occur in various places or to various people. But I assume *weather patterns, ocean warming,* and *climate changes*, including *high and low pressures* and *jet streams,* may play a part in natural disasters.

However, most people assume these natural disasters happen a certain way and to certain people. They assume so because they believe our Supreme God is trying to get our attention. And I believe they also know that most people aren't giving enough attention to God.

Most people believe that our Great Supernatural God wants us to turn away from ungodliness. And it's because most people realize the God of creation isn't happy with us when traveling down a dead-end road filled with uncleanness and ungodliness.

For example, I assure you Sodom and Gomorrah were on a dead-end road concerning the direction of this world. This true analogy statement reveals a warning example to the rest of this world and every generation after Sodom's natural disaster destruction.

Positively, it's quite obvious God got the attention of the homosexual people living in Sodom and Gomorrah. And I believe He's using the wicked cities of Sodom and Gomorrah as a hopeful deterrent to the unclean lifestyle.

However, I know and want you to know the difference between an assumption and knowing the truth. My Great Supernatural God of Heaven and Earth told Abraham beforehand that a natural God-made disaster would happen to Sodom and Gomorrah.

Therefore, this revealing in advance eliminates the possibility of chance occurrence or of the disaster being happenstance. But I assume none of our spiritual leaders today are told in advance that a natural disaster will occur in a specific place.

Anyway, I would like to know the reason; some people assume it's always the hand of God rather than by fate or by chance occurrence. But everyone is allowed to express their opinion, even if it's wrong.

After writing this personal analogy story concerning natural disasters, I believe I'll make a logical analogy about myself. And I believe by the time this story about natural disasters and making assumptions ends.

I'll be a sorrowful man who's made too many assumptions, just as unsubstantiated assumptions blind others who state their opinion. And it's a fact concerning the reason for natural disasters. Most of us talk too much when we shouldn't be talking at all.

However, after reading this personal analogy story concerning the reason for natural disasters. I hope everyone everywhere, including me, will be more careful about making assumptions since it's a character flaw if we let our imagination make assumptions.

I firmly believe all flesh and blood people share a characteristic flaw, and most of us are prone to making unsubstantiated assumptions. However, man's imagination is a runaway train without good brakes, and I am saying assumptions parallel to a runaway train wreck.

Just as the men talking to Jesus were assuming when they asked Him if the Galileans were killed by the hand of God because of their sins, and Jesus, the all-knowing Son of God, who never makes assumptions, had to inject reality into the situation.

Therefore, the wise Son of God replied to the assumers, who assumed terrible disasters were caused by sin and immorality. And Yeshua said the cruel sinners were not killed because of their sins, nor were they killed by the hand of God.

Indeed, this is how the story goes, and you can decide for yourself instead of me making an assumption. But before I tell you this story, I want you to know that it would be better to believe in the Son of God rather than make assumptions.

Luke 13:1 There were present at that season (time) <u>some</u> (men) that told <u>Him</u> (Jesus) of the Galileans, whose blood Pilate had mingled (on the altar to false gods) with their sacrifices. (Human sacrifices).

Luke13:2 And Jesus answering said unto them, <u>suppose</u> (means ye think or assume) that these Galileans were sinners,

Luke 13:2 above all the (other) Galileans, because they <u>suffered</u> (means were the victims of retaliation or judgment from above for) such things?

Luke 13:3 (Jesus said unto them), I tell you <u>nay</u> (means no, these men were not killed because of their sins): But, except <u>ye repent</u> (of your sins), ye shall all likewise perish.

Luke 13:4 Or those eighteen, upon whom the tower of Siloam fell, and slew them, <u>think</u> (means do you assume) that they were sinners <u>above</u> (means more so than) all men that dwell in Jerusalem?

Luke 13:5 (Jesus said), I tell you nay: But <u>except</u> (means unless) ye <u>repent</u> (for your sins), ye shall all likewise perish.

Jesus makes it clear the Galileans weren't being punished for sin. But neither does He say we'll not be punished for sin. And this means every individual situation is different with our Great God, and He reacts to the severity of situations.

It's easy to assume things about the handiwork of God, but an assumption is guessing work. And it's easy to conclude guesswork is entwined with a great big imagination. Even though it's not a good practice, it's like playing the odds or a poker game.

Indeed, some of the men gathered around Jesus were curious, and they were compelled to assume things. They assumed a wrathful death sentence was decreed upon the sinful Galileans because they participated in human sacrifice like many people do today.

They assumed the sinner men were killed because of their own great and horrible sins, and God was taking revenge on them. Sadly, these same men assumed the tower of Siloam purposely fell on the men at Jerusalem.

They assumed it was because of the Galatians' human sacrifices and because they were ungodly, and their sins were great. And most likely, these same kinds of men, or similar to them, assume all-natural disasters are the handiwork of God.

However, Jesus makes it clear it was an assumption for them to think the sinner men were killed because of their sins. It was also an assumption to believe the fallen tower at Siloam was the handiwork of God as if He pushed the tower down on them.

Again, I do say, and maybe it's not fair for me to use the fallen tower and human sacrifice as an example of assumptions. And mainly because those happenstance disasters were not the same as natural disasters decreed from the Heavens above.

Truly, I say, and without assuming, many of the disasters happening to men today aren't related to natural disasters. But I know that God's wrath doesn't have to entwine with a natural disaster; if the disaster isn't related to nature, it isn't natural.

Because I believe plagues and diseases are a form of wrath from above. But how would I know for certain the reason things happen? Since I do not know the mind of God, or when, or why, or how He delivers judgment on sinner men.

Although I believe God does deliver judgment on sinner men, I believe sinner men anger God to the point of wrath. Bible examples prove God has been known to stir up adversaries against certain people for certain reasons. Immorality and rebellion to His word are usually the reasons for incurring His anger.

I assume one assumption may be as valid or invalid as another, and I am certain all men everywhere will continue to make assumptions until the end of time. And it would be as hard to quit eating as it would to quit making assumptions.

Although, I assume our Supreme God is trying to get the attention of men and women in various ways. And I am certain a potential death situation will cause many to examine their lifestyle and promise God they'll change for the better.

However, if I said for a fact, He uses natural disasters to get the attention of men and women. Then, it would be an assumption on my part, and I shouldn't be making any unproven statements. Indeed, to prove my vulnerability, this story is entwined with assumptions.

However, I assume earthquakes and hurricanes get the attention of men and women caught in the midst of them. And since earthquakes and hurricanes are raging out of control, supernatural disasters.

Then, I assume, many men and women believe these natural disasters are the handiwork of our Supreme God. And I am certain that some men and women assume God allows them to happen for a reason. And it's because they are a natural disaster.

Anyway, I sincerely say it's not an assumption for me to make a few matters-of-fact statements and say for certain. *Number one* > God does want all men and women to repent of their sinful, carnal, immoral, and unclean ways of the flesh.

Number two > It's not an assumption that natural disasters will cause some men and women to self-examine their lifestyles. And within these two statements, I am revealing a fact, and they cannot be considered an assumption.

It's undeniable that the wicked first Earth age, immoral and violent, had three different bloodlines. Bible history reveals that it was destroyed by the natural disaster of a great cleansing flood, which covered the whole Earth in deep water.

It's also a fact, and bible history reveals the great cleansing flood was a judgment call from the supernatural God of Heaven and Earth. And it wasn't fate or by chance occurrence. And He didn't tell Noah to build a boat because He assumed a flood might happen.

Truly, I am not assuming it when I say God sent the great flood to destroy the violent and ungodly sinner men upon the Earth during the time of Noah. And He did tell Noah to build a boat to His specifications because He knew a great flood would happen.

My Great God is extremely supernatural, and He controls all the natural elements upon this Earth and in the Heavens above. And He sent the great cleansing flood because the rebellious angels and the children of wicked angels were unholy, violent, sensual, and living a lifestyle of shameful and degrading passions.

The rebellious angels and their children were certainly disobedient and corrupt, and they weren't willing to repent and change their sinful ways. It's a fact God did destroy them with a natural disaster, and it was because of sinful immorality.

It's also an undeniable fact, and it's not an assumption. And this fact is recorded within the book of Genesis, chapter nineteen, verse thirteen. And we should realize there is a potential for the wrath of a similar sort to happen again.

The homosexual cities and the homosexual people of Sodom and Gomorrah were destroyed by the wrathful hand of God. And it's easy to conclude because God tells us their destruction happened using a natural disaster.

Furthermore, the bible reveals Sodom and Gomorrah as examples of God-imposed wrath. These two wicked cities illustrate the same reasons: the great cleansing flood destroyed the sinful and violent first Earth age.

It's also an undeniable fact, and it's not an assumption. The wicked cities of Sodom and Gomorrah were marked and singled out for destruction, and it was because of immorality and sin. And fire came down from Heaven and precisely hit its intended target.

It's also an undeniable fact, and it's not an assumption. Our revengeful and righteous Supreme God visited the land of Egypt during the time of Moses. Bible history proves that all of Egypt could not escape from paying the high price tag for sin.

God plagued the land of Egypt, exceedingly great, with nearly ten plagues of natural disasters before the cruel Pharaoh would let the children of Israel leave Egypt. And bible scriptures reveal that no Hebrew person had to fight for their freedom.

It's also an undeniable fact, and it's not an assumption. The Hebrew children of our Supernatural God crossed the Red Sea on the dry bottom until they reached the other side. And sadly, I must tell you, the bloodthirsty Egyptians were foolish to follow them on the sea floor.

It's also an undeniable fact, and it's not an assumption to say God was watching and orchestrating the situation. And the waters closed back on the Egyptians and drowned them all after the last Hebrew person climbed upon the other side of the Red Sea.

Regardless of how amazing it sounds, the deep red sea was parted by our Supernatural God, who rules in the Heavens and upon this Earth.

And I want you to know that Bible history proves He also creates natural disasters.

It's an undeniable fact, and it's not an assumption. The proof and powers of a Supernatural God are proven true because of His ability to create natural disasters. And again, I am telling you, bible history proves God creates different sorts of natural disasters.

Indeed, His Supreme authority is proven true by all of His recorded supernatural events, which only a Supernatural Orchestrator God can do. Our bible records plenty enough of His supernatural accomplishments, and they prove His ability to control everything.

It's not an assumption to say natural disasters are one of the tools our all-mighty Supreme God uses occasionally. And especially when He decides to get the attention of rebellious sinner men and sinner women on this Earth.

It's an undeniable fact, and it's not an assumption to say the hands of man do nothing supernatural since we are incapable of creating natural disasters. And it's not an assumption to say nothing supernatural happens by accident, nor is it fate or by chance occurrence.

Because everything supernatural is orchestrated by our Great Supernatural Supreme God, who personifies the definition of supernatural, I want you to know that the word orchestrator entwines with His supernatural powers.

Beyond the shadow of a doubt, His unique abilities allow Him to do the extraordinary and control the seemingly uncontrollable forces. And sometimes, He uses natural disasters to get the attention of men and women.

I guarantee you, because of their ability to destroy, terrible supernatural disasters get the attention of all men and women. And it's regardless of whether or not it's the intentions of our wonderful Supreme Supernatural God.

It's an undeniable fact, and it's not an assumption that God expects all men to put a difference between the holy and the unholy. And He expects us to put a difference between the clean and the unclean, and the just and the unjust. And He does implement wrath against humankind sometimes.

Certainly, it's an undeniable fact, and it's not an assumption to say my all-mighty Supreme God will set His face against you or me if we give Him an ungodly reason to oppose us. And especially if we hate, reject, and despise His principles and beautiful Ten Commandments. And His excellent and wonderful, well-intended decrees.

Therefore, if we are anti-godly people and do not believe in Him, we are fierce opposers of godliness. I assure you that troubles of various kinds, including pre-designed curses and natural disasters, will follow us through life.

Furthermore, if we turn our hearts away from God, give place to the ways of the devil, and embrace sinful immorality. Then we are making God angry; we may incur His wrath and suffer from some God-imposed disaster.

It's an undeniable fact, and it's not an assumption, because Jesus said so in the book of Matthew, within chapter twenty-four. And chapter twenty-four includes verse seven, saying, nation shall rise against nation and kingdom against kingdom.

Jesus tells us there shall be <u>famines</u> (means hunger), <u>pestilences</u> (means diseases), and <u>earthquakes</u> (means natural disasters) in <u>diverse</u> (means various places). And I conclude that because Jesus says so, natural disasters are prophesized to occur.

The wonderful Son of God tells us all these troubles and natural disasters are the beginning of sorrows. And apparently, they are caused by the hand of God, or at the least, He allows them to happen. But it's for certain; God knows they are coming upon us.

Furthermore, if you open your eyes and look around, it's easy to see this world is in trouble with God, and it's because of sin. As we can easily see, these natural disasters seem to be picking up speed and happening more frequently than before.

Maybe, and I do not know for certain, natural disasters are increasing for a specific reason. And maybe it's because the unclean, the unjust, the unholy, and acts of sinful immorality are becoming more dominant in this corrupt world.

Indeed, it appears there's a parallel happening among the nations turning their back on God. And the parallel between ungodly nations and natural disasters seems to coincide. And I ask you, consider the world's condition and tell me, is there a parallel happening?

Furthermore, the speed of natural disasters appears to accelerate as nations become more liberal, corrupt, and passive toward ungodly things. Maybe we can accredit this acceleration to our Great God of Heaven and Earth, and maybe we cannot.

King David was much more than the king of Israel and was a prophet of God. And David tells us there's no reward for sinfulness, and calamities will follow after the wicked. And wickedness will increase as this world becomes more ungodly and unclean.

Indeed, when an uncaring nation allows sinfulness, evil, immorality, and uncleanness to grow within the midst of its population, then calamities of all sorts and natural disasters will plague the sinful nation until it returns to the all-mighty God of Heaven and Earth.

My assumption may not be correct, but it does seem reasonable to assume we can make educated assumptions if there's a pattern to what's happening. Although patterns can change from situation to situation, be wise enough to look ahead.

Therefore, I want you to know I am going out on a limb to assume some places might not be spared natural disasters. And it's because they truly are sinful, immoral, wicked, and similar to the ungodly homosexual cities of Sodom and Gomorrah.

The loyal prophet Jude was a servant and friend to the wonderful Son of God, and he revealed a Bible-recorded truth we need to understand when he tells us the destruction of Sodom and Gomorrah wasn't a natural event, nor did it happen by chance occurrence.

However, the destruction of Sodom and Gomorrah was an example of vengeance, and God imposed wrath on sinful immorality. The next informative scripture reveals the words of Jude, and he entwines a certain natural disaster to wrath from the Heavens above.

Jude 7 Even as Sodom and Gomorrah, and the cities about them in like manner, giving themselves over to fornication,

Jude 7 <u>and</u> <u>going</u> <u>after</u> <u>strange</u> <u>flesh</u> (which means strange flesh, and maybe various animals, and homosexuality combined) are set forth, for example, suffering the <u>vengeance</u> (which means punishment from God) of eternal fire.

Indeed, the revealing words we read from the book of Jude concerning a God-imposed disaster aren't an assumption; fire and brimstone from Heaven was the wrathful tool of vengeance used by my Great Creator God.

Therefore, the wicked and unclean homosexual people of Sodom and Gomorrah brought the wrath of God upon themselves. And they were destroyed by the elements from Heaven and by the hand of God because of sinful immorality.

Positively, it's a proven fact and not an assumption that the God of Heaven and Earth charges a price tag for sin, and wrath is His way of collecting a debt on sin. Some cities and some people are not spared from natural disasters, and it's because of sinful immorality.

Furthermore, I assume some natural disasters could be a form of punishment from our Great God, and some natural disasters happen because of too much wickedness and sinful immorality. The old phrase, walking on thin ice, applies to the ungodly person.

However, once again, I must tell you the above statement is an assumption based on past judgment events, which I assume is correct. And I am already sorry; I've assumed a connection between Bible-related judgments and natural disasters occurring in our time.

As much as I wish I did, I do not know when our Supernatural God has seen enough of sinfulness. Nor do I know when He'll pour out His wrath on extreme sinners or cause ungodly nations to feel His wrath and suffer recompense from above.

None of us know when He'll release His fury on sinful and ungodly people who've turned away from Him for the ungodly and unclean pleasures of this Satan-controlled world. But the thin ice analogy could collapse under the ungodly person at any time.

Truly, I am getting tired of making assumptions, but if I make another assumption, I probably shouldn't. I assume that no one knows why natural disasters occur or if all-natural disasters or some natural disasters happen by the hand of God.

Nor do we know if natural disasters happen randomly or occur by chance. But I know for certain we should reverence God and keep His commandments. This truth is the conclusion to the whole matter and the will of God concerning His expectations of us.

Anyway, if I were you reading this story, I couldn't believe my or anyone else's assumptions. Simply because assumptions have too much variableness, and they haven't enough evidence to make assumptions absolute.

Indeed, if I were you, I wouldn't give one hundred percent credibility to any assumption at all. And especially about what is and what isn't, the handiwork of our Great Supernatural God concerning natural disasters.

Now, after expressing my analogy of natural disasters, I am finished assuming things, and I should've quit assuming things at least five hundred words earlier. But I know that nearly all of my analogies were merely an assumption, assumed from a curious mind.

Furthermore, I am not a naïve person, and I realize I do not have the wisdom to say everything I've assumed in this story is a fact. Nor do I have the understanding to know if hurricanes, floods, and earthquakes are caused by the hand of God.

Nor do I know if natural disasters are incidents, or by chance occurrence, or if God is using them to get our attention. But because of all my studies, I know we should give our attention to our great God of Heaven and Earth daily.

Indeed, because of all my studies, I know that our wonderful Supreme God is supernatural. And I know for certain my Great Creator can cause earthquakes, hurricanes, and fire and hail to fall from the sky if He wants to do wrath.

Knowing the above statement is true, I believe no one other than Him knows exactly why natural disasters happen. And I believe when others say it happened because of sinful immorality, they make an assumption.

However, maybe it's a correct assumption they are making, but who knows other than our Great God? Anyway, I thought I'd already quit assuming things. But I assume we, mortal flesh and blood people, do not entirely understand the ways of God.

And now that you've read my story concerning the many reasons for natural disasters. It would help if you concluded that your assumptions concerning natural disasters are as valid or invalid as my many assumptions. However, of course, I am making another assumption.

Anyway, I want you to know whether or not any of my assumptions were true or not true; they cannot be proved, one way or another. But if I were you, I would give our Great God much attention and get on fire for His beautiful word.

Indeed, I must say, honestly, this next statement I declare is the absolute truth simply because I am an ordinary flesh and blood man. Therefore, without going out on a limb or reaching into the unknown part of my mind and making another imaginary assumption.

I encourage you to believe that I, Paul Douglas Castle, a bible story writer, cannot tell you the reason for natural disasters. And I want you to know that my thoughts and analogies were inconclusive but merely assumptions from my limited intelligence.

Truly, again, I will say assumptions have the power to hurt people's feelings regardless of whether they are correct or incorrect assumptions. And when natural disasters occur and hurt and kill people, brotherly love is the best response.

Conclusively, during times of disaster, we can prove we are our brother's keeper to some unknown degree. But we can only be our brother's keeper if our heart isn't hardened by a holier-than-thou assumption, prohibiting compassionate feelings for people in need.

Indeed, I must say, before this explanation story ends, the wisest thing we can do is live by the perfect and excellent word of God. Then, we'll not have to worry about provoking His wrath by assuming this and that are the handiwork of God because of sin and rebellion against Him.

Conclusively, this concerns you and me and God's story, reaching into the unknown, called the reason for natural disasters. It isn't meant to persuade you one way or the other concerning the cause of natural disasters or the reason for wrath from above.

However, because I care about the place, you'll spend eternity. I want you to realize this story is meant to get your attention and advise you not to provoke God's wrath. Simply because He can cause all sorts of disasters, and He can individualize them too. And I conclude we are foolish people to treat the Ten Commandments as unimportant and live ungodly.

Chapter Twenty-Eight
CLOSE TO GOD

Within this enlightenment story, every concerned person must understand I am calling *Close To God*. It reveals where we should be in our spiritual walk, throughout every moment of every day, during the entirety of this life in the flesh.

Furthermore, if we want to ride upon the high places of this Earth and walk within the will of God, then we must delight ourselves in putting God first. Simply because it's God allowing us to walk with Him, know Him, and ride upon the high places of the Earth as we walk through this life.

Positively, I hope and pray every Christian man and woman alive will please God, and He'll allow them to ride upon the high places of the Earth. And I hope our merciful God will feed every believer in Christ with the heavenly heritage of Jacob, a chosen prince of God.

However, I want you to know before anyone can ride upon the high places of the Earth and have the same heavenly heritage as Jacob, they must be close to my great God. And I am telling you, we'll have to know the formula for pleasing Him.

However, if we are at a distance and do not know our Great Creator God, we do not know what pleases Him. Then, sadly, I must tell you, we cannot ride upon the high places of this Earth. And maybe we cannot have the same heritage as Jacob, Moses, and Elijah.

Indeed, getting close to my loving God is the first step every Christian must accomplish before they can claim to ride upon the high places of the Earth. And we will have to fulfill a few requirements before we can ride upon the high places of the Earth.

Therefore, if we desire to know God and be extremely close to Him, we want to please Him and be a permanent part of His family. Then we must know it pleases Him when He sees men and women keeping His righteous and perfect Ten Commandments.

Positively, it pleases God to see His followers teaching their children to obey and keep His extremely important Ten Commandments, which He recorded in stone. And I firmly believe commandment keeping pleases Him more than anything else.

I assure you, three important requirements matter immensely to God if we want to get close to Him. And without doing these three important things, we might never get as close to our Creator God as we would like.

I am positive we may never ride upon the high places of this Earth, as every Christian should ride, unless we do these three special things. And the second special thing that matters immensely to God is an important part of the Ten Commandments.

Indeed, many Christians aren't well-studied and Bible-savvy and tend to overlook this second requirement. And for some illogical reason, they fail to see the importance of observing His holy set apart separated day.

I am certain we cannot be obedient to His word and commandments unless we do this second thing I will tell you about. This second requirement is extremely important to God, and He expects Christians to do it and keep it throughout all generations.

Indeed, this second special requirement is to observe the fourth commandment, specifically stipulating the seventh day of the week. The second important requirement is keeping the authentic seventh-day Sabbath Day, rest day, holy day, and worship day of the Lord.

Truly, I want you to know a certain fact for your benefit: I know nothing more pleasing to our Great Creator God than seeing men and women happily keeping His commandments and The required seventh-day Sabbath Day.

Furthermore, I warn you, unless we keep His blessed and holy day, as He commands us to do. Then there's no way to be obedient to our wonderful Creator God, get close to Him, and ride upon the high places of the Earth.

I assure you if we keep His commandments, and His one and only, sacred and holy, on Sabbath Day's seventh day. Then it pleases God so much that He tells us, whoever we are, we know Him because we keep His required and beautiful commandments.

He also says that we do not know Him if we do not keep His commandments; we are liars if we say we know Him. And the Apostle

John, who passionately loved the Son of God like a brother, tells us how we can be certain that we know God.

> **John 2:3** And <u>here-by</u> (means by this way) we know that we know <u>Him</u> (our wonderful Supreme God, and Jesus Christ) if we keep His commandments.

Over and over, and time after time, many Christian believers, males, and females everywhere, all over this world, look for various ways to please God, get close to God, and know our Great God on a personal basis.

The Apostle John assures us the solution is extremely simple, not grievous, and is not a mystery hard to figure out. And sometimes, the formula is so easy to know we somehow overlook it. And I conclude that a lack of bible knowledge restricts us from knowing important matters.

Positively, many professing Christians do not seem to realize the absolute solution to knowing the God of Heaven and Earth well. Simply because all they have to do is keep His beautiful commandments and the God-appointed seventh-day Sabbath Day.

Furthermore, they must resist eating unclean foods because they can destroy the living temple of the Holy Ghost. But anyone can keep their temple clean, and it's accomplished by not eating unclean swine and other unclean foods.

Some preachers emphasize the importance of seed money, as if seed money is the key to divine supernatural blessings. Some preachers want us to believe giving seed money for unique favors to preachers and churches matters the most to God.

Assuredly, we can give slick-talking preachers all the money we want to, and it will not make us any closer to our creator God. Indeed, money isn't the formula for closeness to the King of Kings, nor do any of His Ten Commandments mention exchanging money for favors.

However, if we keep His Ten Commandments and His special seventh-day Sabbath Day, we'll resist eating the unclean. Then, we can know we know God and be assured we are doing the will of God.

Some preachers claim planting seed money with them will secure us special favor from our Great Creator God. And yet, they omit telling us we need to know the God that judges everyone. And they will not tell us that not planting seed money doesn't restrict us from receiving favor from Him.

Positively, the Apostle John clarifies that we know God simply by keeping His commandments. And as for myself, I believe the Apostle John knows more about the word of God than these preachers, who ask for seed money for uncommon favors.

Furthermore, the Apostle John would have something to say to these money-hungry preachers who sell uncommon favors to their congregation. And I am certain John wouldn't pat them on the back or tell them to keep asking for seed money for favors.

I believe the Apostle John would boldly tell them to their face. They are common thieves and liars and shouldn't use God to fill their pockets with money. This next scripture puts a definition to liars.

> **John 2:4** He (means anyone) that saith, I know Him (Jesus Christ), and keepeth, not His commandments is a liar, and the truth is not in him (the commandment breaker).

I believe that if the wise Apostle John or any other apostles were alive today, these seed money preachers said unto them. The God of creation talked to me last night, and then they claimed to have a divine message for any Christian or the entire congregation.

Then, I am certain the Apostle John, or any other apostles, would be outraged over their false teaching, lying lips, and false statements. And the apostles would label them as liars, deceivers, and charlatans who do not know the God that created them.

The Apostle John's words concerning God's beautiful commandments shouldn't be taken lightly or ever forgotten. And they should be considered a warning to any Christian believer guilty of denying God's required Ten commandments.

The fourth commandment proves that calling the counterfeit Sun-day Sabbath Day on the first day of the week the Lord's Day is wrong. It's not the Sabbath Day of our Lord, but it's a lie. And Christians should not believe a lie or submit themselves to anything counterfeit.

The wonderful word of God assures us that Sun-day is just another day, similar to any other day of the week except for the seventh day. But Saturday, the seventh day of the week, is the holy, sacred, and hallowed Sabbath Day of the Lord.

The loyal Apostle John says that any Christian who claims they know their creator God but keepeth not His commandments is a liar. And these excellent and truthful warning words of wisdom, the Apostle John speaks to us through the above scriptures.

They aren't meant for the unbelievers and the God deniers, who believe nothing is holy, godly, or sacred. And mainly because the unbelievers are not the children of God, and the seventh day, Sabbath Day, means nothing to them.

Therefore, these words the Apostle John speaks in the New Testament should have a lot of impact on every Christian because the words of John are meant for the Christians and are specifically meant for the believers who keep the counterfeit Sabbath Day.

Indeed, after defiling His rest day, the Sun-day Christians treat Saturday, the seventh day of Sabbath Day, as if it's just another normal day. And no matter how controversial the subject of the Sabbath Day is among men, God will not hold men blameless for commandment breaking.

Especially if they deny His seventh-day Sabbath day, and His seventh-day Sabbath Day is valid and documented throughout the bible. The bible scriptures do not justify a substitute counterfeit and imitation of the first day of the week, Sun-day Sabbath Day. And it's because the Sunday Sabbath Day is invalid and never will be recognized by God.

The Sun-day Sabbath Day is undocumented, not God-inspired, and unspoken of anywhere in the bible. And there's no such thing as a Sun-day Sabbath Day of the Lord, but thanks to the deviousness of men, there is an ungodly manufactured Sun-day Sabbath Day.

Assuredly, it doesn't take much research or study for any Christian to know the truth concerning the fourth commandment. And if anyone tells us it doesn't matter which day we keep the Sabbath, they are speaking against the authentic word of God.

Mainly because there's nowhere in the bible, throughout the scriptures, where the Father, the Son, or any apostle changed the Sabbath Day, nor are there any prophets throughout the bible saying it doesn't matter what day we call the Sabbath Day of the Lord.

Therefore, the Roman authority and church were instrumental in establishing the ungodly Sun-day Sabbath Day. Not to say, they were the first ones to defect from the truth and change the Sabbath Day of the Lord to a counterfeit Sabbath Day.

Maybe they were and weren't entirely responsible, but they were instrumental in the changing process. And if we do not like what the Roman church, the Pharisees, or any other church has done to the holy seventh-day Sabbath Day of the Lord.

Then we can change ourselves, not go with the flow, and not be a commandment breaker, week after week. And if you look around, you cannot see the supernatural power of God working through your Sun-day church or prayer answered.

Suppose you can recognize the counterfeit and imitation of Sun-day Sabbath Day as an ungodly and hurtful deviation from the truth. Then, at this point, you are becoming aware of how harmful the manufactured traditions of men are to you and your church.

Indeed, you'll know for certain your walk with God and your relationship with Him has a problem. And if your relationship with Him has been compromised because of rejection of the fourth commandment, you aren't happy with your situation.

It could be possible you'll feel deceived and even be angry at the preachers in the pulpit. Because you've been misled, they do not preach and teach the authentic and hallowed seventh-day Sabbath Day of the Lord.

Especially when you find out you've been keeping a counterfeit Sun-day Sabbath Day, not considered biblical. And especially if you've not been told about it from the pulpit by a preacher you've trusted and believe he's leading you in the right direction.

Then, I invite you to be a member of the living church of God. And it's because the living church is a major part of the kingdom of God; therefore, if you aren't happy about compromising the true Sabbath Day of the Lord and the fact you've been accepting an ungodly counterfeit Sabbath Day.

The Son of God created the wonderful living church of God, and it walks and talks and exists in all four corners of this Earth. And it keeps the required commandments of God and His hallowed seventh-day Sabbath Day.

The living church of God isn't a building, and it's not made of wood, stone, or brick. But it's a many-membered body of believers, and it's made up of people on the street corners, in the fields, and throughout homes worldwide.

I believe God's living church is the greatest in this world, and I know no other denomination cannot equal it. It's made of people walking to and fro on the streets, living in the cities, and living in the country.

I assure you, the living church of God is everywhere, and it's with us if we worship our Creator God. And it's regardless of the hour or the day when we meet another Christian, or an unbeliever, who doesn't believe in God.

Mainly because we believers in the wonderful Son of God are His living church, and we carry His word forth to the saved and the unsaved, and we sleep with it at night. And sometimes, we have dreams revolving around His excellent word.

Positively, First Corinthians 3:16 tells us, You and I are the redefined living temple of God. And for the sake of godliness, the beautiful Holy Spirit of God lives within us and teaches within us. And we will become godlier people because of His presence.

He lives within us *if* the Spirit dwells within us. But if any man has not the Spirit of Christ, he is none of His. The Apostle Paul tells us this message, written in Romans 8:9. And I warn you, God will destroy us if we defile the temple. 1 Corinthians 3:17.

We, believers in Christ, are God's many-membered living church. And this means if we do what we should, we carry His cross correctly. Then we'll spread the gospel of God to whosoever crosses our path and to whosoever desires to hear it.

However, it would be great if the living church of God didn't have to be in the fields all the time and on the highways and the byways because it would be great to have a church made from wood, stone, and brick that truly worships God on the seventh day Sabbath Day of the Lord.

However, the Living Church of God doesn't have to have a manufactured building to worship God within because the living kingdom of God is better than a building made by man's hands and ruled by men's authority.

Furthermore, I want you to realize we cannot claim for certain that everyone who worships God inside a manufactured building is saved. But I believe I am correct to say everyone belonging to God's living church is saved.

The living church of God is the primary church of God, mainly because the Holy Ghost is the teacher in the living church of God. And regardless of how well some of us teach the word of God, the Holy Ghost is the best teacher.

I assure you the words of the Apostle John are true and accurate, and no man has the right to challenge them. But the word of God is challenged by men, who prefer to keep men's traditions rather than the accurate word of God.

Indeed, I challenge any person, or any Sun-day Christian, to prove to me that the traditions of men supersede the word of God. This challenge includes the counterfeit Sun-day Sabbath Day versus the authentic God-designed Seventh-day Sabbath Day.

Suppose uncaring men within the church prefer to keep men's traditions rather than God's original word. The other choice is for Christians who desire to preserve their close and personal relationship with God. It's to separate yourself from the compromisers and belong to the living church of God.

Furthermore, if we want to know God and have a close friendship with Him, then I am telling you, we must keep the holy seventh day, Sabbath Day. Since it's a specially designed fellowship day, God set aside for us and Him.

The seventh day, Sabbath Day, is a special sign, indicating closeness between our Great God and us. And it reveals love, loyalty, and obedience to His word. And the Apostle John clarifies that the fourth commandment needs to be observed by believers in Christ.

I believe God's word is true, and nothing is false about Him. And the loyal Apostle John reveals the way for us to know God. But there is falseness and untruthfulness in the traditions of men, and within the first day of the week, Sun-day Sabbath keeping.

I want you to know the excellent promise taken from the great book of Isaiah and the mouth of the Lord. It's a wonderful promise to the seventh-day Sabbath Day keepers, who prefer to ride upon the high places of the Earth.

The wonderful promise includes anyone; God feeds with the heritage of Jacob, and you can find His promise in **Isaiah 58:13 & 14**. And it's for certain when we ride upon the high places of the Earth, we've found favor with our wonderful Supreme God.

I assure you when our wonderful Supreme God feeds us with Jacob's heavenly heritage, we are considered invites to the wedding feast of the Lamb. We will be glad; we are devout commandment keepers when the wedding begins.

Positively, we, believers in Yeshua, have a goal to achieve and a prize to secure. And when God feeds us with the heritage of Jacob, we'll have a promised home in the kingdom of God. Jacob's home is the kingdom of God, and it's the preferred place to live when our spirit leaves this world.

I guarantee you Jacob's heritage is extremely special, and we'll be glad to share in its specialness simply because it's a wonderful habitation place where our Supreme loving God and His Son, Yeshua, live. And our new habitation place waits for you and me on the other side of the rainbow.

Therefore, and please remember, getting close to our Great God requires at least three things of the utmost importance. Number one is basing our lifestyle and the works of our hands upon the righteous Ten Commandments of God.

Number two is by delightfully keeping the holy, blessed, and sacred seventh-day Sabbath Day. Number three is keeping our redefined body temple clean and not allowing it to be contaminated by the unclean swine and various sins.

The excellent King James Bible consists of approximately seven hundred and eighty thousand words. And according to my analogy, all those seven hundred and eighty thousand words are mostly summed up in six words.

Indeed, I want you to know these six important words are more serious than all others. And these six words are a universal message from the God of Heaven and Earth. And I believe they are given to the angels in Heaven and everyone on this Earth.

Above and beyond all other messages, I want you to know that the greatest and most helpful message from the Heavens above is The Conclusion to the Whole Matter. And so, you'll know His greatest message; the conclusion to the whole matter is revealed below.

I assure you that God didn't want His greatest message to be a puzzle or a complex mystery. And for this reason, it's a simple message. But it's written with a pen of iron and easy for everyone to understand. *#1 Reverence #2 God # 3 and # 4 keep # 5 His # 6 Commandments*!

The wonderful and righteous conclusion to the whole matter is a simple message; most Christians already know it. But being told the importance of it confirms the degree of emphasis my great God puts on the conclusion to the whole matter.

Furthermore, I want you to realize if we live by the conclusion to the whole matter, then we are a member of the living church of God. And it's for certain; we can be sure we know God. And it's because we base our lifestyle on the conclusion to the whole matter.

This serious story is called *Close to God*. It reveals the right formula for getting and staying close to Him. But the fact remains not everyone desires to be close to God. And very little can be done to change a heart not yearning for closeness to Him.

Therefore, observing most people reveals that anyone not desiring to be close to God will wander through the wilderness of sin and lust. And they'll waste their life doing vain things until their time in the flesh is finished.

I am certain, and I wish it weren't true. But sadly, I must tell you, the above analogy sums up most people in this world. And it's because they'll fail to find God. And what does a man profit if he pleasures himself all the days of his life and loses his soul?

Truly, as this story ends, I want my Savior, called Yeshua, to get the last say. And the wonderful Son of God tells us man does not live by bread alone, but by every word proceeding from the mouth of our Creator God.

Conclusively, please consider that man can lean on the gift of grace, expand its definition, and believe it absolves all sins. But the wonderful Son of God tells us we should live by every word God gives us.

Furthermore, I want you to know that God's wonderful gospel is the image of God. And the word of our Great Creator God was made flesh and dwelt among us. And I have one last conclusion to declare, and it proves greatness.

The word of God is the highest pinnacle of intelligence, and the definition of greatness is illuminated and revealed through the works and words of God. And I want you to know that this statement's analogy means God is the great pinnacle of intelligence!

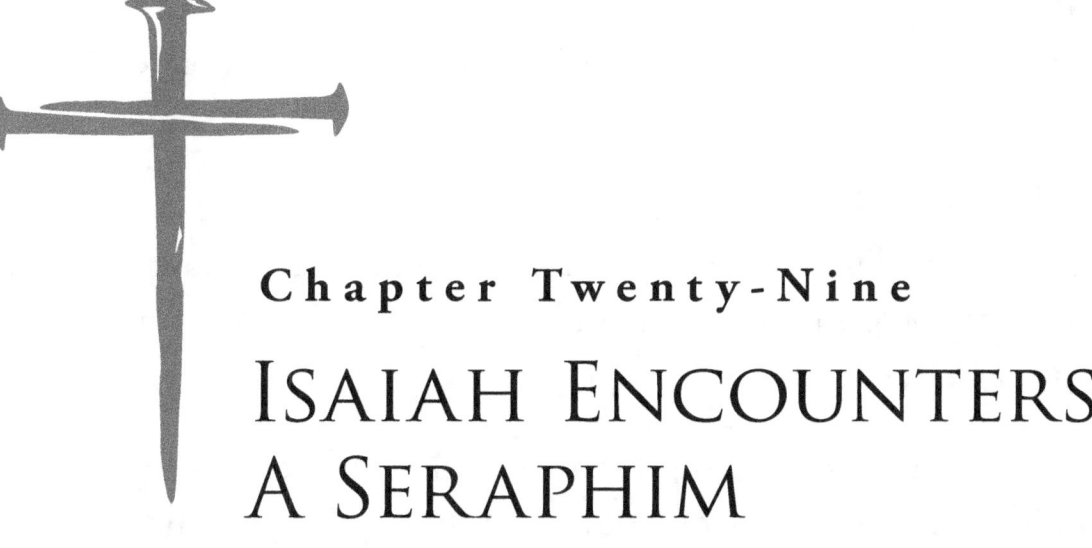

Chapter Twenty-Nine

ISAIAH ENCOUNTERS A SERAPHIM

In an exciting vision, terrific beyond comparison, it was revealed in the Old Testament and during a rare visitation moment. The excellent and loyal prophet Isaiah found himself standing inside the beautiful temple of God upon God's holy mountain.

It was a great honor of the highest degree and a much grander privilege than being a king on Earth. And all of a sudden, compliments of God. The spirit of Isaiah stood before the throne of God in a vision; most of us can only wish for the privilege. But most likely, we'll never receive it.

I am certain that many of us believers in the flesh would like to receive an invitation to look at Heaven and see our God sitting on His throne. And especially at the temple in Heaven and on the mountain of God, where the robe on His back fills the whole temple.

The temple of God was filled with smoke, but not the kind of smoke we are used to seeing. And I believe the smoke in the temple of God, upon the mountain of God, was similar to a beautiful blue misty cloud on a lovely day. And someday, when we go to Heaven, we'll see the creative wonders of God.

Isaiah, a privileged nobleman in service for my Great God, caught between two worlds, was slightly stunned and frightened. And he realized he was surrounded by the greatest of God and angels and said, Woe unto me, I am a man of unclean lips!

The prophet Isaiah hadn't seen heavenly creatures before, had six wings, and could fly inside the great temple of God. And the scriptures reveal the Seraphins stationed themselves somewhere around the throne of the God of creation, and they could talk.

While in their stationed position, somewhere close to our Great God, during the prophet Isaiah's visit. One of the unusual Seraphim cried to the other and said, holy, holy, holy is the Lord of hosts; the whole Earth is filled with His glory.

The glory of the Earth is all His unique creations, including the trees, grass, animals, us, and much more. And when our Great God of creation looks down from the Heavens above, He sees the glory of His accomplishments.

It's for certain all of us living upon this Earth in the flesh are mostly men and women having unclean lips! And I know it would frighten us if God called us up and we stood inside God's temple and saw the heavenly creatures and the out-of-the-ordinary living things the prophet Isaiah saw.

Isaiah 6:6 Then flew one of the <u>Seraphim's</u> (means one of the celestial beings in Heaven) unto <u>me</u> (Isaiah), having a <u>Live</u>

Coal (means a Living Coal from off the altar of God) in his hand, which he had taken with the tongs from off the altar.

Please notice closely when one of the heavenly creatures handled the Living Coals of Fire, the creature did so with a set of tongs. This procedure reveals the Living Coals of Fire weren't touched or handled in the palm of their hand.

> **Isaiah 6:7** And <u>he</u> (the Seraphim) laid <u>it</u> (the Live Coal) upon my mouth, and said, lo, <u>this</u> (coal) hath touched thy lips, and <u>thine</u> (means Isaiah's) <u>iniquity</u> (means sin and uncleanness) is taken away,

> **Isaiah 6:7** and thy sin <u>purged</u> (means the sins of Isaiah have been forgiven and taken away).

Please remember that after the Son of God was taken to Heaven, he said He would work through the wonderful Holy Ghost. The supernatural and powerful Holy Ghost has the authority to use supernatural articles from within the temple of Heaven.

I believe the wonderful Holy Ghost will often use the Living Coals of Fire upon the altar of God, upon the mountain of God. And they and He will work together and accomplish many supernatural missions.

Furthermore, I believe the Holy Ghost is entwined constantly with the Living Coals of Fire, who live upon the altar of God. And it's for certain: the Living Coals of Fire, who live upon the altar of God, are one of the heavenly creations from the Ancient of Days. And sometimes, the Lord uses them to purify and improve men.

The definition of purify means to be free from guilt, sin, and corruption, and it's one of the cleaning abilities of the Living Coals of Fire. And in Isaiah's vision, the heavenly Seraphim touched the lips of Isaiah with a Living Coal of Fire, taken from off the altar of God, upon the mountain of God.

However, I am certain none of us are familiar with the appearance of the Seraphims. But I believe the Seraphims must be extremely powerful supernatural creations. And it's for certain: they are extremely special celestial beings and have a much different appearance than the image of anything we can imagine.

The scriptures reveal when they <u>cry</u> <u>out</u> (means when they speak) in Heaven, the posts on the temple's doors, upon the mountain of God, move. The logical reason is that the posts on the temple's door in Heaven move when the Seraphim cries out.

It must be because the holy temple upon the mountain of God is a living temple, and it's as much alive as anything else. And I believe because the supernatural is commonplace in Heaven, we'll be surprised by how many things are alive in the Kingdom of God.

The Seraphims are holy creatures, completely trustworthy and loyal to their creator God. And it's easy to conclude that they do as the Lord commands them, and administering the Living Coals of Fire is one of their duties.

I believe the primary reason is that the Seraphim used tongs to carry the Living Coals of Fire to touch the lips of Isaiah. It's because the Seraphim didn't want to drain any of the energy from the Living Coals of Fire before they were used to touch Isaiah's lips.

The holy Seraphim touched the mouth of Isaiah with one of the Living Coals of Fire, who lives upon the altar of God, and his unclean lips were purified. This exposure story, *Isaiah Encounters a Seraphim*, reveals some of the power of the Living Coals of Fire.

This unusual story also reveals the dwelling place of the Living Coals of Fire, who reside in the living temple of God and upon the altar. And living upon the altar of God proves their value and connection to the Father, the Son, and the Holy Ghost.

Beyond the shadow of a doubt, the beautiful altar of our Great God, inside the temple of God, has a parallel connection. Indeed, it's similar to the holy of holies in the inner chamber of Solomon's temple, the holiest place in the whole temple.

The animal skin tent tabernacle in the desert housed the Ark of the Covenant, and Solomon's temple housed the Ark of the Covenant. And I want you to know that the Ark of the Covenant was considered holy in both places.

Positively, the sacred altar of God, inside the temple of Heaven, has Living Coals of Fire upon its altar. And I want you to know that the Holy Ghost of God is the Holy of holies. And the Holy Ghost entwines with the Father, His Son, and the Living Coals of Fire.

Furthermore, if the Holy Ghost of God lives within me and you, we also entwine with the Father, Son, and Living Coals of Fire. This truth means a small portion of the God element lives within us, allowing us a brief moment of life in the flesh.

Chapter Thirty

CLOVEN TONGUES ON FIRE

I am certain the supernatural Seraphims are just one of many heavenly creatures in Heaven, among others never mentioned. And we know that the supernatural Cloven Tongues on Fire at the God-inspired Pentecost Revival came from the above Heavens.

We can be certain when these divided Cloven Tongues on Fire came down from Heaven and sat upon the twelve apostles at the Pentecost Revival. Then, the hand of Jesus commanded the apostles to be purified and filled with God's wonderful, supernatural Holy Ghost.

> **Acts 2:4** And <u>they</u> (the twelve apostles) were all filled with the <u>Holy</u> <u>Ghost</u> (means with the living Spirit of God), and they began to <u>speak</u> (means talk) with other <u>tongues</u> (means in different languages),

> **Acts 2:4,** as the Spirit gave them <u>utterance</u> (means words to speak).

Men from everywhere dwelled at Jerusalem, out of every nation under Heaven, and present at the Pentecost Revival. And this means men from every nation under the sun heard the twelve apostles speak in their native language.

Beyond the shadow of a doubt, it was an astounding supernatural miracle when the foreigners listened to the apostles speak in Hebrew. But to the ears of the men from different nations, it was their native language they heard the apostles speak.

Indeed, the supernatural voice of one language was heard and understood in many different languages. And beyond the shadow of a doubt, supernatural creations from Heaven were making a difference at the Pentecost Revival.

Please consider the amazement and the complexity of a supernatural miracle. And especially when all the foreigners understood the Hebrew language, spoken by the apostles at the Pentecost Revival. And this is one of many miracles attributed to my Great Supernatural God.

Positively, the language feat alone was an extraordinary miracle. And surely, it should be called a God-made spectacular miracle. But it was just one of many miracles accomplished at the Pentecost Revival, and it was accomplished with the help of the Living Coals of Fire.

> **Acts 2:7** And <u>they</u> (the foreigners at Pentecost) were all amazed and marveled, saying, one to another, behold, are not all <u>these</u> (apostles) Galileans?

> **Acts 2:8** And how we hear every man in our <u>tongue</u> (means in their language), wherein we were born?

The answer to the above stunning question concerning the supernatural and an extremely unusual accomplishment originates with the power of God. The accomplishment of Hebrews speaking in one tongue and being understood in many different tongues.

I want you to know that this accomplishment can only be attributed to our Supernatural Father, His Supernatural Son, the Supernatural Holy Ghost, and the Living Coals of Fire, who lives upon the altar of God in Heaven.

Truly, the spectacular and unusual things happening at the Pentecost Revival were beyond the abilities of flesh and blood men to comprehend. And all the miracles they saw happened because everything is possible when our Supreme Supernatural God in Heaven gets involved.

Indeed, it's because nothing supernatural can happen through the natural abilities of the flesh and blood person unless the awesome and transferable power of the Holy Ghost of God decides to work through the flesh and blood person.

I am sure without the apostles having the wisdom and the supernatural abilities of God to enhance their works at the Pentecost Revival. Then, the Pentecost Revival would not have found its place in history and within the scriptures of the bible. And it's highly probable we would not know about the Pentecost Revival today.

Beyond the shadow of a doubt, the Holy Ghost of God was responsible for gathering men together at Pentecost. And I believe the Holy Ghost and the Living Coals of Fire were the Cloven Tongues on Fire, who sat upon the apostles at the Pentecost Revival.

Because the wonderful and excellent Holy Ghost of God, the Cloven Tongues, and the Living Coals of Fire are the same, but I believe different names identify them, similar to the holy trinity being three individuals.

Even though there was a language barrier between the men at the Pentecost Revival, the barrier consisted of various languages. The Supernatural Holy Ghost easily removed the language barrier. And doing it reveals His power and influence over our brains.

He allowed every man to hear the same message of the twelve apostles in the language he was born in his own country. And the fast-moving wind, the men thought rushed in at the Pentecost Revival, probably was the invisible and Supernatural Holy Ghost.

The wonderful Holy Ghost of God rushed in, and He filled the entire house at Pentecost with His Spirit, and it was felt by every man present. And when the Cloven Tongues on Fire came down to the Pentecost Revival, they were full of the powerful Holy Ghost.

Furthermore, when they sat upon each of the apostles, they were similar to fire from Heaven, but not the kind of fire we are used to seeing. They were similar to fire from Heaven because they were the Living Coals of Fire from Heaven.

Without a doubt, the Supernatural Cloven Tongues on Fire were living celestial beings from the kingdom of God. They came down to this Earth in their wonderful and helpful supernatural form to reveal another kingdom because they were concerned about the well-being of humankind.

The celestial creations from Heaven want us to understand that our Supreme God of Israel is a real God with real supernatural powers. The

Cloven Tongues on Fire was a supernatural example, saying Heaven is a real kingdom. And God offers it freely to all men and women determined to believe in Him.

The wonderful Supernatural Holy Ghost at the Pentecost Revival inspired the twelve apostles to deliver the message spoken by the prophet Joel. And I believe, because of overwhelming ungodliness, the time of its revealing is close at hand.

Indeed, the God-inspired message at the Pentecost Revival was an end-time message meant for the last days. And probably, shortly before the great tribulation time, before the wicked prisoners from Hell are released upon this Earth.

I assure you, the end-time message is an important one you and I should be aware of and understand because you and I are living in the last days before the second return of Jesus Christ, and I believe we'll be involved in the end-time proclamation.

Therefore, the end-time message they delivered at the Pentecost Revival has everything to do with our generation. And the supernatural God-inspired message is meant for you and me, and we should absorb every word of this prophecy.

Indeed, I hope you and I are one of the many participants in these last days' events and are willing warriors for the glory of God. Luke is thought to be the author of acts, and this next explanation of scripture reveals the end-time message for us in the last days.

Although, I want you to know the end-time message written in the book of Acts isn't the only last day's message. But it's an important end-time sign to remember, and recognizing it will prove that the end time has begun its countdown.

Furthermore, it could be possible the language barrier will disappear again in the last days after the Spirit of God is poured out on all flesh. But whether it does or not, the Spirit of God will bring God into remembrance before all men.

> **Acts 2:17** And it shall come to pass in the last days, saith God, I will pour out My <u>Spirit</u> (means the Holy Ghost) upon all flesh:

> **Acts 2:17** And your sons and your daughters shall <u>prophesize</u> (means speak out and declare, or predict divine things about God), and your young men shall see visions, and your old men shall dream dreams:

I hope to be one of my Great God's hot and on fire people in the last days, whom He pours His Spirit upon. Because I want to see visions and dream dreams, I want to be a part of my wonderful God's last day's plan.

I would certainly like a Cloven Tongue on Fire to sit upon me or touch my lips with a Live Coal of Fire. And I hope you have the same hope as me, and I hope your desire comes true, and a Cloven Tongue on Fire sits upon you.

I sincerely testify that the Spirit of God is strong in me, and I am compelled to write about my God only. And beyond the shadow of a doubt, this special story I am revealing to the world proves the Spirit of God is working through me.

Nothing else upon this Earth, or in the Heavens above, is as important for me to write about as my wonderful God. And the next informative scripture reveals another part of the end-time message from the apostles and the beautiful Holy Spirit of God.

> **Acts 2:18** And on My <u>servants</u> (as I am) and on My handmaidens, I (God) will pour out in those <u>days</u> (the last days) of My Spirit;

> **Acts 2:18** and they (means His servants and maidens) shall <u>prophesize</u> (means speak the word of God, and declare, or predict God inspired divine things).

The Conclusion to the Whole Matter was a big part of the end-time message, which the apostles emphasized at the Pentecost Revival. And the conclusion to the whole matter always entwines with all God-inspired messages.

The Conclusion to the Whole Matter is the greatest message ever given to humankind and angels. And I conclude, regardless of the generation we live within, race, color, gender, or the God-inspired event taking place.

I want you to know that the Old Testament and the New Testament reveal The Conclusion to the Whole Matter is an every-generation message. And it should be a daily message, equally as important as the air we breathe.

I truly testify I am a hungry and willing volunteer, and I am glad to spread the gospel of God of my own free choice. And I sincerely testify, saying I want to be a servant and friend to our Supreme God in this generation and Heaven, and I am happy to do His work.

I am bound by love for His righteousness, illuminated by the Ten Commandments God uses to reveal His covenant with me. I immensely desire to know the meaning and complete definition of His beautiful and important words and understand His mysteries.

I assure you, I passionately write for His glory in all my stories because I sincerely love Him with all my heart. And maybe we cannot be a resident in Heaven unless we love Him with all our heart, mind, and soul.

Furthermore, simply because of the important work I do, entwined with Him, one way or another. I believe He's already poured out His Holy Spirit upon me. Mainly because I do not believe I could understand and write my stories without the guidance of the wonderful Holy Ghost.

Soon to come, in these last days we live in now, there will be a new parallel to the Pentecost Revival. And possibly, it'll involve the Cloven Tongues on Fire and the Living Coals of Fire. I am certain a great revival is coming because acts of ungodliness have increased.

Including the Holy Ghost and men and women everywhere on fire for the word of God, the same way I am. And the next explanation, scripture, reveals more things to come in the last days. And mainly because our wonderful God tells us they'll come to pass.

Acts 2:19 I will show wonders in the Heaven above, signs in the Earth beneath; blood, fire, and vapor of smoke.

Suppose the end-time signs our Creator God just described are natural disaster signs. Then, it could be possible Yehovah is talking about meteors, earthquakes, and volcano eruptions. And please remember that He controls the Heavens and Earth elements and can fulfill end-time signs.

Even though I call these signs natural disaster signs, they probably should be called; God made spectacular disaster signs. Especially if we consider the next sign's meaning depth, it sounds like a spectacular God-made sign.

> **Acts 2:20** The sun shall be turned into darkness, and the moon into blood, before the great and notable day of the Lord to come:

> **Acts 2:21** And it shall come to pass, that whosoever shall call on the name of the Lord (Yeshua, Jesus Christ) shall be saved.

The great and notable day of the Lord, strong and wrathful, will be the second return of Jesus Christ. And it'll be a special time when He returns to this Earth in all His supernatural glory as King of kings! And I assure you, He will return at a spectacular time.

Therefore, the message the apostles recite to us at the Pentecost Revival, which is truly prophetic and a warning in advance, will be a last day's message. And it concerns the time to come, before His return on the great and notable day of the Lord. And I want you to know even the gates of Hell are opened before the Son of God returns.

Indeed, the definition of the word *memorable day* means the events going on during the special day will be the center of everyone's attention. The Lord looked into the future approximately two thousand years ago at the Pentecost Revival, and He said.

This Pentecost Revival event is for an end-time message and much more, including revealing the supernatural abilities of heavenly creations.

And to prove its importance, He sent His loyal servants upon this Earth, divine help from the Heavens above.

The end-time message is given so His loyal servants and friends will know what events are expected in the last days. But I believe bewilderment will be the reaction of whosoever isn't familiar with the written word of God.

However, regardless of the last days, God made spectacular events predicted to happen, and His miracles at the Pentecost Revival. Still, the last message to be preached on this Earth will be The Conclusion to the Whole Matter.

The great book of Revelation, filled with prophecy, mysteries, and warnings, was written by John on Patmos Island. It assures us that The Conclusion to the Whole Matter is the greatest message, regardless of our generation.

The conclusion to the whole matter will be preached by one hundred and forty-four thousand men of God, pure and undefiled. And before preaching ends, they'll say, fear the God of Heaven and Earth, and give glory to Him, for the hour of His judgment comes.

Indeed, the wonderful Holy Ghost of God wants you and me to know for certain. These spectacular things and events, prophesized by the apostles for the last days, will come true. And as for you and me, we are told in advance to be ready.

Indeed, when we see these supernatural changes happening in the Heavens above and the Earth beneath, we should know that His second coming is near the door. And we will realize this fact if we've studied prophecy at all.

Any person who calls upon the name of the Lord in the last days shall be saved from the judgment fires of Hell. The loyal Apostle Peter tells us this truth, written in the book of Acts, chapter two, verse twenty-one.

About three thousand souls from every nation under Heaven were visiting the Pentecost Revival event. And the heart and tongue of every apostle were on fire for the Lord, and because He loves us, the Holy Spirit of God called on everyone's heart to accept Christ.

Indeed, the Holy Ghost of God performed many spectacular miracles and wonders. And He illustrated signs through His apostles, proving His ability to do what He tells us He'll do in the last days. And during the last days, the ungodly will suffer from judgment poured out by the seven angels.

I am certain the revival was a well-planned event, specifically designed so all the Pentecost Revival people would have increased faith in God. And it's obvious that God had a divine message; He wanted it to go forth throughout the world and didn't want it forgotten.

Therefore, He decided to speak through His loyal apostles, and He did with the help of the Holy Ghost and the heavenly Cloven Tongues on Fire. And I assure you, no other revival hasn't equaled the Pentecost Revival.

> **Acts 2:38** Then, Peter said unto <u>them</u> (everyone at the Pentecost Revival), repent and be baptized, every one of you in the <u>name</u> (means in authority),

Acts 2:38 of Jesus Christ for the remission of sins, and ye shall receive the gift of the Holy Ghost (the Spirit of God).

Water baptism is for the remission of sins, and the remission of sin is a promise to all believers determined to believe in the wonderful Son of God. And when submerged under water, we are expected to rise from the water a new person in Christ.

Indeed, anyone or everyone who believes in the wonderful Son of God is called into the family of God. And because God cares about our souls, believers are saved from the perverse ways of sin in every generation until His wonderful Son returns.

This truth means the promise to be cleansed of sin through repentance and water baptism is for every believer in Christ. And it includes every man, woman, and child on this Earth, not just the people at the Pentecost Revival.

The Great Pentecost event was an extremely special revival. And it had supernatural heavenly creations gladly taking part in the revival. And the people saved at the Pentecost Revival received the baptism of the Holy Ghost. And afterward, they became teachers of the perfect word of God.

Indeed, the lives of everyone present at the Pentecost Revival were changed by the miracles they saw happen among them. And even if we haven't seen the miracles they have seen, the things they have seen inspire us to be a changed person, too.

Positively, after the great Pentecost Revival was over, a newness of heart changed their thinking, and their lives were never the same again, especially after having contact with the Holy Ghost of God and witnessing supernatural miracles firsthand.

I am certain if we had seen the supernatural miracles the people at the Pentecost Revival witnessed. Then, neither would our life be the same again, and we would live out the rest of our days doing the good works of the God of Heaven and Earth.

Certainly, fear, reverence, and respect came upon every one of them after witnessing the many supernatural wonders never before seen by any man or woman. And supernatural wonders include the many signs performed by the apostles at the Pentecost Revival, accomplished through the power of the Holy Ghost.

After the amazing Pentecost Revival was over, all the changed men present at the revival, including foreigners from other nations worldwide. They sold their material possessions and divided their goods among all men, as every man had need.

Afterward, the men who were saved and filled with the Holy Ghost at the Pentecost Revival continued teaching daily in the temple. And they went from house to house, determined to share the true gospel of God with everyone, willing to listen to them.

The people receiving the believers in Christ shared in the breaking of bread and ate their food with the happiness of the heart. They lived each day with the same purpose in their mind, and sharing the wonderful gospel of salvation was their new purpose in life.

Indeed, a concrete belief in the God of Israel was permanently established inside their heart because of the Pentecost Revival event. And it's quite obvious, because of the changed people, the wonderful Pentecost Revival started a domino effect.

I assure you, the converted Christians from every nation under Heaven had many supernatural things they could witness. And after the Pentecost Revival was over, the living church of God grew much faster and stronger than it normally would've.

The presence of the Holy Ghost and the heavenly creations made the Pentecost Revival the greatest revival on this Earth. And I am certain that no revival can compare to the Pentecost Revival. And none ever will unless heavenly creations decide to have another revival.

It was a great day at Pentecost, and I am certain all the hosts in Heaven will remember it forever. Simply because, on Pentecost Day, all the hosts in Heaven witnessed the Holy Ghost fill the meeting place with His Spirit, and they watched Him convince unbelievers to be believers.

Even for all the hosts in Heaven, it was amazing for them to watch the living heavenly creations in the form of cloven tongues rest upon the flesh and blood apostles. And I fully believe the cloven tongues were visible on this special occasion, as a witness to remember.

I am certain that on the extremely special Pentecost Day, the Father, the Son, the Holy Ghost, and the watchers, including all the holy ones in Heaven, were watching from above. They witnessed sinner men gladly being saved from the probability of damnation.

Truly, the sinner's hearts were changed, and they were filled with love for God through the power and the supernatural examples of the Holy

Ghost. And I believe every heavenly creation in His kingdom rejoiced when they witnessed sinner men being saved.

The next revealing scripture portrays the results of sinner men when they discover their need to be close to our wonderful and righteous God. And I want you to know that they discovered the treasure of eternal life; all men and women must discover.

> **Acts 2:41** Then they that gladly received <u>his</u> (Peters) <u>word</u> (about Jesus Christ) was baptized: And the same day was added unto <u>them</u> (the disciples of Christ) about three thousand souls.

God so loved the world and everyone in this world, and for the sake of love, He sent us His best representative from Heaven. He sent His only begotten Son onto this Earth as a man born flesh and blood. And He came here to teach us His Father's truthful and life-saving word.

The excellent and wonderful Son of God came into this world mainly to call us out of sin through repentance and water baptism. And repentance and change will convert us into a new person, according to the excellent word of God.

Therefore, the promises of God and eternal salvation aren't only for the Jews anymore, and everyone is invited to be a Child of Christ. And because of this fact, it's become clear that God is no respecter of persons, regardless of color, gender, or nationality.

However, in every nation that <u>feareth</u> (means reverence and worships) Him, and <u>worketh</u> (means doeth) righteousness. They are accepted as sons and daughters of God because they believe in the name of Jesus Christ.

Therefore, male or female believers in Christ are pardoned by the blood of the Lamb and receive forgiveness for sins. And the next informative scripture reveals how instrumental the Holy Ghost is when men hear and love the word of God.

> **Acts 10:44** While Peter yet spake these <u>words</u> (about the remission of sin to whosoever believeth on the name of Jesus), The Holy Ghost fell on all who heard the word.

Therefore, men in love with the wonderful word of God are not alone on this Earth because the beautiful Holy Ghost is deeply involved within the heart of every believing person. And He enters into believers after they fall in love with His required word.

The indiscriminate Holy Ghost, determined to be helpful, inspires every believer in God to do the righteous works of our Great God. And because He loves everyone, it's regardless of what nation they live within or the color of their skin.

I assure you that salvation is a gift to everyone if they are determined to believe in the death, burial, and resurrection of Jesus Christ. And this means salvation is secured and can be claimed by believing in the sacrifice of Jesus Christ.

Truly, the Cloven Tongues on Fire, the Living Coals of Fire, and the Holy Ghost are closely related to each other in their works. I am not sure; one can be separated from the other. And it appears for certain all three have the power of transformation.

This truth means they can be anything they want or a person in the flesh when they leave the holy and sacred temple in Heaven and visit this Earth.

And as for you and me, we'll never know they are observing and walking among us here.

Therefore, the Cloven Tongues on Fire, the Holy Ghost, and the Living Coals of Fire seem the same. So, do the Living Coals of Fire, the essence of pure energy, the spark of life, the breath of life, and the powerful God element seem the same too?

It's for certain, and it appears correct to believe that multiple names for heavenly beings aren't uncommon among them. And our main example is our Creator Father and His wonderful Son, who most certainly have multiple names.

Furthermore, so does the Holy Ghost of God, also called the Spirit of God. This truth implies the Living Coals of Fire also have multiple names. And I believe the Living Coals of Fire and the wonderful Holy Ghost are the same heavenly creation.

Most likely, the Supernatural Cloven Tongues on Fire was a visible appearance of the Holy Ghost. And the many Cloven Tongues on Fire, visiting the Pentecost Revival, were just a dividing transformation of the Spirit of God.

I believe everyone at the Pentecost Revival who needed healing did receive healing, and the miracle of healing was the work of the Holy Ghost. And I believe only part of the supernatural accomplishments recorded at the Pentecost Revival have been revealed to us.

I also believe the wonderful Holy Ghost, who made His appearance at the Pentecost Revival, is still with us today. Teaching men and women the right way is His priority, and we believers in Christ are proof of His works.

It's for certain because the bible says so; the Holy Ghost lives within the clean heart of every hot and on fire believer. And He's the reason the wonderful kingdom of God lives within us. This truth means we believers are noble saints in the family of God. Furthermore, if the Holy Ghost lives within every believer, His Spirit can divide and enter millions of people.

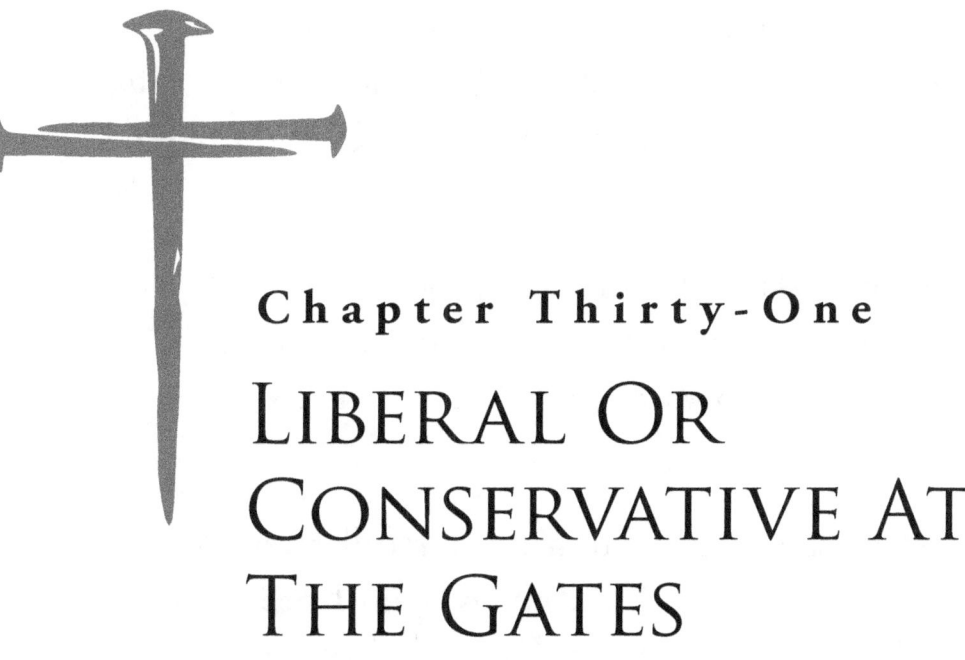

Chapter Thirty-One

Liberal Or Conservative At The Gates

This informative story concerns two types of people, liberals, and conservatives, standing at one or the other gate. It refers to the gates of heaven and the gates of Hell. And someday, we'll stand before the Gates of Heaven or Hell.

Please be aware it's not my intention to stereotype the liberals or the conservatives in a certain way because all liberals and all conservatives are not the same in every respect. But still, liberal is ungodly and worldly, and conservative is godly.

Furthermore, it takes more than talking to prove ourselves a liberal or a conservative. A pattern can be established, but not a one hundred percent pattern. This truth means when I describe the liberals and the conservatives.

I am expressing a general description, entwining most of them from my point of view. And not only from my point of view but from a conservative point of view, based upon the conservative gospel of my Great Creator God only.

Furthermore, please be aware our choice of being a liberal or a conservative is a definitive statement concerning our character. And this means being a liberal or a conservative reveals how we feel about various controversial issues.

Positively, these controversial issues, requiring our full attention, are subjects all of us are faced with in this world today. And I believe many conservatives lie about their position concerning liberal or conservative issues.

I believe this world is full of liberals masquerading as conservatives, and they say they are a conservative when they are liberals at heart. And I also believe many counterfeit conservatives lie about their position on controversial issues.

I also believe many imitation conservatives are masquerading as real conservatives when they are liberals at heart. In the last days, before Yeshua returns, this world will be in great distress and confusion, and liberalism will majorly contribute to the chaos.

Indeed, this unstable world will mostly be liberal and ungodly, and it'll be driving down the wide road of destruction. And the next warning scripture reveals a glimpse of the imbalance between Christian conservatives and ungodly liberals.

Therefore, the next informative scripture perfectly highlights the barometer of godliness and ungodliness. It has illustrated phrases like the straightway versus the crooked way, the narrow way, the broad gate, and the narrow gate.

However, please keep in mind the crooked way and the broad gate is entwined together with destruction to the soul. And sadly, I must tell you, the ungodly liberals walk on the crooked road leading to the broad gate designed to accommodate heavy traffic flow.

> **Matthew 7:13** Enter ye in at the <u>straight</u> (means the narrow) gate: For wide is the gate, and broad is the way, that leadeth to <u>destruction</u> (means to the pits of Hell), and <u>many</u> (lawless and liberal sinners,

> **Matthew 7:13,** which puts no difference between the clean and the unclean, and the holy and the unholy, and the righteous and the unrighteous, and many ungodly liberals) there be which go in there at.

Although, the road going to Hell is invisible, not detectable by eyesight. It does still exist, and many ungodly liberal people use it daily. And wherever there are cities, towns, and people, then the invisible liberal road to Hell is there also.

Without a doubt, angels stand at the crossroads, directing traffic up or down. The concerned Son of God clarifies that the broad road is ungodly, leading to the soul's destruction and a downward place called Hell.

Observation of this mainstream world and the characteristics of ungodly liberal and cold and lukewarm people living in it proves there will be many liberal people determined to take the broad way through life and enter through the wide-open gates to Hell.

All because they are too liberal-minded, too passive, and too indifferent. And because they oppose the righteousness of God, as it's expressed through His required word and illustrated by the perfect Ten Commandments of God.

Positively, the sincere word of God reveals that opposition to God's required word has serious consequences for the soul. And this life-threatening problem needs to be recognized before it's too late to get on the narrow road.

Opposition defines the liberal-minded person as a cold or lukewarm individual. And our God-inspired bible tells us that God will reject them and not allow them to live in His kingdom. And I warn you; we better not end our life cold or lukewarm.

The next explanation scripture, requiring much consideration, reveals an important metaphor example. And it indicates only a few, compared to many, will find the narrow road with the narrow gate going to Heaven.

> **Matthew 7:14** Because <u>strait</u> (means narrow) is the <u>gate</u> (to the kingdom of God), and narrow is the <u>way</u> (means the path) which leadeth unto <u>life</u> (means to the kingdom of Heaven),

> **Matthew 7:14** and <u>few</u> (means only hot and on fire religious conservatives) there be that find it.

Indeed, the reason for the broad gate, and the narrow gate, and the broad road, and the narrow road. It's because the broad road with the broad gate is built for the ungodly liberals, who have a cold temperature or are lukewarm for the ways of God.

Therefore, the narrow road, having the narrow gate, is built for god-fearing conservatives, who are determined to be hot and on fire for the word of God. But being liberal and accepting anything as long as it doesn't affect you is considered broad and ungodly liberal thinking.

However, at the least, being liberal-minded is considered not caring about the Bible-quoted ways of our righteous God. Liberalism is one of the reasons that only a few men and women will find their way into the kingdom of Heaven.

I assure you that it's for our benefit when the Son of our Supreme God tells us something since His words are always important. And when He talks, we should listen closely and intensely to His extremely important words of wisdom and obey them.

Indeed, in the above scripture, Jesus says the road to Hell is built much broader and wider to accommodate more traffic. This truth means the wide road to Hell is more traveled than the narrow and righteous road, with the narrow gate taking us to Heaven and eternal life.

Surely, Jesus's statement means there are more ungodly than righteous and god-fearing people on this Earth. This analogy is made from a godly, conservative point of view and a heavenly point of view coming from the throne of God in Heaven.

Seeing so many liberal-minded people putting this world's unclean and immoral ways before God's clean and righteous ways is stunning. And when men and women become this passive, we can correctly say they are liberal.

Indeed, the mistake of being too ungodly liberal, cold, and lukewarm to the word of God is like walking down the broad road and going through the wide gate and not realizing you've gone through the gate into Hell.

Even if you realize you've taken the wrong turn in life. It doesn't matter too much until after the death of the flesh. But after the death of the flesh, you cannot turn back because it's a one-way road after you've gone through the gates of Hell.

From the definition of the last two scriptures, there are two avenues of travel after the death of the flesh. And I want you to know that the choices we had before our death disappear after our death. And choosing the narrow road, or the broad road, must be decided as we live and breathe.

Because an angel delivers us to one gate or the other, we go through the gate alone, which is a one-way gate. And this means life's test is over, and only judgment or reward remains. And sadly, I must tell you, the clock cannot be turned backward for the liberal unbelievers.

It's sad to realize there's a greater number of people who fit the definition of liberal, concerning the holy and the unholy, the godly and the ungodly, and the just and the unjust, designated to go through the wide gate.

I guarantee you that traveling on the wide road means cold and lukewarm people aren't using the required word of God for their road map. And sadly, I must tell you, they aren't seeking to travel and stay on the godly and narrow conservative road.

Indeed, when conservative men and women arrive at the gates of Heaven and enter through the gates of Pearl, it'll be because they are hot and on fire conservatives, and they've journeyed through this life on the narrow road.

For this reason, they'll enter the wonderful kingdom of God. And I am certain, after the death of the flesh, the moral conservatives will be happy they lived a conservative lifestyle in conjunction with the word of God.

Although I am certain when the ungodly liberals enter through the gates of Hell, there will be weeping and gnashing of teeth. And at this point, I believe, the ungodly liberals, who put no difference between the clean and the unclean, and the holy and the unholy.

They will wish they had been a godlier conservative concerning the issue between the holy and the unholy. But for some illogical reason, people alive and doing well do not want to rock the boat or be hot and on fire for the wonderful word of God.

Indeed, the informative story example in the Bible to illustrate the destiny of Lazarus and the rich man should be considered an illustration, illustrating two different destination places at the end of life. And we want to be conservative and not go where the ungodly rich man went, too.

The revealing story concerning the poor Lazarus and the rich man proves a fact. It proves the gate we pass through after the death of the flesh doesn't allow course changes or the option to repent and change after someone is delivered down to Hell.

Surely, the prize of immortality and living in the kingdom of God should inspire men and women to walk on the narrow road. But popular television movies portraying the persona of casual sex and immoral lifestyles as normal and acceptable inspire ungodliness.

Inspiring ungodliness proves there must be a bad case of spiritual blindness enveloping the world, causing people to make illogical decisions simply because this entire world seems to be emulating the lifestyles of the immorality of ungodly movies.

Therefore, I must warn you: Lucifer is this world's immoral, ungodly dark prince. And acts of immorality are his greatest influence on society. And he encourages immorality, ungodliness, uncleanness, and unfaithfulness to the required word of God.

Furthermore, he's the stumbling block between us and the prize of salvation, and he doesn't want us to receive the great gift of immortality. And we must overcome Lucifer and his prevalent ungodly lifestyle before we can be the children of God.

Simply because the loyal children of God have to separate themselves from the ungodly, liberal, and rebellious ways of the wicked Lucifer, and I want you to know, this is one of the required expectations my all-mighty God expects from every believer.

Nor can anyone be a child of God and a child of Lucifer, and the wisest decision is to be a hot and on-fire believer in God. And mainly because the hot and on fire children of God are the only ones able to pass beyond the gates of pearl and win the prize of immortality.

Positively, the gift of immortality is a special prize I hope to win, and I hope you do, too. But we must give our heart to God, travel the narrow road, and go through the narrow gate before the prize is ours to claim.

This revealing story, concerning everyone looking for the right way, called *liberal or conservative at the gate*, is saying liberalism coincides with the definition of being passive or indifferent to the excellent word of our Great God.

Positively, everyone guilty of being passive and indifferent to the required word of God will not get through the gates of Pearl at the end of the narrow road. But I guarantee you, hot and on fire passionate Christians, easily get through the gates of pearl.

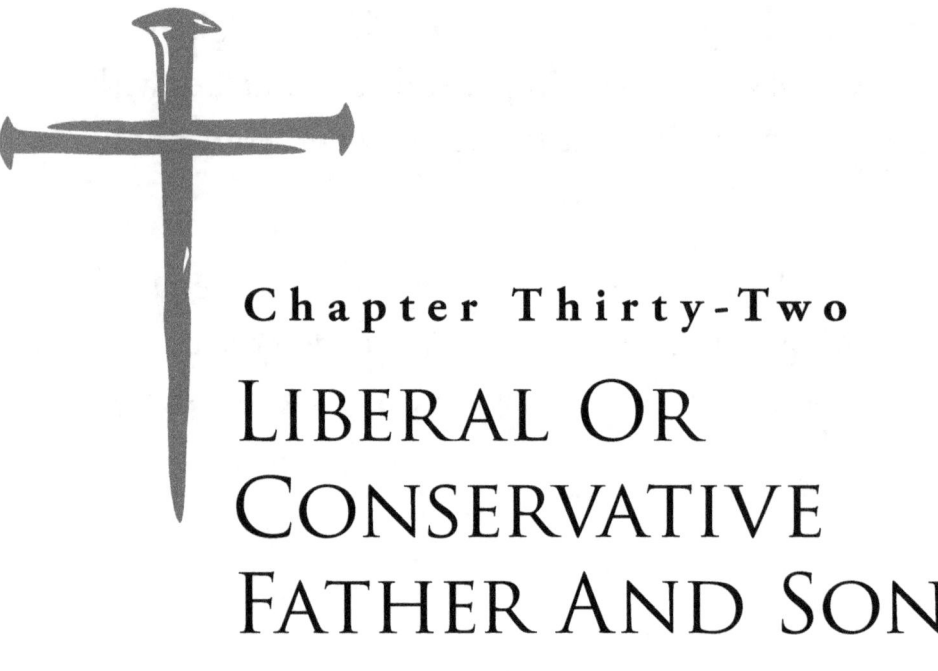

Chapter Thirty-Two

LIBERAL OR CONSERVATIVE FATHER AND SON

I want you to know that salvation and immortality are the grand prizes at the end of our lives, and we should be serious about winning the prize. And for perfect fairness, the Father, the Son, and the Holy Ghost are the contest Judges.

Furthermore, I want you to realize that if we do not entwine our lifestyle to their commandments, we'll lose the grand prize of immortality. And for this reason, I strongly suggest we abide by the *conclusion rules* to win the gift of eternal salvation.

Positively, the conclusion rules are the excellent Ten Commandments of God. The conclusion rules are our testing challenges if we want to be a winner of salvation instead of a loser who will receive the judgment of damnation.

Indeed, it wouldn't hurt to ask ourselves every time we do something if God would approve of our actions. And if we think the God of Heaven and Earth would approve, we should do it. But if we think our supreme God wouldn't approve, we shouldn't do it.

Furthermore, if I only had two words to describe our Supreme God, the Son of God, and the Holy Ghost. I have a choice of two words to choose from to describe them, and the two words are liberal or conservative.

Then, I would describe God, the Son of God, and the Holy Ghost as extremely strong conservatives. And I am positive there's no way they can be described as easygoing, non-caring, open-minded, and lukewarm passive liberals.

I sincerely doubt if God, the Son of God, and the Holy Ghost could be considered liberals in any analogy. And especially when distinguishing between the holy and the unholy, the clean and the unclean, and the just and the unjust.

Therefore, I seriously doubt if the Father, the Son, and the Holy Ghost would buy into the equal rights argument today. And especially if the equal rights argument gives place to the unholy, unclean, and ungodly liberal freedom, opposing righteousness and morality.

I assure you, our Supreme God didn't make liberal commandments, and He didn't say you can keep them if you want to observe them. But He tells us to keep His commandments if we love Him. And if we do not keep His commandments, we do not love Him.

The Apostle John assures us that His conservative commandments are not grievous or burdensome to anyone claiming to love Him. We cannot be liberal-minded concerning the perfect word of God and still care about His conservative commandments, too.

All liberalism, sinfulness, corruption, and uncleanness are connected through similarities. And this means they are connected by policies, habits, and lifestyles contrary to righteousness.

Positively, liberalism is expressed by people choosing to be corrupt, drink, party, and live a rebellious lifestyle. And by liberal people, willing to fornicate, who see nothing wrong with sodomy, same-sex marriage, and legalized abortion of babies.

Therefore, I am positive my God of creation is a red-hot conservative. And He'll not foolishly accept liberalism or any changes to His conservative words and laws, nor will He change His serious commandments or relax their value.

Furthermore, His excellent commandments will not conform to the liberal and ungodly traditions of men. Nor does He care about the desires of ungodly liberals who have no desire to obey His rules and His perfect Ten Commandments.

I am certain the Son of God believes the same as His Father and supports the same conservative values as His wonderful Father. And this means He's not liberal concerning the traditions of men and the foolish and unclean ways of this world.

The wonderful Son of our Supreme God tells us straight up and to the point. Only a few people will find the narrow road leading to eternal life in the kingdom of God. And it's not because the narrow road, with the narrow gate, is harder to find.

The narrow way isn't hidden from anyone if they seek to find and walk on it, although it seems hidden because most people prefer the broader road with the wider gate. Since the broader road with the wider gate is considered more liberal, lewd, and lawless.

Indeed, as illogical as it is to choose the broad road, most people in this unstable world prefer it. And it must be because it's a do-anything wide-open road. And it's filled with the pleasures of sin and a compatible group of ungodly men and women.

However, if you are looking for a better road where godliness matters, I want you to know that the pleasures of sin aren't on the narrow, conservative road with the narrow gate. But sadly, I must tell you, the narrow road is considered much too conservative for the liberals.

Truly, the narrow road and the narrow gate have similarities, and it coincides with the eye of the needle. And it's a more conservative road with conservative rules and where God-fearing men and women prefer to travel.

And I want to enlighten you that only repented sinners travel on the narrow road. The narrow road, having the narrow gate, is an invisible highway going through all four corners of this Earth. It has restrictions and doesn't allow the ungodly liberals access unless they repent, change, and pick up the cross of Jesus.

For certain, love for the gospel of God wins us the key to the narrow gate, and God lovers are the only ones given the key to His gates. And mainly because they love to avoid liberalism, lewdness, uncleanness, and ungodly men in love with the liberal pleasures of sin.

Positively, all men and women determined to travel on the narrow road do not travel the narrow road because they are forced to travel it. But they travel on the narrow road because it is the only road they love and desire to travel.

The narrow road is the only road they prefer to travel every day. And it's because they love to obey God's words and commandments, and they take His word seriously. And I assure you, they despise the wide road with the wide gate with a passion.

Simply because loyal and faithful Christians like, enjoy, and agree with the righteous ways of God because it's the righteous ways of God, pleasing to them. And I conclude that conversion to Christianity means the narrow road is our choice highway.

It's quite obvious: the narrow road and the liberal road are opposite types of roads. And it's easy to conclude they have two different types of people traveling on them even though the narrow road would create a perfect world.

Think not; lovers of the wonderful word of God want to travel on the broad road, having a wide gate. But the loyal God lovers who love the word of God warn the ungodly liberals to change course before it's too late.

The liberal road is the broad road, where the soul is in jeopardy, and the heat is extremely hot. The liberal road is where passive people and ungodly nations put no difference between one God and another god.

Character characteristics prove that the liberals serve and worship false gods and bow their knees before strange gods. And some ungodly liberals might be so liberal they proudly call themselves atheists and feel like no supernatural God of creation exists.

It's the liberals guilty of not putting a difference between same-sex marriage and God-inspired marriage, consisting of a man and a woman. And I assure you, evolving onto the wide road of ungodliness amounts to the same thing as drifting further away from God and the prize of immortality.

Indeed, the ungodly liberals establish a predictable pattern, and it's the ungodly liberals who support ungodly laws. And ungodly laws allow men with men to expand their ungodliness and openly practice same-sex marriage.

However, moral conservatives put a difference between a God-inspired marriage and same-sex marriage devised by the liberals. And moral conservatives do not evolve to accept more ungodliness. But they stand for what's right, based on the perfect word of God.

Furthermore, I want you to realize that a conservative doesn't put a difference between same-sex marriage and traditional marriage. Then the conservative lies and truly isn't a conservative but is a liberal, masquerading as a conservative.

However, we all have free will to choose, and we can be a godly conservative or an ungodly liberal. And best of all, our Great Supreme God will not stand in our way nor interfere with our choice of principles and lifestyles.

Therefore, I am a little indecisive, and I believe we shouldn't let the liberals bother us with their ungodliness. And maybe we shouldn't stand in the way of the ungodly liberals or care about their next habitation place if they lust men for men.

Maybe we should let them marry each other and walk down the broad road straight through the gates of Hell. And especially if they are unconcerned about their soul. And liberals, unconcerned about God's infallible word, purposely oppose and hate it.

After all, the ungodly liberals can choose their road as they journey through this complicated life. And regardless of whether we like it, the excellent and perfect gift of free will applies to the ungodly liberals, too.

I assure you, Christians aren't dictators; we cannot wear someone else's shoes for them or change another person's free will. But we can be separated from the ungodly liberals and not do the ungodly things they do.

The main thing is for Christians not to be forced to bend their beliefs because Christians shouldn't accommodate ungodly values. This truth means religious conservatives shouldn't be forced to get involved with ungodliness and shouldn't be asked to support ungodly values.

Nor should any government authority force conservatives to be a part of ungodly liberalism or the liberal agenda. But beware, this corrupt and passive world system mostly belongs to Lucifer. And he and his servants of darkness support ungodly liberalism.

Maybe we should count our blessings and be glad ungodly liberalism will not be a part of the next world. And for our benefit and the sake of perfect righteousness, we'll not be bothered with liberalism in the perfect kingdom of God.

Beyond the shadow of a doubt, we all make the bed we lay in, and the bed we make has the choice of two covers. One cover is illuminated by light, and the other by darkness. And we can walk in the light, or we can walk in the dark.

In other words, the narrow road, having the narrow gate, is illuminated by the brightness of God. And because of lifestyle, the ungodly liberals cannot stand the light. But because the ungodly liberals love darkness, Lucifer provides the light haters a dimly lit road.

This truth means the wide road having the wide gate is a dark road, and ungodly people travel it. And it's because ungodly people prefer to be unclean and liberal and walk in darkness. And this analogy means the liberals walk with Lucifer, and the conservatives walk with God.

This extremely serious story is called *Liberal* or *Conservative Father and Son*. It purposely revolves around our Father in Heaven, His excellent Son, and the righteous word they give this confused world.

We shouldn't have to ask if our heavenly Father and His wonderful Son are liberal or conservative. And it's because bible scriptures prove, beyond the shadow of a doubt, that the values they support are conservative.

Furthermore, I advise you that if they support conservative values, we should too if we are passionate, hot, and on-fire Christians. And I want you to realize the Book of Life records our conservative values and the liberalism you and I submit ourselves to daily.

Positively, the perfectly kept book of life will be opened against you and me someday. And I am certain that our deeds and actions will be reviewed accurately. And I am also certain we'll be glad to have conservative values written about us in the Book of Life.

Indeed, you and I will be overjoyed on Judgment Day if our recorded life reveals a hot and on-fire Christian, a loyal conservative Christian who wasn't ashamed to be passionately in love with the wonderful word of God.

I am certain I will be proud to stand before my wonderful God of Heaven and Earth as a loyal God lover and be identified as a warrior for His excellent word. And I hope you are strong in God and will stand before Him the same way.

This testimonial story is called Liberal or Conservative Father and Son. It coincides with the greatest message given to us by the Father and the Son. And their message breaks the boundaries of perfection, and no other words come close to being as meaningful as them.

Beyond the shadow of a doubt, their greatest message is the required Ten Commandments. And I guarantee you all of His commandments are conservative commandments. And they reveal the highest pinnacle of greatness and the Great Creator of greatness.

Positively, none of His righteous commandments express a liberal point of view, nor should you and I express a liberal point of view. And every decision we make should entwine with His conservative Ten Commandments.

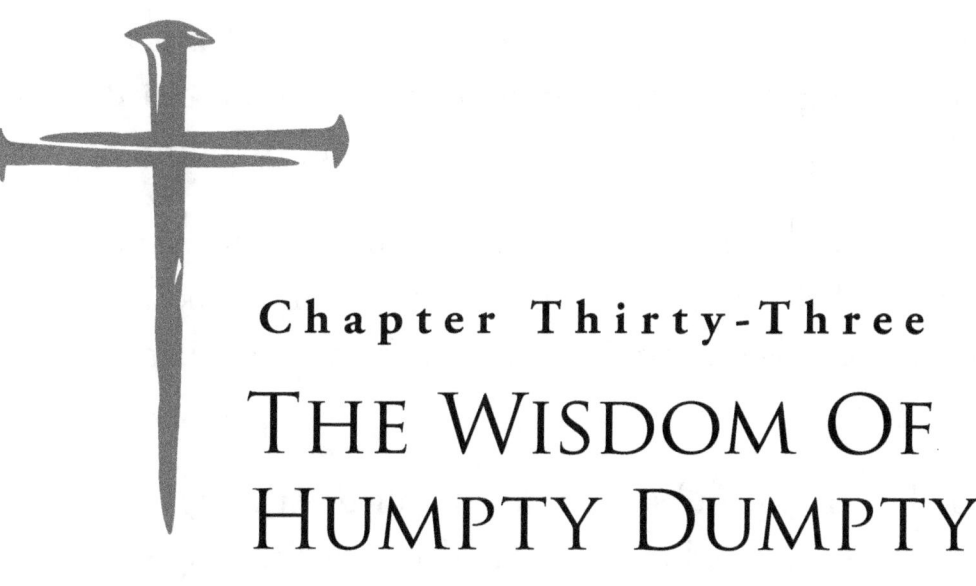

Chapter Thirty-Three

THE WISDOM OF HUMPTY DUMPTY

Throughout the portals of time, a message has been hidden, and the world has been waiting on an egg with the wisdom of Solomon to come alone and recite the truth for the human race. Then, one day near the king's palace, an egg stood on the wall with a bible in his hand and said I have a message for you.

Before this parallel story starts, I want you to know that Humpty Dumpty sat on a wall, always content and happy, until he had a great fall. Then, all the king's horses and all the king's men couldn't put Humpty Dumpty back together again.

This paralleling to us story, Humpty Dumpty, is a metaphor that relates to many relationships. And this means relationships between God and Lucifer, us and God, husbands and wives, and children and parents.

I am certain Humpty Dumpty was a good old egg, traveled much, dressed well, and bred to be a gentleman. He crossed the sea and traveled around the world, and there wasn't an egg as wise as or frailer than him.

Humpty Dumpty was a vulnerable egg, concerned about his frailty. And he always worried about his shell and knew a fall would end him. And the metaphor part of this story reveals that strained relationships are similar to a cracked eggshell.

Sometimes, our mood is serious, and sometimes, it's filled with laughter. Indeed, the first part of this story is humorous, and it's easy to laugh at Humpty Dumpty. But the rest of this story isn't so humorous and funny, and it's much more serious than a cracked eggshell.

I want you to know the rest of this story entwines with a warning, and I am telling you, husbands and wives, mothers and daughters, fathers and sons. Beware, and do not crack the eggshell. Because sometimes, our relationships cannot be mended and be put back together again.

This truth means stepping on toes gains nothing but sore toes. And we better treat our relationships carefully and be cautious about our decisions. And base everything we do on righteousness and fairness, or we'll take a great fall.

Characteristics of character matter, and so does how we treat our fellow person. And this means if we do too much harm to one another, our relationships will coincide with the end of Humpty Dumpty. And all the king's horses and all the king's men couldn't put Humpty Dumpty back together again.

I hope you enjoy this metaphor story, designed especially to make us consider everything we do and say when talking to all our friends and acquaintances and everyone we meet along the way. And I want you to know we are our brother's keeper to some unknown degree.

Positively, this story isn't really about Humpty Dumpty, but it's about you and me, and our actions and reactions, and considerations and inconsideration, and the consequences of our choices. And I want to say Humpty Dumpty was teaching the right way before he fell off the walk.

Chapter Thirty-Four
PINPOINTING EXPECTATIONS

This revealing story concerning us looking for the right way is called *Pinpointing Expectations*. It gets personal, illuminates His highest expectation of us, and His greatest expectation is summed up in two hundred and ninety-five righteous words.

These extremely important two hundred and ninety-five words place a dividing line between righteousness and unrighteousness. And I want you to know they pinpoint God's expectations concerning His created children.

If we are created equal in the eyes of God, and He shows no difference of persons, and we are in the driver's seat of our destiny? And if we were His sons in Heaven and knew Him personally before being born here through a woman's womb?

Then surely, all of us are bound by the same requirements. And this means we haven't any special exemptions concerning God-given stipulations. And if the above two sentences are true, I believe they are true, then no favorites are the best way to portray us all.

This impartial story, requiring our full attention, is called pinpointing expectations. It portrays our Creator God as a fair and righteous Judge, not swayed by color or gender. But I want you to know He's extremely serious about His requirements.

This impartial story illustrates the expectations of God, and they are the same for everyone who lives on this Earth. And I assure you, personal favors to certain people aren't a part of His selection process, and God will treat us equally if we love Him.

However, I want you to realize that *commandment keeping* and *love for the wonderful gospel of God* are a special part of His selection process, and I guarantee you these two important requirements reveal His expectations.

The excellent and wonderful bible, entwined with all its wonderful scriptures, is designed to point men toward righteousness, and living righteous pinpoints His expectation of us. And you and I should be glad to live a righteous lifestyle.

Synopsis

Everything has a beginning, including our Supreme God, and most likely, the Living Coals of Fire, who lives continually upon God's altar, are His beginning. And they were here first, the beginning of life and the beginning of God. They are the pure essence of universal energy, love, and holiness.

Most likely, all creation has a parallel source of life channeled through God. And everything was given life through the spark of the pure and powerful energy of the Living Coals of Fire, not known to burn to the touch. And they live upon the altar of God and do not harm anything.

It could be possible and most likely is a true analogy since there isn't any other analogy. Our Supreme God was chosen and formed from the pure energy within the midst of the Stones of Fire, and He was the first to rise from their creation.

Truly, God is the essence of pure energy, life, love, and holiness. And I am certain He's the Tree of Life for every living thing in the Heavens above and upon the Earth. And upon the mountain of God, inside the temple is the special place where the Mystery of Life will be revealed.

Indeed, men, women, and children gather everywhere in the temples, at the church houses, and before the altar, and they pray to our Supreme God. And they do it without realizing it's the Living Coals of Fire, who live upon the altar of God in Heaven, and the Living Coals of Fire hear their prayers too.

The Living Coals of Fire, who live upon the altar of God, are a part of the body of God and a part of His glory. And the Mystery of God, and the mystery of the Living Coals of Fire who live on the altar of God, are the greatest mystery of all mysteries, men can only speculate about.

Surely, the Holy Ghost of God and the Living Coals of Fire are one. And the sacred altar of God, located inside their temple, is their special dwelling place. And I believe God's sacred altar is the centerpiece of attention in Heaven.

www.ingramcontent.com/pod-product-compliance
Lightning Source LLC
Chambersburg PA
CBHW080946120626
46546CB00010B/2852